HINGE HOURS for ADVENT

Psalms, Canticles, and Readings on the Christian Life

a meditation rendering by
Stephen Joseph Wolf

idjc press

www.idjc.org

THE MORNING BEGINNING: PSALM 51:17

+ Lord, open my lips
and my mouth will declare your praise.

Glory to the Father and to the Son and to the Holy Spirit
As it was in the beginning, is now, and will be forever. Amen.

INVITATION ANTIPHONS

Through December 16

Come and worship the Lord, the King who is to come.

December 17 through December 23:

The Lord is close at hand; come and worship.

December 24:

Today you will know the Lord is coming,
and in the morning you will see his glory.

INVITATION PSALM to Adonai (*ah-duh-'nigh*)

PSALM 100

Shout for joy to Adonai, all you earth!
Serve Adonai with gladness!
Come into the presence with joyful song.

Know that Adonai is God, who made us,
whose people we are,
in whose pasture we are the sheep.

Enter the gates with thanksgiving,
go into the courts with praise!
Give thanks and give praise to the Name!

Good is Adonai, and loving to forever,
and faithful through generations and generation.

Glory to the Father and to the Son and to the Holy Spirit
As it was in the beginning, is now, and will be forever. Amen.

← The antiphon is traditionally repeated.

THE EVENING BEGINNING: PSALM 70:2

\+ God, come to my assistance;
make haste, Adonai, to help me!

Glory to the Father and to the Son and to the Holy Spirit
As it was in the beginning, is now, and will be forever. Amen.

Hinge Hours for Advent

For the holy name YHVH or Yahweh,
the Hebrew word for "my Lord" (***Adonai***) is used,
pronounced ***ah-duh-nigh'***.
See page 445
for the other choices made in this meditation rendering.

Icons are by Stephen Joseph Wolf

ISBN 978-1-937081-17-1

printed and distributed by Ingram Books
published by idjc press
www.idjc.org

THE FOUR-WEEK REPEATING CYCLE FOR MORNING & EVENING

Hinge Hours for Ordinary Time ISBN 978-1-937081-16-4
Hinge Hours for Advent ISBN 978-1-937081-17-1
Hinge Hours for Christmas ISBN 978-1-937081-31-7
Hinge Hours for Lent and Easter ISBN 978-1-937081-30-0
Hinge Hour Singer, the songs used in the Hinge Hours prayer books

ONCE-A-DAY PRAYER THROUGH THE LITURGICAL YEAR

A Simple Family Breviary, updating the Psalms of Saint Francis of Assisi

ONE-WEEK REPEATING CYCLE FOR MORNING & EVENING

In Health & In Healing, encouraging passages for the ill & depressed
Work Hours, drawn from the daytime hours, for morning & afternoon
Best of the Psalter, drawn from commons of the saints, includes IHIH & WH

SPECIAL PURPOSE PRAYER

Gospel of Life Prayer Cycle, a prayer for peace and justice study groups
Gone Before Us, praying for the dead

Hinge Hours for Advent

ADVENT
VIGILS OF SUNDAY (Saturday Evening)

Cre-a-tor of the stars of night,
Your peo-ple's ev-er-last-ing light,
Re-deem-er Je-sus, save us all,
And hear your ser-vants when we call.

You griev-ing that the an-cient curse
Should doom to death a u-niv-erse,
Find now the med-i-cine of grace,
To save and heal the hu-man race.

See now the Bride-groom of the bride,
As drew the world to eve-ning tide;
Pro-ceed-ing from a vir-gin shrine,
As ful-ly hu-man and div-ine.

This Awe-some Name, ma-jes-tic now,
All knees to bend and hearts to bow;
All things ce-les-tial God does own,
And things ter-res-trial, God a-lone.

To God the Fa-ther, God the Son,
And God the Spir-it, Three in One,
Laud, ho-nor, might, and glo-ry be
From age to age e-ter-nal-ly.

Text: 7th Century unknown author; translated by John M. Neale, 1852, altered
Music: CONDITOR, LM; *Conditor Alme Siderum*, Sarum plainsong, Mode IV

PSALMS & CANTICLES
WEEK I, go to page 68
WEEK II, go to page 156
WEEK III, go to page 258
WEEK IV, go to page 354

READING **1 THESSALONIANS 5:19-24**

Do not quench the Spirit. Do not despise prophecies. Prove all things and hold fast to the good. Abstain from every form of bad doings. May the God of peace, God's own self, completely sanctify you and may your entire spirit and soul and body be kept without blame in the presence of our Lord Jesus Christ. The Caller is faithful and will indeed do it.

RESPONSORY Ps 85:7

Lord, show to us...

...your mercy and unfailing love.

And grant us your salvation...

GOSPEL READING OF THE DAY (or use the **Canticle of Mary** from page 452)

Antiphon, Week I .. See the Lord coming from afar;
his splendor fills the earth.

Antiphon, Week II .. Come to us, Lord,
and may your presence be our peace.

Antiphon, Week III .. There was no "god" before me
and after me there will be none.

Antiphon, Week IV: *See the Evening Prayer antiphon for Dec. 17-24.*

EVENING PRAYER INTERCESSIONS AND CLOSING PRAYER, see page 453.

ADVENT
SUNDAY MORNINGS

O come, O come, Em-man/\\-u-el,
And ran-som cap-tive Is\\\\-ra-el,
That mourns in lone-ly ex\\-ile here
Un-til the Son of God/\\ ap-pear.

Re-joice! Re-joice! Em-man /\\ -u-el
Shall come to you, O Is \\\\ -ra-el.

(17th) **O** come now Wis-dom of our God Most High,
With love and ten-der strength, Cre-a-tor Guide;
To us the path of true know-ledge show,
And teach us in her sa-ving Way to go.
Rejoice!...

(18th) **O** come great Lord of an-cient Is-ra-el,
Who in the fire to Mos-es showed your-self,
And gave the Law up-on Si-nai height;
Stretch out your hand and
free us by your might.
Rejoice!...

(19th) **O** come raise up, deep Root of Jes-se's tree,
A sign for peo-ple seek-ing to be free,
Be-fore whom na-tions' rul-ers will bow,
Come save with-out de-lay to keep your vow.
Rejoice!...

(20th) **O** come, O Key of Da-vid, Roy-al Pow'r,
And o-pen gates to end our cap-tive hour;
For all be-hind a dark pris-on wall
Re-move the fear that blocks your sac-red call.
Rejoice!...

(21st) **O** come, O Ra-diant Dawn, e-ter-nal light,
Come shine and put the fear of death to flight.
In splen-dor o-ver dwell-ings of shade
The sun of Jus-tice has our full debt paid.
Rejoice!...

(22nd) **O** come, O King of na-tions, migh-ty arc,
Au-then-tic joy of ev-'ry hu-man heart;
O Key-stone, true foun-da-tion to trust,
Come save us whom you
fash-ion from the dust.
Rejoice!...

(23rd) **O** come, de-sire of all the na-tions, bind
In one the hearts and souls of hu-man-kind;
Come make our sad di-vis-ions to cease,
And be, Em-man-u-el, our King of Peace.
Rejoice!...

Text: Combined from O Antiphons, 12th C.?; translated by John M. Neale, 1851, altered
Music: VENI EMMANUEL, LM with refrain; 15th C.; adapt. by Thomas Helmore, 1856

PSALMS & CANTICLES
WEEK I, go to page 78
WEEK II, go to page 168
WEEK III, go to page 266
WEEK IV, go to page 364

READING **ROMANS 13:11-12**

Know that this is the kairos-time,
the hour for you to be raised out of sleep,
for now our salvation is nearer
than when we became believers.
The night has advanced and the day draws near.
Let us cast off therefore the deeds of the darkness,
and let us put on the armor of the light.
As in the new day, let us walk
not in revellings to drunken bouts,
not in sex to excesses, not in strife to jealousy,
but put on the Lord Jesus Christ,
and as for the flesh, give its lust no room to think.

RESPONSORY Luke 18:13, 22:69

Lord Jesus Christ, Son of the living God…
…have mercy on us.
You are seated at the right hand of the Father…

GOSPEL READING OF THE DAY (or use the **Canticle of Zechariah** from page 451)

Antiphon, Week I . . The Holy Spirit will come upon you,
Mary; you have no need to be afraid.

Antiphon, Week II . . I am sending my angel before me
to prepare the way for my coming.

Antiphon, Week III .. John sent two of his disciples to ask:
Are you the One whose coming was
foretold, or should we look for another?

Antiphon, December 17-24:

Let everything within you watch and wait,
for the Lord our God draws near.

MORNING PRAYER PETITIONS FOR THE CONSECRATION TO GOD OF THE DAY AND ITS REST

For the Church and her ministry and apostolates...
For secular authorities and all serving as stewards...
For people who are poor or sick or in sorrow...
For peace and the basic needs of each human being...
In gratitude for blessings and grace...
For those who have asked for my prayer...
For those for whom I have promised to pray...
For those who weigh on my heart...

CLOSING PRAYER FOR MORNING AND EVENING

Our Fa-ther,
who art in heav-en,
hal-lowed be thy name.
Thy king-dom come,
thy will be done
on earth as it is in heav-en.
Give us this day our dai-ly bread
and for-give us our tres-pass-es,
as we for-give those who tres-pass a-gainst/ us,
and lead us not in-to temp-ta/-tion,
but de-liv-er us from e\-vil.
A-men.

ADVENT
SUNDAY EVENINGS

On Jor-dan's bank the Bap-tist's cry
An-nounc-es that the Lord is nigh;
A-wake and heark-en, for he brings
Glad ti-dings of the King of kings.

Then cleansed be ev-'ry soul from sin;
Make straight the way of God with-in,
Pre-pare we in our hearts a home,
Where such a migh-ty guest may come.

For you are our sal-va-tion, Lord,
Our ref-uge and our sure re-ward;
Shine forth, and let your light re-store
Our souls to heav'n-ly grace once more.

All praise, e-ter-nal Son, to thee
Whose ad-vent set your peo-ple free,
Whom with the Fa-ther we a-dore
And Ho-ly Spir-it ev-er-more.

Text: Charles Coffin, d.1749; translated by John Chandler, d.1876, altered
Music: WINCHESTER NEW, CM, *Musikalisches Handbuch*, Hamburg, 1690;
adapted by William H. Havergal, d.1870

PSALMS & CANTICLES
WEEK I, go to page 83
WEEK II, go to page 177
WEEK III, go to page 273
WEEK IV, go to page 371

READING **PHILIPPIANS 4:4-7**

Rejoice in the Lord always; again I will say, rejoice.
Let your forbearance be known to all human beings.
The Lord is near. Be anxious about nothing,
but in everything, by prayer and thanksgiving petition,
let your requests be made known to God.
And the peace of God which surpasses all understanding
will guard your hearts and your thoughts in Christ Jesus.

RESPONSORY Ps 85:7

Lord, show to us...

...your mercy and unfailing love.

And grant us your salvation...

GOSPEL READING OF THE DAY (or use the **Canticle of Mary** from page 452)

Antiphon, Week I .. Do not be afraid, Mary,
you have found favor with God;
you will conceive and give birth to a Son,
alleluia.

Antiphon, Week II .. Blessed are you, O Virgin Mary,
for your great faith.

Antiphon, Week III .. Tell John what you see:
the blind have their sight restored,
the dead are raised to life,
the poor hear the good news.

Antiphon, Week IV: *See the Evening Prayer antiphon for Dec. 17-24.*

EVENING PRAYER INTERCESSIONS AND CLOSING PRAYER, see page 453.

ADVENT, *before December* 17
MONDAY MORNINGS

Come, Thou long ex-pect-ed Je-sus
Born to set your peo-ple free;
From our fears and sins re-lease us,
Let us find our rest in thee.

Is-rael's strength and con-so-la-tion,
Hope of all the earth you are;
Dear de-sire of ev-'ry na-tion,
Joy of ev-'ry long-ing heart.

Born your peo-ple to de-liv-er,
Born a child and yet a king,
Born to reign in us for-ev-er,
Now your gra-cious king-dom bring.

By your own e-ter-nal Spir-it
Rule in all our hearts a-lone;
By your all suf-fic-ient mer-it,
Raise us to your glo-rious throne.

Text: Charles Wesley, *Hymns for the Nativity of our Lord,* 1745, altered
Music: 87 87 D, STUTTGART, Christian F. Witt, 1715;
adapted by Henry J. Gauntlett, d.1876
An Alternate Melody: HYFRYDOL, Rowland H. Prichard, 1830,
Love Divine All Love Excelling

PSALMS & CANTICLES
WEEK I, go to page 88
WEEK II, go to page 182
WEEK III, go to page 280
WEEK IV, go to page 376

READING **ISAIAH 2:3-4**

Come, let us go up to the mountain of Adonai,
to the house of the God of Jacob,
who will teach us the ways so we may walk in the path.
Indeed, from Zion the law will go out
and from Jerusalem the word of Adonai,
who will judge between the nations
and settle disputes for many peoples.
They will beat their swords into plowshares
and their spears into pruning hooks.
Nations will not take up the sword against nations,
and they will train for war no more.

RESPONSORY

Your light will come, Jerusalem...
...the Lord will dawn on you in radiant beauty.
The glory of the Lord you will see within you...

GOSPEL READING OF THE DAY (or use the **Canticle of Zechariah** from page 451)

Antiphon, Week I . . Lift up your eyes, Jerusalem,
Mt 8:5-11 and see the great power of your King;
your Savior comes to set you free.

Antiphon, Week II . . The Lord proclaims: Repent,
Lk 5:17-26 the kingdom of God is upon you, alleluia.

Antiphon, Week III .. From heaven he comes,
Mt 21:23-27 the Lord and Ruler;
in his hand are honor and royal authority.

MORNING PRAYER PETITIONS AND CLOSING PRAYER, see page 453.

ADVENT, *before December* 17
MONDAY EVENINGS

Draw near to your Je-ru-sa-lem, O Lord,
Your faith-ful peo-ple cry with one ac-cord;
Ride on in tri-umph; Lord, be-hold we lay
Our stub-born hearts and proud wills in your way!
Your road is read-y and your path made straight;
With long-ing ex-pec-ta-tion is our wait.

Ho-san-na! wel-come to our hearts! for here
You have a temp-le, too, as Zion dear;
O en-ter in, dear Lord, un-bar the door;
And in that temp-le dwell for-ev-er-more.
Your road is read-y and your path made straight;
With long-ing ex-pec-ta-tion is our wait.

Text: Jeremy Taylor, *Festival and Penitential Hymns*, 1655;
abridged in *Sarum Hymnal*, 1868, altered
Music: 10 10 10 10 10 10 UNDE ET MEMORES, William H. Monk, 1823-1899
Popular melody for: *Lord, Who At That First Eucharist Didst Pray*

PSALMS & CANTICLES		
	WEEK I, go to page 94	WEEK III, go to page 287
	WEEK II, go to page 190	WEEK IV, go to page 384

READING **PHILIPPIANS 3:20b-21**

And we await a Savior,
the Lord Jesus Christ,
who will change the body of our humility,
conforming it to the body of his glory,
as it is his ability to subject
even all things to himself.

RESPONSORY Ps 146:7; 63:3; 67:2

Come and set us free…
…Lord God of power and glory…
Let your face shine upon us and we will know salvation…

GOSPEL READING OF THE DAY (or use the **Canticle of Mary** from page 452)

Antiphon, Week I . . The angel of the Lord
brought God's message to Mary,
and she conceived
by the power of the Holy Spirit,
alleluia.

Antiphon, Week II . . See, your King comes,
the master of the earth;
he will shatter the yoke of slavery.

Antiphon, Week III . . All generations will call me blessed:
The Lord has looked with favor
on his lowly servant.

EVENING PRAYER INTERCESSIONS AND CLOSING PRAYER, see page 453.

ADVENT, before December 17
TUESDAY MORNINGS

The ad-vent of our\ King
Our/ thoughts must\ now em-ploy;
Then let us meet him on/ the/ road
With songs of\ ho-ly joy.

The co-e-ter-nal\ Son
A/ maid-en's\ off-spring see;
A ser-vant's form Christ did/ put/ on,
To set his\ peo-ple free.

In glo-ry from his\ throne
A/-gain will\ Christ de-scend,
And sum-mon all who are/ his/ own
To joys that\ nev-er end.

Our joy-ful prais-es\ sing
To/ Christ, who\ set us free;
As trib-ute to the Fa/-ther/ bring,
And Ho-ly\ Ghost, to thee.

Text: Charles Coffin, d.1749; translated by Robert Campbell, d.1868, altered
Music: 66 86 ST. THOMAS (WILLIAMS); Aaron Williams, d.1776

PSALMS & CANTICLES
WEEK I, go to page 99
WEEK II, go to page 197
WEEK III, go to page 293
WEEK IV, go to page 390

READING **GENESIS 49:8-10**

You, Judah, will your brothers praise; your hand
on the neck of your enemies, the sons of your father
will bow to you. Judah, lion cub, my son, you return
from prey, crouching, lying like a lion and like a lioness;
who will rouse? The scepter will not depart from Judah
nor the ruling staff from between his feet
until when he comes, the one whose it is,
and to that one is the obedience of the peoples.

RESPONSORY

Your light will come, Jerusalem...
...the Lord will dawn on you in radiant beauty.
The glory of the Lord you will see within you...

GOSPEL READING OF THE DAY (or use the **Canticle of Zechariah** from page 451)

Antiphon, Week I .. From the root of Jesse a bud will blossom,
Lk 10:21-24 the glory of the Lord will fill the earth,
and all creation shall see
the saving power of God.

Antiphon, Week II .. Rejoice and be glad, O daughter of Zion;
Mt 18:12-14 I will come and make my dwelling in you,
says the Lord.

Antiphon, Week III .. Arise, arise, Jerusalem;
Mt 21:28-32 wake from your slumber!
shake the chain from your neck,
captive daughter Zion.

MORNING PRAYER PETITIONS AND CLOSING PRAYER, see page 453.

ADVENT, before December 17
TUESDAY EVENINGS

Im-mac-u-late Ma-ry, your prais-es we\ sing.
You reign now in heav-en with Je-sus our\ King.
A-ve, A-ve, A-ve, Ma-ri-a! A-ve, A-ve, Ma-ri/\-a!

In heav-en the bless-ed your glo-ry pro\-claim;
On earth we your chil-dren in-voke your fair\ name.
A-ve, A-ve, A-ve, Ma-ri-a! A-ve, A-ve, Ma-ri/\-a!

We pray for our Mo-ther, the Church up-on\ earth,
And bless, Ho-ly Ma-ry, the land of our\ birth.
A-ve, A-ve, A-ve, Ma-ri-a! A-ve, A-ve, Ma-ri/\-a!

Text: anon. in *Parochial Hymn Book;* Boston, 1897;
rev. of *Hail Virgin,* by Jeremiah Cummings,, altered
Music: 11 11 LOURDES HYMN with refrain, trad. Pyrenean Melody,
pub. Grenoble, 1882; altered by Augustus Edmonds Tozer, d.1910

PSALMS & CANTICLES
WEEK I, go to page 106 WEEK III, go to page 301
WEEK II, go to page 206 WEEK IV, go to page 397

READING **1 CORINTHIANS 1:4-9**

I give thanks to God always concerning you,
on the grace of God given to you in Christ Jesus,
because in everything you were enriched in him,

in all speech and all knowledge,
as the testimony of Christ was confirmed in you,
that you be lacking in no gift,
awaiting the revelation of our Lord Jesus Christ,
who will also confirm you to the end,
blameless in the day of our Lord Jesus Christ.
Faithful is God, through whom you were called
to communion (*koinonia*) with God's Son
Jesus Christ our Lord.

RESPONSORY Ps 146:7; 63:3; 67:2

Come and set us free…

…Lord God of power and glory…

Let your face shine upon us and we will know salvation…

GOSPEL READING OF THE DAY (or use the **Canticle of Mary** from page 452)

Antiphon, Week I .. Seek the Lord while he may be found;
call on him while he is near, alleluia.

Antiphon, Week II .. A voice is heard crying in the wilderness:
Prepare the way of the Lord;
make straight the path of our God.

Antiphon, Week III .. Before Mary and Joseph
had come together,
they learned that Mary was with child
by the power of the Holy Spirit,
alleluia.

EVENING PRAYER INTERCESSIONS AND CLOSING PRAYER, see page 453.

ADVENT, *before December* 17
WEDNESDAY MORNINGS

The/ King shall come when/ morn-ing dawns,
And light tri-umph\-ant/ breaks;
When/ beau-ty gilds the east-ern hills,
And/ life/ to joy\ a-wakes.

O/ bright-er than that/ glo-rious morn
Shall this fair morn\-ing/ be,
When/ Christ, our King, in beau-ty comes,
And/ we/ his face\ shall see.

The/ King shall come when/ morn-ing dawns,
And light and beau\-ty/ brings:
Hail/, Christ the Lord! your peo-ple pray,
Come/ quick/-ly, King\ of kings.

Text: author unknown; translated from Greek by John Brownlie,
Hymns of the Russian Church, 1907
Music: MCKEE, CM; African American Spiritual,
arranged by Harry T. Burleigh, 1866-1949
Popular melody for: *In Christ There Is No East or West*

PSALMS & CANTICLES WEEK I, go to page 111 WEEK III, go to page 307
WEEK II, go to page 211 WEEK IV, go to page 402

READING **ISAIAH 7:10-15**

Adonai spoke again to Ahaz to say, "Ask for a sign from
your God Adonai; ask to dig deep or to go high above."
But Ahaz said, "I will not ask, I will not test Adonai."
So Isaiah said, "Hear now, house of David!
Is it enough for you to try the patience of humans?
Will you also try the patience of my God?
And so the Lord will give to you a sign to see:
the virgin with child, bearing a son,
and she will call his name Immanu-El!
He will be eating curds and honey
when he knows to reject the bad and choose the good."

RESPONSORY

Your light will come, Jerusalem...
...the Lord will dawn on you in radiant beauty.
The glory of the Lord you will see within you...

GOSPEL READING OF THE DAY (or use the **Canticle of Zechariah** from page 451)

Antiphon, Week I .. The One who is coming after me
Mt 15:29-37 is greater than I; I am not worthy
to untie the strap of his sandals.

Antiphon, Week II .. He will be enthroned in David's place
Mt 11:28-30 to be king for ever, alleluia.

Antiphon, Week III .. Be comforted, my people, be comforted,
Lk 7:18b-23 says the Lord your God.

MORNING PRAYER PETITIONS AND CLOSING PRAYER, see page 453.

ADVENT, before December 17
WEDNESDAY EVENINGS

Com-fort, com-fort, O my peo-ple,
Speak of peace, thus says our God;
Com-fort those who sit in dark-ness,
Mourn-ing un-der sor-row's load;
Speak un-to Je-ru-sa-lem
Of the peace that waits for them;
Tell her all her sins I cov-er,
And that war-fare now is o-ver.

For the her-ald's voice is cry-ing
In the des-ert far and near,
Call-ing peo-ple to re-pen-tance
Since the king-dom now is here.
Now that warn-ing cry o-bey!
Now pre-pare for God a way!
Let the val-leys rise to meet him,
And the hills bow down to greet him.

Make now straight what long was crook-ed,
Make the rough-er pla-ces plain;
Let our hearts be true and hum-ble,
As be-fits the ho-ly reign.
For the glo-ry of the Lord
Over earth is shed a-broad.
Hu-man be-ings, see the to-ken
That God's word is ne-ver bro-ken.

Text: based on Isaiah 40:1-8 for the Feast of John the Baptist,
Johann G. Olearius, 1611-1684, translated by Catherine Winkworth, 1827-1878, altered
Music: 87 87 77 88, GENEVA 42, Claude Goudimel, *Geneva Psalter*, 1551

PSALMS & CANTICLES	WEEK I, go to page 117	WEEK III, go to page 315
	WEEK II, go to page 218	WEEK IV, go to page 409

READING **1 CORINTHIANS 4:5**

Judge not anything before the time,
until the coming of the Lord,
who will shed light on our dark and hidden things
and will show forth what goes on in human hearts.
Then will be the praise to each one from God.

RESPONSORY Ps 146:7; 63:3; 67:2

Come and set us free...
...Lord God of power and glory...
Let your face shine upon us and we will know salvation...

GOSPEL READING OF THE DAY (or use the **Canticle of Mary** from page 452)

Antiphon, Week I .. The law will go forth from Zion;
the word of the Lord from Jerusalem.

Antiphon, Week II .. Zion, you will be renewed, and you will
see the Just One who is coming to you.

Antiphon, Week III .. You, O Lord, are the One
whose coming was foretold:
we long for you to come
and set your people free.

EVENING PRAYER INTERCESSIONS AND CLOSING PRAYER, see page 453.

ADVENT, before December 17
THURSDAY MORNINGS

Come, Re-deem-er of our race,
Choic-est Gift of heav'n-ly grace!
Be the bless-ed vir-gin's Son;
Join your race on earth be-gun.

Both of hu-man blood and birth
And of God he comes to earth
Ho-ly Spir-it breath con-ceived.
God and hu-man, we be-lieve.

Wond-rous, this ex-pect-ed Child
Of the vir-gin un-de-filed!
By the world he'll be dis-owned,
Still to be in heav'n en-throned.

Bright-ly will your man-ger shine!
Glo-rious in its light div-ine:
Let our sin not cloud this light;
Keep our gift of faith thus bright.

Text: Charles Wesley, *Veni Redemptor gentium,* ascribed to Ambrose of Milan, d. 397, trans. to German by Martin Luther, 1523, to English by W.M. Reynolds, 1850, altered
Music: 7 7 7 7 HEINLEIN, Attributed to Martin Herbst, d. 1681
Popular melody for: *Forty Days and Forty Nights*

PSALMS & CANTICLES		
	WEEK I, go to page 124	WEEK III, go to page 319
	WEEK II, go to page 223	WEEK IV, go to page 416

READING **ISAIAH 45:5-8**

I am Adonai and there is no other;
apart from me there is no God.
I will strengthen you though you do not know me
so that they may know there is none besides me,
from the rising of the sun to its setting place.
I am Adonai and there is no other,
forming light and creating darkness,
bringing prosperity and allowing disaster;
I Adonai am the one doing all of these.
Heavens at above, let them rain;
and let clouds shower justice;
let the earth open and let salvation spring up
and with justice; let them grow together,
as I Adonai have created.

RESPONSORY

Your light will come, Jerusalem…
…the Lord will dawn on you in radiant beauty.
The glory of the Lord you will see within you…

GOSPEL READING OF THE DAY (or use the **Canticle of Zechariah** from page 451)

Antiphon, Week I . . I shall wait for my Lord and Savior and
Mt 7:21,24-27 point him out when he is near, alleluia.

Antiphon, Week II . . I will help you, says the Lord.
Mt 11:11-15 I am your Savior, the Holy One of Israel.

Antiphon, Week III . . Arise, arise, Lord;
Lk 7:24-30 show us your power and might.

MORNING PRAYER PETITIONS AND CLOSING PRAYER, see page 453.

ADVENT, before December 17
THURSDAY EVENINGS

Faith of our an-ces-tors, liv\-ing still,
In spite of dun-geon, fire\ and sword;
O how our hearts\ beat high\ with joy
When-'er we hear that glo/-rious Word!

Refrain Faith of our an-ces-tors, ho-ly faith!
We will be true to you till death.

Faith of our fa\-thers, we\ will strive
A-mong all peo-ples, as is our call;
That through the truth\ that comes\ from God,
True free-dom may be found/ by all.

Refrain

Faith of our mo\-thers, we\ will love
Both friend and foe in all\ our strife;
Liv-ing and preach-ing as love\ knows how
By kind-ly words and vir/-tuous life.

Refrain

Text: Frederick W. Faber, *Jesus and Mary*, 1849; refr. by James G. Walton, 1874; altered
Music: ST. CATHERINE, LM with refrain; Henry F. Hemy, 1864;
adapted by James G. Walton, 1874

PSALMS & CANTICLES WEEK I, go to page 130 WEEK III, go to page 325
WEEK II, go to page 231 WEEK IV, go to page 421

READING **JAMES 5:7-11**

And so be patient, brothers and sisters, until the parousia of the Lord. Behold, the farmer awaits the precious fruit of the earth, being patient over it until receiving early and late rains. You also be patient and build up your hearts, because the parousia of the Lord has drawn near. Do not murmur, brothers and sisters, about one another lest you be judged. Behold, the judge stands before the doors. Brothers and sisters, take as an example of suffering and patience the prophets, who spoke in the name of the Lord. Behold we count blessed the ones enduring. You have heard of the endurance of Job, and you have seen the purpose of the Lord, that the Lord is full of compassion and mercy.

RESPONSORY Ps 146:7; 63:3; 67:2

Come and set us free…

…Lord God of power and glory…

Let your face shine upon us and we will know salvation…

GOSPEL READING OF THE DAY (or use the **Canticle of Mary** from page 452)

Antiphon, Week I . . Blessed are you among women,
and blessed is the fruit of your womb.

Antiphon, Week II . . The one who is coming after me
existed before me;
I am not worthy to untie his sandals.

Antiphon, Week III . . All you who love Jerusalem,
rejoice with her forever.

EVENING PRAYER INTERCESSIONS AND CLOSING PRAYER, see page 453.

ADVENT, *before December* 17
FRIDAY MORNINGS

O come, div-ine Mes-si-ah;
The world in si-lence waits\ the day
When hope shall sing its tri-umph
And sad-ness flee\ a-way...

Refrain **D**ear Sav-ior haste! Come, come to earth.
Dis-pel the night and show your face,
And bid us hail the dawn of grace...

O Christ, whom na-tions sigh for,
Whom priest and proph-et long\ fore-told,
Come, break the cap-tive fet-ters,
Re-deem the long\-lost fold... *Refrain*

You come in peace and meek-ness
And low-ly will your cra\-dle be;
All clothed in hu-man weak-ness
Shall we your God\-head see. *Refrain*

O come, div-ine Mes-si-ah;
The world in si-lence waits\ the day
When hope shall sing its tri-umph
And sad-ness flee\ a-way.

Text: Abbe Simon-Joseph Pellegrin, d. 1745; trans. by S. Mary of St. Philip, 1877, altered
Music: 78 76 VENEZ DIVIN MESSIE, Traditional French Carol, 16th C.

PSALMS & CANTICLES
WEEK I, go to page 137
WEEK II, go to page 237
WEEK III, go to page 331
WEEK IV, go to page 426

READING **JEREMIAH 30:21,22**

This Adonai says:
"Their leader will be from them
and their ruler will arise from among them,
and I will bring him near and he will come close to me.
...So you will be my people,
and I will be your God."

RESPONSORY

Your light will come, Jerusalem...
...the Lord will dawn on you in radiant beauty.
The glory of the Lord you will see within you...

GOSPEL READING OF THE DAY (or use the **Canticle of Zechariah** from page 451)

Antiphon, Week I . . Our God comes,
Mt 9:27-31 born a human in David's line,
enthroned as king forever, alleluia.

Antiphon, Week II . . Say to the fainthearted: Take courage!
Mt 11:16-19 The Lord our God is coming to save us.

Antiphon, Week III .. Guard what is good
Jn 5:33-36 and cherish what is true,
for our salvation is at hand.

MORNING PRAYER PETITIONS AND CLOSING PRAYER, see page 453.

ADVENT, before December 17
FRIDAY EVENINGS

Take, Lord, re-ceive my lib-er-ty,
My will en-tire and mem-o-ry,
My un-der-stand-ing, ev-'ry-thing,
Pos-ses-sions all, my off-er-ing.

The giv'n by you I do re-turn;
Con-form my life as is your will.
Suf-fic-ient now, no more to own:
E-nough are love and grace a-lone.

Lord A-do-nai, give love and grace,
Suf-fic-ient these in time and place,
Your love and grace, un-earned and free,
This true a-bun-dance may we see.

Love show-ing more in deed than word,
Love sha-ring in the com-mon good,
I pon-der with a-ffec-tion great
What God has done and does of late.

Text: Suscipe from The Spiritual Exercises of St. Ignatius of Loyola, #234, d. 1556,
inspired by Veneremur, Jesuit Spirituality Center, Grand Coteau, LA, 1957
Music: TALLIS CANON, LM, Thomas Tallis, d. 1585
Alternate Music: OLD HUNDREDTH, LM, Louis Bourgeois, Genevan Psalter, 1551
Popular melody for: Praise God From Whom All Blessings Flow

PSALMS & CANTICLES
WEEK I, go to page 144 | WEEK III, go to page 339
WEEK II, go to page 245 | WEEK IV, go to page 433

READING **2 PETER 3:8b-10**

One day with the Lord is as a thousand years
and a thousand years as day one.
The Lord is not slow on his promise,
as some deem slowness, but is patient with you,
not for the purpose that any perish
but that all people might come to repentance.
But the day of the Lord will come as a thief,
in which the heavens will pass away with rushing sound
and the elements burning will be dissolved
and the earth and its works will be uncovered.

RESPONSORY Ps 146:7; 63:3; 67:2

Come and set us free...
...Lord God of power and glory...
Let your face shine upon us and we will know salvation...

GOSPEL READING OF THE DAY (or use the **Canticle of Mary** from page 452)

Antiphon, Week I .. Out of Egypt I have called my Son;
he will come to save his people.

Antiphon, Week II .. Rejoicing you shall draw water
from the wellsprings of the Savior.

Antiphon, Week III .. Out of Egypt I have called my Son;
he will come to save his people.

EVENING PRAYER INTERCESSIONS AND CLOSING PRAYER, see page 453.

ADVENT, before December 17
SATURDAY MORNINGS

The an-gel Ga-bri-el from heav-en came,
With wings as drift-ed snow and eyes as flame;
"All hail," the an-gel said, "O low-ly place,
Most high-ly fa-vored maid-en, full of grace."
Of her would come the Christ Em-man-u-el;
With all the an-gels, "Glo-ri-a!" we tell.

"**F**or know a bless-ed Moth-er you shall be,
All gen-er-a-tions' praise e-ter-nal-ly;
Your Son shall be Em-man-u-el, fore-told,
Most high-ly fa-vored la-dy, from of old."
Of her would come the Christ Em-man-u-el;
With all the an-gels, "Glo-ri-a!" we tell.

Then gen-tle Ma-ry meek-ly bowed her head;
"To me be as it pleas-es God!" she said.
"My soul shall laud and mag-ni-fy the Name."
Most high-ly fa-vored la-dy, liv-ing flame.
Of her would come the Christ Em-man-u-el;
With all the an-gels, "Glo-ri-a!" we tell.

Text: from *Birjina gaztettobat zegoen*, traditional Basque Carol; translated by Sabine Baring-Gould, d.1924, altered significantly for a different melody
Music: 10 10 10 10 10 10 UNDE ET MEMORES, William H. Monk, d.1899
Popular melody for: *Lord Who At The First Eucharist Did Pray*

PSALMS & CANTICLES
WEEK I, go to page 149 WEEK III, go to page 347
WEEK II, go to page 249 WEEK IV, go to page 438

READING **ISAIAH 11:1-5**

A shoot will come up from the stump of Jesse
and a branch from his roots will bear fruit.
And the Spirit of Adonai she will rest on him,
the Spirit of wisdom and understanding,
the Spirit of counsel and power,
the Spirit of knowledge and fear of Adonai,
and for delight the fear of Adonai.
Not by seeing with eyes will he judge,
and not by hearing with ears will he decide,
but he will judge the needy with righteousness
and decide with justice for poor ones of the earth,
and he will strike the earth with the rod of his mouth
and with the breath of his lips he will slay bad doings.

RESPONSORY

Your light will come, Jerusalem...
...the Lord will dawn on you in radiant beauty.
The glory of the Lord you will see within you...

GOSPEL READING OF THE DAY (or use the **Canticle of Zechariah** from page 451)

Antiphon, Week I . . Banish your fears, O people of Zion;
Mt 9:35-10:1,5a,6-8 God, your own God, is coming to you.

Antiphon, Week II . . The Lord will set up his standard
Mt 17:9a,10-13 in the sight of all the nations,
and gather the dispersed of Israel.

MORNING PRAYER PETITIONS AND CLOSING PRAYER, see page 453.

ADVENT - December 17
MORNING

O come, O come, Em-man/\-u-el,
And ran-som cap-tive Is\\-ra-el,
That mourns in lone-ly ex\-ile here
Until the Son of God/\ appear.
Re-joice! Re-joice! Em-man /\ -u-el shall come to you, O Israel.

O come now Wis-dom of our God Most High,
With love and ten-der strength, Cre-a-tor Guide;
To us the path of true know-ledge show,
And teach us in her sa-ving Way to go.
Re-joice! Re-joice! Em-man /\ -u-el shall come to you, O Israel.

Text: Combined from O Antiphons, 12th C.?; translated by John M. Neale, 1851, altered
Music: VENI EMMANUEL, LM with refrain; 15th C.; adapt. by Thomas Helmore, 1856

PSALMS & CANTICLES go to the day of the week in WEEK III

READING **MATTHEW 1:1-17**

The book of the generation of Jesus Christ
son of David son of Abraham.
Abraham was father to (begat) Isaac, and Isaac was father to Jacob, and Jacob was father to Judas and his brothers, and Judas was father to Perez and Zerah out of Tamar, and Perez was father to Hezron, and Hezron was father to Aram, and Aram was father to Aminadab, and Aminadab was father to Nahshon, and Nahshon was

father to Salmon, and Salmon was father to Boaz
out of Rahab, and Boaz was father to Obed out of Ruth,
and Obed was father to Jesse, and Jesse was father
to David the king.
And David was father to Solomon out of the one
who had been wife to Uriah, and Solomon was father
to Rehoboam, and Rehoboam was father to Abijah,
and Abijah was father to Asaph, and Asaph was father
to Jehoshaphat, and Jehoshaphat was father to Joram,
and Joram was father to Uzziah, and Uzziah was father
to Jotham, and Jotham was father to Hezekiah, and
Hezekiah was father to Manasseh, and Manasseh was
father to Amos, and Amos was father to Josiah, and
Josiah was father to Jechoniah and his brothers at the
time of the Babylonian Exile.
And after the exile to Babylon, Jechoniah was father to
Shealtiel, and Shealtiel was father to Zerubbabel, and
Zerubbabel was father to Abiud, and Abiud was father
to Eliakim, and Eliakim was father to Azor, and Azor
was father to Zadok, and Zadok was father to Achim,
and Achim was father to Eliud, and Eliud was father
to Eleazor, and Eleazor was father to Mathan, and
Mathan was father to Jacob, and Jacob was father
to Joseph, the husband of Mary, of whom was born
Jesus called Christ.
Therefore all the generations from Abraham to David:
fourteen generations,
and from David until the Babylonian Exile:

MATTHEW 1:1-17, continued

fourteen generations,
and from the Babylonian Exile until the Christ:
fourteen generations.

RESPONSORY

Your light will come, Jerusalem...
...the Lord will dawn on you in radiant beauty.
The glory of the Lord you will see within you...

GOSPEL CANTICLE (**Canticle of Zechariah**) see page 451.

Antiphon . . . Believe me, the kingdom of God
is at hand; I tell you solemnly,
your Savior will not delay his coming.

MORNING PRAYER PETITIONS AND CLOSING PRAYER, see page 453.

ADVENT - December 17
EVENING

O come now Wis-dom of our God Most High,
With love and ten-der strength, Cre-a-tor Guide;
To us the path of true know-ledge show,
And teach us in her sa-ving Way to go.
Re-joice! Re-joice! Em-man /\ -u-el shall come to you, O Israel.

Text: Combined from O Antiphons, 12th C.?; translated by John M. Neale, 1851, altered
Music: VENI EMMANUEL, LM with refrain; 15th C.; adapt. by Thomas Helmore, 1856

PSALMS & CANTICLES go to the day of the week in WEEK III or IV

READING **JEREMIAH 23:5-8**

"See, days are coming," declares Adonai, "when I will raise up to David a righteous branch, and he will reign as king, and he will be wise and do justice and right in the land. In his days Judah will be saved and Israel will live in safety, and this is his name that Adonai will call him: Our Righteousness. So see, days are coming," declares Adonai, "when they will no longer say, 'Adonai lives who brought the sons and daughters of Israel up from the land of Egypt,' but rather, 'Adonai lives who brought up and brought back descendants of the house of Israel from the land of the north and from all the countries where they were banished,' and then they will live in their land."

RESPONSORY Ps 85:7

Lord, show to us...

...your mercy and unfailing love.

And grant us your salvation...

GOSPEL CANTICLE (**Canticle of Mary**) see page 452.

Antiphon, Dec. 17 .. **O Wisdom**, O holy Word of God, you govern all creation with your strong yet tender care. Come and show your people the way to salvation.

EVENING PRAYER INTERCESSIONS AND CLOSING PRAYER, see page 453.

ADVENT - December 18
MORNING

O come, O come, Em-man/\-u-el,
And ran-som cap-tive Is\\-ra-el,
That mourns in lone-ly ex\-ile here
Until the Son of God/\ appear.
Re-joice! Re-joice! Em-man /\ -u-el shall come to you, O Israel.

O come great Lord of an-cient Is-ra-el,
Who in the fire to Mos-es showed your-self,
And gave the Law up-on Si-nai height;
Stretch out your hand and free us by your might.
Re-joice! Re-joice! Em-man /\ -u-el shall come to you, O Israel.

Text: Combined from O Antiphons, 12th C.?; translated by John M. Neale, 1851, altered
Music: VENI EMMANUEL, LM with refrain; 15th C.; adapt. by Thomas Helmore, 1856

PSALMS & CANTICLES — go to the day of the week in WEEK III or IV

READING **MATTHEW 1:18-25**

Now thus was the birth of Jesus Christ.
When his mother Mary was betrothed to Joseph,
before they came together
she was found having in womb by the Holy Spirit.
Now Joseph her husband, being just,
and not wishing to hold her up as an example,
resolved secretly to dismiss her.

But while thinking on these things, behold an angel
of the Lord appeared to him by a dream saying,
"Joseph son of David,
do not fear to take Mary as your wife.
For in her is the begotten of the Spirit that is Holy.
And she will bear a son,
and you shall call his name Jesus,
for he will save his people from their sins."
Now all this occurred that might be fulfilled what was
spoken by the Lord through the prophet saying,
Behold the virgin in womb will have and will bear a son,
and they will call his name Emmanuel,
which is being interpreted, *God with us.*
Then Joseph being raised from his sleep
did as the angel of the Lord greeted him,
and took his wife.
And he did not know her until she bore a son,
and he called his name Jesus.

RESPONSORY

Your light will come, Jerusalem...
...the Lord will dawn on you in radiant beauty.
The glory of the Lord you will see within you...

GOSPEL CANTICLE (**Canticle of Zechariah**) see page 451.

Antiphon . . . Let everything within you watch and wait
for the Lord our God draws near.

MORNING PRAYER PETITIONS AND CLOSING PRAYER, see page 453.

ADVENT - December 18
EVENING

O come great Lord of an-cient Is-ra-el,
Who in the fire to Mos-es showed your-self,
And gave the Law up-on Si-nai height;
Stretch out your hand and free us by your might.
Re-joice! Re-joice! Em-man /\ -u-el shall come to you, O Israel.

Text: Combined from O Antiphons, 12th C.?; translated by John M. Neale, 1851, altered
Music: VENI EMMANUEL, LM with refrain; 15th C.; adapt. by Thomas Helmore, 1856

PSALMS & CANTICLES go to the day of the week in WEEK III or IV

READING **JUDGES 13:2-7,24-25a**

A certain man of Zorah, from the clan of the Danite, was named Manoah, and his wife was sterile and did not bear a child. An angel of Adonai appeared to the woman and said to her, "See now! You are sterile and have not born a child; but you will conceive and you will bear a son, and see now that you drink no wine or fermented drink and you eat nothing unclean, because, see, conceiving you will bear a son and no razor may go on his head, because the boy will be a Nazirite of God from the womb and he will begin to deliver Israel from the hand of the Philistines. Then the woman went and told her husband,

"The man of God came to me, an appearance appearing like an angel of God, very awesome. I did not ask him from where he came and he did not tell me his name. But he said to me, 'See, conceiving you will bear a son; now to then drink no wine or fermented drink and eat nothing unclean, for the boy will be a Nazirite of God from the womb until the day of his death."
And the woman bore a son and she called his name Samson, and the boy grew and Adonai blessed him, and the Spirit of Adonai, she began to stir him.

RESPONSORY Ps 85:7

Lord, show to us...

...your mercy and unfailing love.

And grant us your salvation...

GOSPEL CANTICLE (**Canticle of Mary**) see page 452.

Antiphon, Dec. 18 . . **O Sacred Lord** of ancient Israel,
who showed yourself to Moses
in the burning bush,
who gave him the holy law
on Sinai mountain:
come, stretch out your mighty hand
to set us free.

EVENING PRAYER INTERCESSIONS AND CLOSING PRAYER, see page 453.

ADVENT - December 19
MORNING

O come, O come, Em-man/\-u-el,
And ran-som cap-tive Is\\-ra-el,
That mourns in lone-ly ex\-ile here
Until the Son of God/\ appear.
Re-joice! Re-joice! Em-man /\ -u-el shall come to you, O Israel.

O come raise up, deep Root of Jes-se's tree,
A sign for peo-ple seek-ing to be free,
Be-fore whom na-tions' rul-ers will bow,
Come save with-out de-lay to keep your vow.
Re-joice! Re-joice! Em-man /\ -u-el shall come to you, O Israel.

Text: Combined from O Antiphons, 12th C.?; translated by John M. Neale, 1851, altered
Music: VENI EMMANUEL, LM with refrain; 15th C.; adapt. by Thomas Helmore, 1856

PSALMS & CANTICLES go to the day of the week in WEEK III or IV

READING **LUKE 1:5-25**

There was in the days of Herod, king of Judea, a certain priest by the name of Zechariah of the course of Abijah, and his wife of the daughters of Aaron, and her name was Elizabeth. And they were both righteous before God, going blameless in all the commandments and ordinances of the Lord. And they had no child, because Elizabeth

was barren, and both were advanced in their days.
It came to pass while he served as priest in the order of his course before God, it was his lot according to the custom of the priesthood to enter into the temple of the Lord to burn incense, and all the multitude of the people were praying outside at the hour of incense. And there appeared to him an angel of the Lord standing on the right of the altar of incense. And seeing this, Zechariah was troubled, and fear fell upon him. But the angel said to him, "Fear not, Zechariah, because your request was heard, and your wife Elizabeth will bear to you a son, and you shall call his name John, and you shall have joy and gladness, and many will rejoice over his birth, for he will be great in the eyes of the Lord, and wine and strong drink by no means may he drink, and he will be filled with the Holy Spirit even from the womb of his mother, and he will turn many of the sons of Israel to the Lord their God, and he will go before the Lord in the spirit and power of Elijah, to turn the hearts of fathers to children and disobedient ones to the understanding of the just, to prepare for the Lord a people prepared."
And Zechariah said to the angel, "By what shall I know this? For I am old and my wife has advanced in her days."
And answering the angel said to him, "I am Gabriel, the one standing before God, and I was sent to speak to you and to announce to you these things. And behold you shall be being silent and not able to speak until the day when these things happen, because you did not believe

LUKE 1:5-25, continued

my words, which will be fulfilled in their time."
And the people were expecting Zechariah, and they marvelled when he delayed in the temple. And going out he was unable to speak to them, and they knew that he had seen a vision in the temple, and he was beckoning to them and remained dumb. And it came to pass when days of his service were fulfilled, he went away to his house. And after these days, his wife Elizabeth conceived, and hid herself for five months, saying, "Thus has the Lord done to me in days in which he looked upon me to take away my reproach among humans."

RESPONSORY

Your light will come, Jerusalem...
...the Lord will dawn on you in radiant beauty.
The glory of the Lord you will see within you...

GOSPEL CANTICLE (**Canticle of Zechariah**) see page 451.

Antiphon ... Like the sun in the morning sky,
the Savior of the world will dawn;
like rain on the meadows he will descend
to rest in the womb of the Virgin, alleluia.

MORNING PRAYER PETITIONS AND CLOSING PRAYER, see page 453.

ADVENT - December 19
EVENING

O come raise up, deep Root of Jes-se's tree,
A sign for peo-ple seek-ing to be free,
Be-fore whom na-tions' rul-ers will bow,
Come save with-out de-lay to keep your vow.
Re-joice! Re-joice! Em-man /\ -u-el shall come to you, O Israel.

Text: Combined from O Antiphons, 12th C.?; translated by John M. Neale, 1851, altered
Music: VENI EMMANUEL, LM with refrain; 15th C.; adapt. by Thomas Helmore, 1856

PSALMS & CANTICLES go to the day of the week in WEEK III or IV

READING **ISAIAH 7:10-14**

Adonai spoke again to Ahaz to say, "Ask for a sign from
your God Adonai! Ask to the deep or at high above!"
But Ahaz said, "I will not ask; I will not test Adonai."
Then Isaiah said, "Hear now, house of David!
Is it enough for you to try human patience?
Will you also try the patience of my God?
And so the Lord will indeed give to you a sign:
See the virgin with child and bearing a son,
and she will call his name Immanu-El."

RESPONSORY Ps 85:7

Lord, show to us...

...your mercy and unfailing love.

And grant us your salvation...

GOSPEL CANTICLE (**Canticle of Mary**) see page 452.

Antiphon, Dec. 19 . . **O Flower** of Jesse's stem, you have been raised up as a sign for all peoples; kings stand silent in your presence; the nations bow down in worship before you. Come, let nothing keep you from coming to our aid.

EVENING PRAYER INTERCESSIONS AND CLOSING PRAYER, see page 453.

ADVENT - December 20
MORNING

O come, O come, Em-man/\-u-el,
And ran-som cap-tive Is\\-ra-el,
That mourns in lone-ly ex\-ile here
Until the Son of God/\ appear.
Re-joice! Re-joice! Em-man /\ -u-el shall come to you, O Israel.

O come, O Key of Da-vid, Roy-al Pow'r,
And o-pen gates to end our cap-tive hour;
For all be-hind a dark pris-on wall
Re-move the fear that blocks your sac-red call.
Re-joice! Re-joice! Em-man /\ -u-el shall come to you, O Israel.

Text: Combined from O Antiphons, 12th C.?; translated by John M. Neale, 1851, altered
Music: VENI EMMANUEL, LM with refrain; 15th C.; adapt. by Thomas Helmore, 1856

PSALMS & CANTICLES go to the day of the week in WEEK III or IV

READING **LUKE 1:26-38**

Now in the sixth month the angel Gabriel was sent from God to a city of Galilee named Nazareth, to a virgin betrothed to a man named Joseph, of the house of David, and the virgin's name was Mary. And entering to her he said, "Hail, favored one, the Lord is with you." And she was greatly disturbed at the saying, and considered of what sort this greeting might be. And the angel said to her, "Fear not, Mary, for you have found favor with God. And behold you will conceive in womb and bear a son, and you shall call his name Jesus. This will be great, and will be called Son of the Most High, and the Lord God will give him the throne of David his father, and he will reign over the house of Jacob to the eons, and of his kingdom there will not be an end." And Mary said to the angel, "How will this be, since I know not a man?" And answering the angel said to her, "The Holy Spirit will come upon you, and the power of the Most High will overshadow you, and this one being born holy will be called Son of God. And behold your relative Elizabeth has also conceived a son in her old age, and this is the sixth month for her who was being called barren, because no not any word will be impossible with God." And Mary said, "Behold, the handmaid of the Lord; may it be to me according to your word." And the angel went away from her.

RESPONSORY

Your light will come, Jerusalem...
...the Lord will dawn on you in radiant beauty.
The glory of the Lord you will see within you...

GOSPEL CANTICLE (**Canticle of Zechariah**) see page 451.

Antiphon . . . The angel Gabriel was sent
to the Virgin Mary,
who was betrothed to Joseph.

MORNING PRAYER PETITIONS AND CLOSING PRAYER, see page 453.

ADVENT - December 20
EVENING

O come, O Key of Da-vid, Roy-al Pow'r,
And o-pen gates to end our cap-tive hour;
For all be-hind a dark pris-on wall
Re-move the fear that blocks your sac-red call.
Re-joice! Re-joice! Em-man /\ -u-el shall come to you, O Israel.

Text: Combined from O Antiphons, 12th C.?; translated by John M. Neale, 1851, altered
Music: VENI EMMANUEL, LM with refrain; 15th C.; adapt. by Thomas Helmore, 1856

PSALMS & CANTICLES go to the day of the week in WEEK III or IV

READING **SONG OF SONGS 2:8-14**

Sound of my lover, look, there he comes!
Leaping across the mountains, bounding over the hills,
my lover like to a gazelle, or to young deer of the stags.
Look, here standing behind our wall,
gazing through the windows, peering through the lattices!
My lover spoke and said to me,
"Arise, you my darling, my beautiful one, and come!
For see, the winter passed, the rain is over, it went!
The flowers appear on the earth, the song season has
come, and the dove sound is heard in our land.
The fig tree forms her early fruits
and the vines blossom and spread their fragrance!
Arise and come, my darling, my beautiful one and come!
My dove in clefts of rock, in mountainside hiding places,
show me your face! Let me hear your voice!
For your voice is sweet and your face is lovely!"

RESPONSORY Ps 85:7

Lord, show to us...
...your mercy and unfailing love.
And grant us your salvation...

GOSPEL CANTICLE (**Canticle of Mary**) see page 452.

Antiphon, Dec. 20 .. **O Key of David**, O royal Power of Israel, controlling at your will the gate of heaven: come, break down the prison walls of death for those who dwell in darkness and the shadow of death; and lead your captive people into freedom.

EVENING PRAYER INTERCESSIONS AND CLOSING PRAYER, see page 453.

ADVENT - December 21
MORNING

O come, O come, Em-man/\-u-el,
And ran-som cap-tive Is\\-ra-el,
That mourns in lone-ly ex\-ile here
Until the Son of God/\ appear.
Re-joice! Re-joice! Em-man /\ -u-el shall come to you, O Israel.

O come, O Ra-diant Dawn, e-ter-nal light,
Come shine and put the fear of death to flight.
In splen-dor o-ver dwell-ings of shade
The sun of Jus-tice has our full debt paid.
Re-joice! Re-joice! Em-man /\ -u-el shall come to you, O Israel.

Text: Combined from O Antiphons, 12th C.?; translated by John M. Neale, 1851, altered
Music: VENI EMMANUEL, LM with refrain; 15th C.; adapt. by Thomas Helmore, 1856

PSALMS & CANTICLES go to the day of the week in WEEK III or IV

READING **LUKE 1:39-45**

And rising up in those days Mary went with haste
to the mountain country to a city of Judah
and entered the house of Zechariah
and greeted Elizabeth.

And it came to pass
when Elizabeth heard Mary's greeting,
the baby in her womb leaped,
and Elizabeth was filled with the Holy Spirit,
and she called out with a great cry and said,
"Blessed are you among women,
and blessed is the fruit of your womb.
And how to me this,
that the mother of my Lord comes to me?
For behold
when the sound of your greeting entered my ears,
the baby in my womb leaped in gladness.
And blessed the one believing
because there will be a completion to the things
spoken to her from the Lord."

RESPONSORY

Your light will come, Jerusalem...
...the Lord will dawn on you in radiant beauty.
The glory of the Lord you will see within you...

GOSPEL CANTICLE (**Canticle of Zechariah**) see page 451.

Antiphon . . . There is no need to be afraid;
in four days our Lord will come to us.

MORNING PRAYER PETITIONS AND CLOSING PRAYER, see page 453.

ADVENT - December 21
EVENING

O come, O Ra-diant Dawn, e-ter-nal light,
Come shine and put the fear of death to flight.
In splen-dor o-ver dwell-ings of shade
The sun of Jus-tice has our full debt paid.
Re-joice! Re-joice! Em-man /\ -u-el shall come to you, O Israel.

Text: Combined from O Antiphons, 12th C.?; translated by John M. Neale, 1851, altered
Music: VENI EMMANUEL, LM with refrain; 15th C.; adapt. by Thomas Helmore, 1856

PSALMS & CANTICLES — go to the day of the week in WEEK III or IV

READING — **1 SAMUEL 1:24-28**

Hannah took the young boy Samuel with her
just as she weaned him,
with a three year old bull,
an ephah of flour, and a skin of wine,
and she brought him to the house of Adonai at Shiloh.
When they slaughtered the bull,
they brought the boy to Eli,
and she said,
"My lord, as sure as my soul is alive, my lord,
I am the woman who stood beside you here
to pray to Adonai for this child.

I prayed and Adonai granted to me my request.
So now I give him to Adonai;
all the days that he lives are given to Adonai."
And he worshiped Adonai there.

RESPONSORY Ps 85:7

Lord, show to us...

...your mercy and unfailing love.

And grant us your salvation...

GOSPEL CANTICLE (**Canticle of Mary**) see page 452.

Antiphon, Dec. 21 .. **O Radiant Dawn**,
splendor of eternal light,
sun of justice: come,
shine on those who dwell in the shadows.

EVENING PRAYER INTERCESSIONS AND CLOSING PRAYER, see page 453.

ADVENT - December 22
MORNING

O come, O come, Em-man/\-u-el,
And ran-som cap-tive Is\\-ra-el,
That mourns in lone-ly ex\-ile here
Until the Son of God/\ appear.
Re-joice! Re-joice! Em-man /\ -u-el shall come to you, O Israel.

O come, O King of na-tions, migh-ty arc,
Au-then-tic joy of ev-'ry hu-man heart;
O Key-stone, true foun-da-tion to trust,
Come save us whom you fash-ion from the dust.
Re-joice! Re-joice! Em-man /\ -u-el shall come to you, O Israel.

Text: Combined from O Antiphons, 12th C.?; translated by John M. Neale, 1851, altered
Music: VENI EMMANUEL, LM with refrain; 15th C.; adapt. by Thomas Helmore, 1856

PSALMS & CANTICLES — go to the day of the week in WEEK III or IV

READING **LUKE 1:46-56**

Mary said, "My soul magnifies the Lord,
and my spirit is exulted in God my Savior,
Who looked on the humiliation
of the Lord's own handmaid.
For behold, from now on
all the generations will deem me blessed,
Because the Mighty One did great things to me.

Holy is the name and the mercy
to generations and generations,
the ones fearing the One,
Who with arm and might scattered
ones haughty in the understanding of their heart.
Who pulled down rulers from thrones,
and exalted humble ones,
Who filled hungering ones with good things
and sent rich ones away empty,
Who gave relief to servant Israel to remember mercy,
as spoken to our ancestors,
to Abraham and to his seed forever."
And Mary remained with her about three months,
and returned to her house.

RESPONSORY

Your light will come, Jerusalem...
...the Lord will dawn on you in radiant beauty.
The glory of the Lord you will see within you...

GOSPEL CANTICLE (**Canticle of Zechariah**) see page 451.

Antiphon ... The moment that your greeting
entered into my ears,
the baby in my womb leaped for joy.

MORNING PRAYER PETITIONS AND CLOSING PRAYER, see page 453.

ADVENT - December 22
EVENING

O come, O King of na-tions, migh-ty arc,
Au-then-tic joy of ev-'ry hu-man heart;
O Key-stone, true foun-da-tion to trust,
Come save us whom you fash-ion from the dust.
Re-joice! Re-joice! Em-man /\ -u-el shall come to you, O Israel.

Text: Combined from O Antiphons, 12th C.?; translated by John M. Neale, 1851, altered
Music: VENI EMMANUEL, LM with refrain; 15th C.; adapt. by Thomas Helmore, 1856

PSALMS & CANTICLES go to the day of the week in WEEK III or IV

READING **MALACHI 3:1-4,23-24**

See, I am sending my messenger
who will prepare a way before me;
then suddenly the Lord whom you seek
will come to his temple.
Even the messenger of the covenant you desire,
see him coming, says Adonai of Hosts.
But who can endure the day of his coming?
And who will stand when he appears
who is like the fire of the refiner
or the soap of the launderer?

And he will sit as a refiner purifying silver,
and he will purify the sons of Levi,
and he will refine them like the gold and the silver.
Then they will bring to Adonai
an offering of righteousness
and the offerings of Judah and Jerusalem
will be acceptable to Adonai as in days of time gone by,
as in years of old...
See, I am sending to you Elijah the prophet
before the day of Adonai comes, the great day of dread,
and he will turn hearts of parents to children
and hearts of children to their parents,
lest I come and strike doom on the land.

RESPONSORY Ps 85:7

Lord, show to us...

...your mercy and unfailing love.

And grant us your salvation...

GOSPEL CANTICLE (**Canticle of Mary**) see page 452.

Antiphon, Dec. 22 .. **O King** of all the nations,
the true joy of every human heart;
O Keystone
of the mighty arch of humanity,
come and save the creature
you fashioned from the dust.

EVENING PRAYER INTERCESSIONS AND CLOSING PRAYER, see page 453.

ADVENT - December 23
MORNING

O come, O come, Em-man/\-u-el,
And ran-som cap-tive Is\\-ra-el,
That mourns in lone-ly ex\-ile here
Until the Son of God/\ appear.
Re-joice! Re-joice! Em-man /\ -u-el shall come to you, O Israel.

O come, de-sire of all the na-tions, bind
In one the hearts and souls of hu-man-kind;
Come make our sad di-vis-ions to cease,
And be, Em-man-u-el, our King of Peace.
Re-joice! Re-joice! Em-man /\ -u-el shall come to you, O Israel.

Text: Combined from O Antiphons, 12th C.?; translated by John M. Neale, 1851, altered
Music: VENI EMMANUEL, LM with refrain; 15th C.; adapt. by Thomas Helmore, 1856

PSALMS & CANTICLES go to the day of the week in WEEK III or IV

READING **LUKE 1:57-66**

Now the time for Elizabeth to give birth was fulfilled, and she brought forth a son. Her neighbors and relatives heard that the Lord had shown her magnified mercy, and they rejoiced with her.
And it came to pass on the eighth day, they came to circumcise the child and

were calling him by the name of his father Zechariah.
And answering, his mother said,
"No, but he shall be called John."
And they said to her, "There is no one of your kindred
who is called by this name."
And they nodded to his father,
what he might wish him to be called.
And asking for a tablet he wrote saying,
"John is his name."
And they all marvelled. And his mouth and tongue
were opened instantly, and he spoke blessing God.
And fear came on all those dwelling round them,
and all these facts were talked over
in all the mountain country of Judea,
and all those hearing put them in their heart, saying,
"What then will this child be?"
For indeed the hand of the Lord was with him.

RESPONSORY

Your light will come, Jerusalem...
...the Lord will dawn on you in radiant beauty.
The glory of the Lord you will see within you...

GOSPEL CANTICLE (**Canticle of Zechariah**) see page 451.

Antiphon ... All that God promised to the virgin
through the message of the angel
has been accomplished.

MORNING PRAYER PETITIONS AND CLOSING PRAYER, see page 453.

ADVENT - December 23
EVENING

O come, de-sire of all the na-tions, bind
In one the hearts and souls of hu-man-kind;
Come make our sad di-vis-ions to cease,
And be, Em-man-u-el, our King of Peace.
Re-joice! Re-joice! Em-man /\ -u-el shall come to you, O Israel.

Text: Combined from O Antiphons, 12th C.?; translated by John M. Neale, 1851, altered
Music: VENI EMMANUEL, LM with refrain; 15th C.; adapt. by Thomas Helmore, 1856

PSALMS & CANTICLES go to the day of the week in WEEK IV

READING **GENESIS 49:2,8-10**

Assemble and listen, children of Jacob,
and listen to Israel your father:
Judah, your brothers will praise you;
your hand on the neck of your opponents,
the children of your father will bow to you.
Judah, lion cub, my son, you return from prey.
He crouches and lies like a lion and lioness.
Who rouses him?
The scepter will not depart from Judah,
nor the ruling staff from between his feet
until the one whose it is comes,
and to that one is the obedience of peoples.

RESPONSORY Ps 85:7

Lord, show to us...

...your mercy and unfailing love.

And grant us your salvation...

GOSPEL CANTICLE (**Canticle of Mary**) see page 452.

Antiphon, Dec. 23 .. **O Emmanuel**, king and lawgiver,
desire of the nations, Savior of all people,
come and set us free, Lord our God.

EVENING PRAYER INTERCESSIONS AND CLOSING PRAYER, see page 453.

ADVENT - December 24
MORNING

O come, O come, Em-man/\\-u-el,
And ran-som cap-tive Is\\\\-ra-el,
That mourns in lone-ly ex\\-ile here
Until the Son of God/\\ appear.
Re-joice! Re-joice! Em-man /\\ -u-el shall come to you, O Israel.

Text: Combined from O Antiphons, 12th C.?; translated by John M. Neale, 1851, altered
Music: VENI EMMANUEL, LM with refrain; 15th C.; adapt. by Thomas Helmore, 1856

PSALMS & CANTICLES go to Saturday Morning, WEEK IV, page 438

READING **2 SAMUEL 7:1-5,8b-12,14a,16**

After David the king was settled in his palace and Adonai gave him rest from all around being enemies, the king said to Nathan the prophet, "See me living in a palace of cedars while the ark of God remains inside the tent." And Nathan replied to the king, "All in your heart, go ahead and do, for Adonai is with you." In that night the word of Adonai came to Nathan to say, "You go tell my servant David that this Adonai says: 'Will you build for me a house for my dwelling?... I took you from the pasture after the flock, to be ruler over my people Israel. And I was with you in every place that you went and I cut off your enemies. Now I will make your name great, like the names of the great ones of the earth, and I will provide a place for my people and I will plant Israel so they can stay in their place and be disturbed no longer and sons and daughters of badness will not continue to oppress them as at the beginning. And from the day I appointed leaders over my people Israel, I will give you rest from all who would be your enemies. And Adonai declares to you that Adonai will establish a house for you. When your days are over and you rest with your ancestors, then I will raise up your offspring after you who will come from your bodies and I will establish his kingdom... I will be as father to him and he will be as son to me... Your house and your kingdom will endure to forever. Before your throne he will be established to forever.

RESPONSORY

Tomorrow will be the day of your salvation...
...the sinfulness of earth will be destroyed.
The Savior of the world will be our king...

GOSPEL READING **LUKE 1:67-79**

Antiphon . . . The time has come for Mary
to give birth to her firstborn Son.

And John's father Zechariah
was filled with the Holy Spirit and prophesied saying,
"Blessed be the Lord the God of Israel,
who visited and wrought redemption
for the people of God,
and raised a horn of salvation for us
in the house of David, the servant,
spoken through the mouth of the holy
from the age of the prophets,
salvation out of our enemies
and out of the hand of all the ones hating us,
to perform mercy with our fathers
and to remember God's holy covenent,
the oath sworn to Abraham our father,
to give us fearlessly
out of the hand of our enemies
having been delivered
to serve the Lord in holiness and righteousness
before the Lord all our days.

LUKE 1:67-79, continued

And you also, child,
will be called a prophet of the Most High
for you will go before the Lord to prepare his ways,
to give a knowledge of salvation to the people of God
by forgiveness of their sins,
because of the bowels of God's mercy on us,
whereby will visit a sun rising from the height,
to appear to those sitting in darkness
and in a shadow of death,
to guide our feet into a way of peace."

Antiphon . . . The time has come for Mary
to give birth to her firstborn Son.

MORNING PRAYER PETITIONS AND CLOSING PRAYER, see page 453.

A PRAYER BEFORE A MANGER SCENE

Loving Creator God,
let my gaze on this humble scene
of the fragrant glory of the Incarnation
be heard in my heart
as the touch of the gospel
and a taste of true peace.
Amen.

HINGE HOURS Psalter

Each liturgical year begins on
the Sunday nearest to November 30, the First Sunday of Advent.

The season of Advent concludes
when the season of Christmas begins,
the Vigil of the Solemnity of the Nativity
(Evening Prayer on December 24).

WEEK I
VIGIL OF SUNDAY
(Saturday Evening)

PSALM 4

Antiphon My God, be merciful to me
and hear my prayer.

When I call, answer me, righteous God.
From distress you give me relief.
Be merciful to me and hear my prayer.

Until when, human, will you shame the glory?
Until when will you love delusion and seek the lie?
Know that Adonai set apart the faithful for Adonai
and will hear when I call.

When you are angry, do not sin.
Search in your heart and on your bed, and be silent.
Offer sacrifices of goodness, and trust Adonai.

Many are asking,
"Who can show us good?
Adonai, let the light of your faces shine upon us."

You put joy in my heart, more joy
than when their grain and new wine abound.
In the peace of God's face I will lie down and sleep,
for you alone, Adonai, make me dwell in safety.

Traditional Doxology

Glory to the Father and to the Son
and to the Holy Spirit,
As it was in the beginning, is now,
and will be forever. Amen.

The antiphon is traditionally repeated:

My God, be merciful to me
and hear my prayer.

PSALM 141

Antiphon

Proclaim the good news among the nations:
Our God will come to save us.

Adonai, I call to you; be quick to come to me.
Hear my voice when I call to you.
May my prayer of incense be set before you,
lifting my hands in evening sacrifice.

Set guard, Adonai, over my mouth.
Keep watch over the door of my lips.
Let my heart not be drawn to evil matter,
to join in wicked deeds with their doers
or to eat of their delicacies.

Let the just person strike me with kindness
and rebuke me with oil on my head;
my head will not refuse this,
my prayer is ever against evil deeds.

PSALM 141, continued

Their rulers will drop over cliff edge;
they will learn that my words were well spoken:
"As a plower breaks up the earth
our bones were scattered at the mouth of Sheol."

But on you, Lord Adonai, are my eyes,
and in you I take refuge;
my self you do not give over to death.

Keep me from the hands of the snares
and from the traps of those doing evil.
When they fall together into their nets,
keep me in safety.

Glory...

Antiphon Proclaim the good news among the nations:
Our God will come to save us.

PSALM 142

Antiphon Know that the Lord is coming
and with all the saints;
that day will dawn with a wonderful light,
alleluia.

My voice cries to Adonai;
my voice asks for mercy from Adonai,
before whom I pour out my complaint,
before whom I tell my trouble.
When my spirit grows faint within me
then you know my way.

In the path where I walk they hid a snare for me.
Look right and see: the one with concern for me
has fled away from me for refuge;
there is no one who cares for my life.

I cry to you, Adonai, and say you are my refuge,
my portion in the land of the living.
Listen, El, to my cry, for I am in desperate need.

Rescue me from the strong ones pursuing me;
set my self free from prison to praise your name.
The righteous ones will gather about me
because you will be good to me.

Glory...

Antiphon Know that the Lord is coming
and with all the saints;
that day will dawn with a wonderful light,
alleluia.

PHILIPPIANS 2:6-11

Antiphon The Lord will come with mighty power;
all mortal eyes shall see the Lord.

Christ Jesus, subsisting in the form of God,
did not deem equality with God something to grab,
but emptied himself, taking the form of a slave,
becoming in human likeness.

And being found in human fashion,
he humbled himself,
becoming obedient until death,
and death on a cross.

And so God highly exalted him,
and gave to him the name above every name,
that in the name of Jesus every knee should bend,
of heavenly beings and earthly beings,
and beings under the earth;

And every tongue acknowledge
to the glory of God the Father
that Jesus Christ is Lord.

Glory…

Antiphon The Lord will come with mighty power;
all mortal eyes shall see the Lord.

WEEK I
RESURRECTION VIGIL

ISAIAH 33:2-10

Antiphon In Christ who rose from the dead
our hope of resurrection dawned.

Adonai, be gracious to us; for you we long;
be our strength in the mornings
and our salvation in times of distress.

At the voice of thunder peoples flee,
at your rising the nations scatter
and your plunder is harvested
as a harvesting by the young locust,
like a swarm of locusts pouncing.

Dwelling on the height, exalted is Adonai,
who will fill Zion with justice and righteousness,
who will be the sure foundation for your times,
the rich store of salvation, wisdom and knowledge;
fear of Adonai is the treasure.

Look! Their brave ones cry in the street,
envoys of peace in bitter weeping.
Highways are deserted, road travel ceases,
treaties are broken, cities are despised,
and no one is respected.

ISAIAH 33:2-10, continued

The land mourns and wastes away,
Lebanon withers in shame.
The Sharon is like the Arabah;
dropping are Bashan and Carmel.
"Now I will arise," says Adonai,
"Now I will be exalted,
now I will be lifted up."

Glory...

Antiphon In Christ who rose from the dead
our hope of resurrection dawned.

FOR SUNDAYS OF WEEK 1

MATTHEW 28:1-11,16-20

After the Sabbath,
the first day of the week drawing on,
Mary the Magdalene and the other Mary
came to view the grave.
And behold a great earthquake occurred,
for an angel of the Lord
descended out of heaven
and approaching
rolled away the stone and sat upon it.
His appearance was as lightning,
and his dress white as snow.
The guards, shaken from fear of him, became as dead.
The angel answered the women, saying,
"Fear you not;
for I know that you seek Jesus,
the one crucified.

He is not here,
for he was raised as he said.
Come see the place where he lay.
Go quickly and tell his disciples
that he was raised from the dead,
and behold he goes before you to Galilee.
There you will see him.
Behold, I have told you."
Going away from the tomb quickly,
with fear and great joy,
they ran to announce to his disciples.
Behold, Jesus met them saying, "Rejoice."
Approaching they held of his feet and worshipped him.
Jesus said to them,
"Fear you not;
go announce to my brothers
that they may go away into Galilee,
and there they will see me."
As they were going,
behold some of the guard coming into the city
announced to the chief priests
all the things that happened...
So the eleven disciples went to Galilee,
to the mountain where Jesus appointed them,
and seeing him they worshipped,
but some doubted.
And approaching, Jesus talked with them saying,
"All authority in heaven and on earth
has been given to me.

Go therefore, you disciples, to all the nations,
baptizing them in the name of the Father
and of the Son and of the Holy Spirit,
teaching them to observe all things
whatever I gave command to you.
And behold I am with you all the days
until the completion of the eon."

•

FOR SUNDAYS OF WEEK 5

LUKE 24:35-53

They related the things on the way
and how he was known by them
in the breaking of the bread.
These things being said by them,
he stood in their midst.
But becoming scared and terrified,
they thought they beheld a spirit.
He said to them,
"Why have you been and are being troubled?
And why do thoughts come up in your heart?
See my hands and my feet, that I am myself.
Feel me and see,
because a spirit has no flesh or bones
as you behold me having."
And yet disbelieving from their joy and marvelling,
he said to them,
"Have you any food here?"

LUKE 24:35-53, continued

They handed to him part of a broiled fish,
and taking he ate before them.
He said to them,
"These my words I spoke to you while yet with you,
of the need to be fulfilled
of all the things written concerning me
in the law of Moses and the prophets and the psalms."
Then he opened up their mind
to understand the scriptures,
and said to them,
"Thus it has been written:
the Christ to suffer
and to rise again out of the dead on the third day,
and in his name a proclamation
of repentance unto forgiveness of sin,
to all the nations beginning from Jerusalem.
You are witnesses of these things.
And behold I send forth on you
the promise of my Father,
but sit in the city until you are
clothed out of the height with power."
He led them out to Bethany,
and lifting up his hands he blessed them.
And it came to pass
that while he blessed them
he withdrew from them.
They returned to Jerusalem with great joy,
and were constantly in the temple blessing God.

•

WEEK I
SUNDAY MORNING

PSALM 1

Antiphon See how the cross of the Lord
stands revealed as the tree of life.

Blessings are on the human being
who stands not in wicked counsel,
who walks not on the path of sinners,
who sits not in the seat of mockers,
but rather delights in the law of Adonai
and meditates on it by day and by night.

This blessed one is like a tree
being planted by streams of water
which yields fruit in the season
and its leaf withers not
and prosperity finds what this one does.

Not so those who do wicked,
but rather like the chaff blown in the wind
those who do wicked
will be unable to stand in the judgment
nor sinners in the assembly of the righteous.

Adonai watches over the way of righteous ones
and wicked ways will perish.

Glory…

Repeat antiphon.

PSALM 63:1-8

Antiphon On that day sweet wine
will flow from the mountains,
milk and honey from the hills, alleluia.

God, you are my God; you I earnestly seek.
My soul, she thirsts for you,
my body, he longs for you,
as in a land with no water, dry and weary.

So in the sanctuary I saw you,
beheld you in your power and glory.
Your love is better than life itself;
my lips will glorify you.

So I will praise you in all the ways I am alive;
in your name I will lift up my hands.
As with fatness and richness,
my soul will be satisfied;
with singing lips my mouth will sing praise.

When I remember you on my bed,
through night watches I think of you,
you who are my help;
then in the shadow of your wings I sing.
My very self stays close to you;
your right hand upholds me.

Glory...

Antiphon On that day sweet wine
will flow from the mountains,
milk and honey from the hills, alleluia.

DANIEL 3 :57-90

Antiphon The mountains and hills will sing praise to God;
all the trees of the forest will clap their hands,
for he is coming,
the Lord of a kingdom to last forever.

Bless the Lord, all you works of the Lord,
exalt and sing praise to forever.
Angels of the Lord, bless the Lord,
You heavens, bless the Lord,
All you waters above the heavens, bless the Lord,
All you powers, bless the Lord,
Sun and moon, bless the Lord,
Stars of heaven, bless the Lord.

All you rain and dew, bless the Lord,
All you winds, bless the Lord,
You fire and heat, bless the Lord,
You ice and cold, bless the Lord,
You dews and falling snows, bless the Lord,
You snows and frosts, bless the Lord,
You nights and days, bless the Lord,
You light and darkness, bless the Lord,
You lightning and clouds, bless the Lord.

Let the earth bless the Lord,
exalt and sing praise to forever.
You mountains and hills, bless the Lord,
All things growing in the ground, bless the Lord,
You seas and rivers, bless the Lord,
You springs and rain, bless the Lord,
You sea monsters and all swimmers, bless the Lord,
All you birds of the air, bless the Lord,
All you wild beasts and cattle, bless the Lord,
You sons and daughters, bless the Lord.

O Israel, bless the Lord,
exalt and sing praise to forever.
You priests of the Lord, bless the Lord,
You servants of the Lord, bless the Lord,
You spirits and souls of the just, bless the Lord,
You holy and humble in heart, bless the Lord,
Hananiah, Azariah, and Mishael, bless the Lord,
exalt and sing praise to forever...

Give thanks to the Lord, who is good,
whose mercy endures to forever.
Bless the God of "gods"
all you who worship the Lord;
sing praise and give thanks to the One God
whose mercy endures to forever.

(*No doxology*)

Antiphon The mountains and hills will sing praise to God;
all the trees of the forest will clap their hands,
for he is coming,
the Lord of a kingdom to last forever.

PSALM 149:1-6,9c

Antiphon A great prophet will come to Jerusalem;
of that people he will make a new creation.

Hallelujah! Praise Adonai!

Sing to Adonai a new song,
praise in the assembly of saints.
Let Israel rejoice in their Maker,
let the people of Zion be glad in their King.

Let them praise the name
with dance, tambourine and harp.
Let them make music for Adonai
who delights in Adonai's people.

Adonai crowns humble ones with salvation.
Let the saints rejoice in honor,
Let them sing for joy on their beds...

Hallelujah! Praise Adonai!

Glory...

Antiphon A great prophet will come to Jerusalem;
of that people he will make a new creation.

WEEK I
SUNDAY EVENING

PSALM 91

Antiphon

Have no fear of terror at night;
in the shadow of the Almighty, find rest.

One who dwells in the shelter of Elyon,
in the shadow of Shaddai, will find rest.
I will say of Adonai, my refuge, my fortress:
in my God do I trust.

Surely the Lord will save you
from fowler snare, from deadly pestilence.
With the feather of the Lord you will be covered,
and under those wings you will find refuge,
shield and rampart, the faithfulness of the Lord.

You will have no fear of terror at night
nor of arrows flying by day,
of pestilence stalking in the darkness,
nor of plague that destroys at midday.

A thousand may fall at your side,
and ten thousand at your right hand;
near to you they will not come.

PSALM 91, continued

Observe with your eyes, simply watch;
punishment of wicked ones you will see.
Make Adonai, who is my refuge,
make Elyon your dwelling.

Harm will not befall you,
nor will disaster come near your tent.
God's own Angels, the Lord will command
to guard you in all of your ways.

In their hands they will lift you up;
your foot will not strike against the stone.
Upon lion and cobra you will tread,
you will trample the great lion and serpent.

"Because you love me, I will rescue you,
I will protect all who acknowledge my Name.
You will call upon me and I will answer.
I am with you in trouble;
I will deliver you and honor you.

In length of days I will satisfy you,
and show you my salvation."

Glory...

Antiphon Have no fear of terror at night;
in the shadow of the Almighty, find rest.

PSALM 110:1-6a,7

Antiphon Rejoice, daughter of Zion;
shout for joy, daughter of Jerusalem,
alleluia.

Adonai said to my Lord:
"Sit at my right hand
until I make enmity as a footstool for your feet."

A scepter of your might
Adonai will extend from Zion,
and rule in the midst of enmity!

Your troops are willing on the day of your battle.
In majesties of holiness from the womb of the dawn
to you is the dew of your youth.
Adonai swore and this mind will not change,
"You are a priest to forever
in the order of Melchizedek."

The Lord is at your right hand
and will crush kings on the day of wrath,
will judge the nations…,
and will drink from a brook on the way
with head lifted up because of all this.

Glory…

Antiphon Rejoice, daughter of Zion;
shout for joy, daughter of Jerusalem,
alleluia.

PSALM 114

Antiphon Christ our King will come to us,
the Lamb of God foretold by John.

When Israel came out from Egypt,
the house of Jacob
free from people of another tongue,
Judah became as God's sanctuary,
and Israel God's dominion.

The sea looked and fled, the Jordan turned back.
The mountains skipped like rams
and hills like a flock of lambs.

What to you, sea, that you fled?
Jordan, that you turned back?
Mountains, that you skipped like rams?
You hills, like a flock of lambs?

Tremble, earth, at the presences of the Lord!
Tremble at the presences of the God of Jacob,
the one turning the rock into pools of waters,
hard rock into springs of waters.

Glory…

Antiphon Christ our King will come to us,
the Lamb of God foretold by John.

REVELATION 19:1b,2a,5b,6b,7

Antiphon I am coming soon, says the Lord;
I will give to everyone
the reward his or her deeds deserve.

Alleluia! Praise the Lord!
Salvation and glory and power are to our God,
whose judgments are true and just.

Alleluia! Praise the Lord!
Praise our God, all you slaves of the Lord,
you small and you great, who hold God in awe.

Alleluia! Praise the Lord!
The Lord is reigning, our God, the Almighty.
Let us rejoice and let us exult,
and we will give the glory to the Lord.

Alleluia! Praise the Lord!
The day has come
for the marriage of the Lamb,
and the bride has prepared herself.

Glory...

Antiphon I am coming soon, says the Lord;
I will give to everyone
the reward his or her deeds deserve.

WEEK I
MONDAY MORNING

PSALM 9

Antiphon The Lord is a refuge for the oppressed,
a stronghold in times of trouble,
alleluia.

I will praise Adonai with all my heart;
I will tell of all the wonderful things.
I will be glad and rejoice in you,
I will sing praise to your name, Most High.

When enmity turns back
it stumbles before you
for you upheld my right and my cause;
you sat on the throne judging justly.

You rebuked nations, you destroyed wicked ways;
their name you blotted out to forever and ever.
Enmity is overtaken by endless ruin;
cities are uprooted and their memories perish.

Adonai reigns to forever,
set up on the throne for judgment
to judge the world in righteousness
and to govern peoples with justice.

Adonai is the refuge for the oppressed,
the stronghold in times of trouble.
Those who know your name will trust in you,
for you have never forsaken seekers of Adonai.

Sing praise to Adonai, enthroned in Zion.
Proclaim the deeds among the nations
for the One who can avenge bloodshed remembers
and does not ignore the cry of the afflicted.

Have mercy on me, Adonai,
and see the persecution by enmity.
Lift me up from the gates of death
that I may declare all of your praises
in the gates of your daughter Zion.
I will rejoice in your salvation.

Nations fell into the pit they dug;
in the net that they hid are their own feet caught.
Adonai is known in justice;
wicked ways are ensnared in their handiwork.

The nations forgetting God return to Sheol,
but the needy will not be forgotten
nor will the hope of the afflicted ever perish.

Arise Adonai; let not the human triumph.
Let the nations be judged in your presences.
Strike the nations, Adonai,
and let them know their humanity.

Glory…

Antiphon The Lord is a refuge for the oppressed,
a stronghold in times of trouble, alleluia.

PSALM 5

Antiphon

Lord, you hear my morning voice;
with my morning request before you,
I wait.

Give ear to my words, Adonai;
consider my sighing.
Listen to the sound of my cry for help,
for to you I pray, my King and my God.

Hear, Adonai, my morning voice;
with my morning request before you, I wait.

You are not pleased with evil,
nor can the doer of evil dwell with you.
The arrogant cannot stand before your eyes.
You hate when wrong is done, you destroy lies,
you abhor bloodshed and deceit.

By the greatness of your mercy, Adonai,
I will come into your house,
I will bow toward your holy temple in reverence.

Lead me in your justice, Adonai;
because of enmity
make straight before me your way.

Their mouth is not to be trusted,
their heart is destruction,
their throat an open grave,
and their tongue speaks deceit.

If you, God, declare them guilty
let their fall be by their intrigue;
let them be banished if they have sinned,
if they have rebelled against you.

But let all who take refuge in you be glad;
let them sing for joy forever.
You spread protection over them
that they may rejoice in you and love your name.

You bless the righteous, Adonai,
surrounding them with favor as a shield.

Glory...

Antiphon Lord, you hear my morning voice;
with my morning request before you,
I wait.

1 CHRONICLES 29:10b-13

Antiphon Now, our God,
we praise your name and your glory.

Praise be to you, Adonai, God of Israel,
our Father from everlasting to everlasting.

To you, Adonai, are the greatness and power
and glory and majesty and splendor
for all in the heavens and on the earth.

To you, Adonai, are the kingdom
and exaltation as head over all,
and wealth and honor from before you.

And you rule over all in your hand,
strength and power in your hand,
to exalt and give strength to all.

Now, our God, we give thanks to you
and praise your name and your glory.

Glory...

Antiphon Now, our God,
we praise your name and your glory.

PSALM 29

Antiphon Worship the Lord in the holy splendor.

Ascribe to Adonai, mighty ones.
Ascribe to Adonai glory and strength.
Ascribe to Adonai the glory of the name.
Worship Adonai in holy splendor.

The voice of Adonai over the waters,
the God of glory thunders.
Adonai over mighty waters,
the voice of Adonai in power,
the voice of Adonai in majesty,
the voice of Adonai breaking cedars,

Adonai breaks the cedars of Lebanon
and makes Lebanon skip like a calf
and Sirion like the son of a wild ox.

The voice of Adonai strikes flashes of lightning,
the voice of Adonai shakes the desert,
Adonai shakes the desert of Kadesh.

The voice of Adonai makes the deer give birth
and strips the forests bare,
and all in the temple cry, "glory."
Adonai sits over the flood
and King Adonai is enthroned to forever.

Adonai gives strength to the people;
Adonai blesses the people with peace.

Glory...

Repeat antiphon.

WEEK I
MONDAY EVENING

PSALM 7

Antiphon Lord, my God, save me;
I take refuge in you.

My God, Adonai, in you I take refuge;
save me and deliver me from all who pursue me.
Like lions they want to tear me up,
rip my self to pieces with no one to rescue me.

My God, Adonai, if I deserve this,
if there is guilt on my hands,
if I did wrong to one at peace with me
or if I robbed without cause from an enemy,
then let that one pursue my self
and overtake my life
and trample my honor to the ground;
let that one put me to sleep in the dust.

Arise, Adonai, rise up in your anger
against the rages of enmity.
Awake, my God, and decree your justice
and let the assembly of peoples surround you;
rule over us from the height.
Let Adonai be the judge of the peoples.

Judge me, Adonai, as you judge me in justice,
as you judge my integrity, Most High.
May violence end now and the righteous be secure;
search our minds and hearts, righteous God.
My shield, God Most High, saves the upright heart,
and judges each day with justice, threatening wrath.

If none repent, they will sharpen their sword
and bend their bow with string and make ready
with weapons of death and flaming arrows.
See, trouble is conceived and evil is pregnant,
then comes to birth disillusionment.

They dig holes and scoop them out
but fall into the pits they made.
Their trouble recoils on their heads;
on their heads their violence makes landing.

I give thanks for Adonai's righteousness
and sing praise to the name of Most High Adonai.

Glory...

Antiphon Lord, my God, save me;
I take refuge in you.

PSALM 11

Antiphon Blessed are you poor,
for yours is the kingdom of God.
Luke 6:20b

In Adonai I take refuge.
How can you say to my self,
"Flee, bird, to your mountain

for look, doers of bad now bend their bow,
they set their arrow on the string
to shoot from the shadow at the upright of heart.
When the foundations are destroyed,
what can the righteous do?"

Adonai is in the holy temple,
on Adonai's throne in the heavens
with eyes observing, examining
the sons and daughters of humanity.

Adonai examines the righteous,
hating in the soul the love of violence,
will rain onto wicked ways coal and sulphur on fire
and scorching wind, the lot of their cup,

for righteous is Adonai, loving justice;
we will see the faces of the upright One.

Glory...

Antiphon Blessed are you poor,
for yours is the kingdom of God.
Luke 6:20b

PSALM 15

Antiphon Blessed are the clean of heart,
for they shall see God.

Matthew 5:8

Adonai, who may dwell in your sanctuary?
Who may live on your holy hill?
One walking without blame, one doing the right,
speaking truth in that one's heart,

whose tongue does not slander,
who does no wrong to a neighbor,
who casts no slur on a mutual human,
in whose eyes vile acts are despised

while those who fear Adonai are honored,
whose sworn oath is not changed even to pain,
who lends money without usury,
and accepts no bribe against the innocent.

One faithful in these
will be unshaken to forever.

Glory...

Antiphon Blessed are the clean of heart,
for they shall see God.

Matthew 5:8

EPHESIANS 1:3-10

Antiphon God gives us a destiny as adopted sons and daughters through Jesus Christ himself.

Blessed be the God and Father
of our Lord Jesus Christ,
who has blessed us in Christ
with every spiritual blessing in the heavens.

God chose us in Christ
before the foundation of the world,
to be holy and free of blemish before him.

In love, God gave us a destiny:
as sons are adopted, through Jesus Christ himself,
in accord with the good pleasure of God's will
to the praise of the glory of grace
by which we are favored as God's beloved.

In Christ we have the redemption
through his blood, the forgiveness of sins,
in accord with the riches of his grace
which he made abound to us.

In all wisdom and intelligence
the mystery of God's will is made known to us
in accord with God's good pleasure and purpose:

A stewardship of the fullness of time,
heading up all things in Christ,
the things in the heavens and the things on earth.

Glory... Repeat antiphon.

WEEK I
TUESDAY MORNING

PSALM 10

Antiphon The Lord hears the desire of the afflicted,
defends the fatherless, and frees the oppressed,
alleluia.

Why, Adonai, do you stand at far off
and hide in times of the trouble?
In arrogance doers of bad hunt the weak;
they are caught in schemes they devise.

Doers of badness boast of what their hearts crave,
blessing the greedy and reviling Adonai.
In pride they point their nose away
and seek God in none of their thoughts.

Their haughty ways prosper at all times,
your laws are kept at a distance,
and they sneer at all their enemies.

They say to themselves
"I will not be shaken, but happy,
untroubled for generations to come."
Their mouths are full of curses and lies and threats,
trouble and bad things kept under their tongue.

PSALM 10, continued

They lie in wait to ambush villages and murder,
their secret eyes on the innocent victim.
They lie in wait to ambush like a lion,
undercover lying in wait to catch the helpless,
they catch and drag the helpless off in their nets.

The victims are crushed and collapse,
falling under their strength.
They say to themselves "El has forgotten,
with faces covered, and sees nothing anymore."

Arise, Adonai! God, lift up your hand!
Do not forget the helpless ones.
For why do those doing bad revile God and say,
to themselves, "God will not call an accounting"?

But you do see trouble and grief,
and consider taking the matter in hand;
to you the victims commit themselves,
to you, the One helping the fatherless.

Stop the arm of the doer of badness;
call to account lest bad things be kept secret.
Adonai is King forever and ever;
the nations will perish from Adonai's land.

You hear, Adonai, the desire of the afflicted;
you encourage their heart and open your ear
to defend the fatherless and the oppressed.
May humanity repeat no terror on the earth.

Glory...

Antiphon The Lord hears the desire of the afflicted,
defends the fatherless, and frees the oppressed,
alleluia.

PSALM 24

Antiphon The pure of heart with clean hands
ascend the hill of the Lord.

The earth and everything,
the world and all who are alive are to Adonai,
who founded the earth on the seas
and established the earth on the waters.

Who may ascend to the hill of Adonai?
And who may stand in the holy place?
The clean of hand and pure of heart
who do not lift the soul to an idol
and do not swear by falsehood
will receive the blessing from Adonai
and vindication from the God who saves.

Such is the generation of ones who seek,
who seek your faces, God of Jacob.

Lift up your heads, you gates;
be lifted up you ancient doors,
that the King of glory may come in.

Who is this King of glory?
Adonai, strong and mighty,
Adonai, mighty of battle.

Lift up your heads, you gates;
lift up, you ancient doors,
that the King of glory may come in.

PSALM 24, continued

Who is this King of glory?
Adonai Sabaoth is the King of glory.

Glory…

Antiphon The pure of heart with clean hands
ascend the hill of the Lord.

TOBIT 13:1b-8

Antiphon Blessed be God and the kingdom forever.

Blessed be God who lives forever
and the kingdom of our God,
who scourges but then has mercy,
casts down to the deepest grave
and brings up from the great abyss.
No one can escape this hand.

Israelites, acknowledge before the nations
God who has scattered you among them
and even there shown you great mercy.

Let God be exalted by every living being
because our Lord is our God,
our Father and God forever.

Though scourged for your iniquities,
mercy will be on you all;
you will be gathered from all the nations
among whom you have been scattered.

With all your heart and soul
turn with honesty to the Lord
who will turn the face to you and no longer hide.

See now what has been done for you,
and with full voice praise Adonai.
Bless the Lord of justice
and exalt the King of the ages.

In the land of my exile I acknowledge the Lord
and make known to a sinful nation
this power and majesty:
"Turn, you sinners, and do right before the Lord,
who may look upon you with favor and mercy."

My God, I will exalt you
and rejoice in the King of Heaven.
Let all speak of this majesty
in Jerusalem with exaltation.

Glory...

Antiphon Blessed be God and the kingdom forever.

PSALM 33

Antiphon The loyal heart will praise the Lord.

Sing joyfully to Adonai, righteous ones,
for praise is fitting for the upright.

Praise Adonai with a harp,
make music on the lyre of ten.
Sing a new song with skill
and play with a shout of joy.

For right is the word of Adonai
and all the faithful deeds done.
Loving righteousness and justice,
the earth is full of Adonai's unfailing love.

The heavens were made by the word of Adonai
and all their hosts by the breath of this mouth,
as one gathers in a heap the waters of the sea,
as one puts into the deep of the storehouses.

Let all the earth, let them fear,
let all alive in the world revere Adonai
who spoke and it came to be,
who commanded and it stood firm.

Adonai foils the plans of the nations
and thwarts the purposes of peoples.
The plan of Adonai stands firm to forever,
heartfelt purpose to generation and generation.

Blessed is the nation for whom Adonai is God,
the people chosen for this inheritance.
From the heavens Adonai looks down and sees
all sons and daughters of Adam and Eve,

and from the place of dwelling watches
all those alive on the earth.
The one who formed our heart
considers all our deeds.

No king is saved by the size of an army;
no warrior escapes by greatness of strength.
The horse is a vain hope for deliverance;
despite greatness of strength it cannot save.

See the eye of Adonai on those who place
their fear and hope in the unfailing love
that delivers them from death
and keeps them alive in the famine.

Our being waits for Adonai,
who is our help and our shield,
in whom our heart rejoices,
the holy name in whom we trust.

Adonai, may you rest on us your unfailing love
even as we hope in you.

Glory…

Antiphon The loyal heart will praise the Lord.

WEEK I
TUESDAY EVENING

PSALM 14

Antiphon

If we say we have no sin,
we deceive ourselves;
if we confess our sins,
God is faithful and forgiving. 1 John 1:8,9

The fool says in the heart, "There is no God."
They are corrupt, vile are their deeds;
no one is doing good.

Adonai looks down from the heavens
on sons and daughters of Adam and Eve
to see if one understands, if one is seeking God.

All turned aside together to corruption;
no one is doing good, not even one.

Will the doers of bad things never learn?
Devouring my people as they eat bread,
they do not call on Adonai.

There they are, in dread of dread,
for God is in the company of the righteous.
They frustrate the plans of the poor,
but in Adonai the poor find their refuge.

Who from Zion could bring the salvation of Israel?
When Adonai restores the fortune to the people,
let Jacob rejoice, let Israel be glad.

Glory...

Antiphon

If we say we have no sin,
we deceive ourselves;
if we confess our sins,
God is faithful and forgiving. 1 John 1:8,9

PSALM 20

Antiphon Now I know that the Lord saves
the Lord's own anointed.

May Adonai answer you on the day of distress.
May the name of the God of Jacob protect you,
send you help from the sanctuary,

support you from Zion,
remember all of your sacrifices,
accept your burnt offerings,
give to you as your heart desires,
and make all of your plans succeed.

We will shout for joy at your victory
and lift a banner in the name of our God;
may Adonai grant all your requests.

Now I know that Adonai saves the chosen anointed
and answers from the holy heavens
with a right hand of saving powers.

Some trust in the chariot
and others in the horses,
but we in the name of our God Adonai.
They kneel and they fall,
but we rise up and stand firm.

Adonai, save the king;
answer us on the day of our call.

Glory...

Repeat antiphon.

PSALM 21 :2-8,14

Antiphon Be exalted, Lord, in your strength;
we sing praise of your might.

In your strength, Adonai, the king rejoices,
and in your victory; how great is the joy!
You granted to him the desire of his heart
and did not withhold the request of his lips.

Indeed, you welcomed him with rich blessings
and placed on his head a crown of pure gold.
He asked from you life
and you gave length of days forever and ever.

Great is the glory through your victory;
on him you bestowed splendor and majesty.
Surely you granted him blessings for eternity
making him glad with joy in your presences,

for the king trusts in Adonai and will be unshaken
through the unfailing love of the Most High...
Be exalted, Adonai, in your strength!
We will sing and we will praise your might.

Glory...

Antiphon Be exalted, Lord, in your strength;
we sing praise of your might.

REVELATION 4:8b,11; 5:9,10,12,13b

Antiphon Lord, out of every tribe and tongue
and people and nation,
you made for our God
a kingdom and priests.

Worthy are you, our Lord and our God,
to receive the glory and honor and power,
because you have created all things,
and by your will all things were created and are.

Worthy are you to receive the scroll
and to open its seals,
because you were slain
and purchased for God by your blood
from every tribe and tongue and people and nation.

You made of them to our God
a kingdom and priests,
and they will reign over the earth.

Worthy is the Lamb, slain to receive
the power and riches and wisdom and strength
and honor and glory and blessing.

Glory…

Antiphon Lord, out of every tribe and tongue
and people and nation,
you made for our God
a kingdom and priests.

WEEK I
WEDNESDAY MORNING

PSALM 18:2-30

Antiphon I love you, Lord, my deliverer,
alleluia.

I love you, Adonai, my strength,
my rock Adonai, my fortress and deliverer;
in my God and Rock I take refuge,
my shield and horn, my salvation and stronghold.

I call out praise to Adonai
and am saved from enmity.

They tangled me in cords of death
and overwhelmed me in torrents of destruction.
Cords of Sheol coiled around me
and snares of death confronted me.

In my distress I called "Adonai,"
I cried for help from my God,
who heard from the temple my voice;
my cry went into those ears.

The earth trembled and quaked
and foundations of mountains shook
and trembled because of anger.
Smoke rose from the nostrils
and fire from the mouth consumed blazing coals.

PSALM 18:2-30, continued

The heavens parted
and dark clouds came down under the feet.
Mounted on the cherub,
flying and soaring on wings of wind,
a canopy of darkness covered all around,
dark waters in the clouds of the skies.

From the brightness of the presence
the clouds advanced hailstone and lightning bolts.
Adonai thundered from the heavens,
the voice of the Most High resounding
as hailstone and lightning bolts.

Arrows shot, scattering them all;
with great lightning bolts they are routed.
Valleys of waters were exposed and laid bare,
foundations of earth at your rebuke.

At the blast of the breath of your nostril, Adonai,
you reached from on high and took hold of me
and drew me out from the deep waters;
you rescued me from enmity
and from powerful foes,
for they were too strong for me.

They confronted me in the day of my disaster
but Adonai was my support,
brought me out to the spacious place,
and rescued me because of delight in me.

Adonai dealt with me as my ways are righteous,
rewarded me as my hands are clean,
for I kept to the ways of Adonai.
Indeed all of God's laws are before me
and I did not turn from those decrees.

Blameless before God, I kept myself from sin
and seen by the eyes of Adonai I am rewarded
as my ways are right and my hands are clean.

You show yourself faithful to the faithful,
to the blameless you show yourself blameless,
and to the pure you show yourself pure,

but to the crooked you show yourself shrewd,
for you save humble people
but bring low the eyes of the haughty.

Indeed you make my lamp burn;
my God Adonai makes light in my darkness.
Indeed with you I can advance against troops,
with my God I can scale a wall.

Glory...

Antiphon I love you, Lord, my deliverer,
alleluia.

PSALM 36

Antiphon Lord, in your light we see light.

An oracle of sin in the midst of my heart:
There is no fear of God in the eyes of a sinner,
whose own eyes are full of self-flattery,
who hates to detect sin.

Words of this mouth are wicked and deceitful:
Ceasing to be wise or do good,
this one plots evil while still in bed
and commits to a course not good
and rejects nothing that is wrong.

Adonai, to the heavens is your love
and your fidelity to the skies.
Your righteous might is like the mountains,
your justice deep and great;
human and beast you preserve, Adonai.

How priceless is your unfailing love.
High ones and humans find refuge
in the shadow of your wings.

They feast on the abundance of your house;
in the river of your delights you give them drink.
With you is the fountain of life,
and in your light we see light.

Continue your love to those who know you
and your righteousness to the upright of heart.
Let the foot of pride not come to me
nor the hand of wicked ways drive me away.

See, doers of evil lie fallen;
they are thrown down, unable to rise.

Glory...

Antiphon Lord, in your light we see light.

JUDITH 16:1,13-15

Antiphon O Lord, you are great and glorious,
wonderful in strength, invincible.

Begin a song to my God with timbrels;
sing to my Lord with cymbals.
Sing to my Lord a new song;
exalt and acclaim the name.

I will sing to my God a new song;
O Lord, you are great and glorious,
wonderful in strength and unbeatable.

Let your every creature serve you,
for you spoke, and they were made.
You sent forth your spirit, and they were created;
no one can resist your word.

Mountain foundations are shaken by waters
and rocks melt like wax at your glance.
But to those who fear you, you show mercy.

Glory...

Antiphon O Lord, you are great and glorious,
wonderful in strength, invincible.

PSALM 47

Antiphon Sing praises to God, sing praise.

All you nations, clap your hands!
Shout to God with cries of joy!
How awesome, Most High Adonai.

The great King over all the earth
subdued nations under us
and peoples under our feet,
and chose for us an inheritance,
the pride of Jacob the beloved.

God ascended with shouts of joy,
Adonai amid sound of trumpet.
Sing praises to God, sing praises.
Sing praises to our King, sing praises.

For God, King of all the earth, sing praises.
God reigns over the nations,
God sits on the holy throne.

Nobles of nations assemble,
the people of the God of Abraham.
God, shield of the earth, is greatly exalted.

Glory…

Antiphon Sing praises to God, sing praise.

WEEK I
WEDNESDAY EVENING

PSALM 17

Antiphon Lord, hold my steps to your paths.

Hear, Adonai, a righteous plea; listen to my cry.
Give ear to my prayer, from lips without deceit.
May my vindication come from you;
may my eyes see right things.

You probe and examine my heart in the night,
you test me and will find nothing.
By resolve my mouth will not sin.

By the word of your lips
my human deeds are kept from violent ways.
Holding my steps to your paths my feet did not slip.

I call on you, El, for you will answer me.
Give your ear to me and hear my prayer.
Show the wonder of your great saving love,
at your right hand those taking refuge from foes.

PSALM 17, continued

Keep me as the apple daughter of your eye.
You hide me in the shade of your wings
from those who assail me in enmity,
surrounding around my life.
They close their callous hearts,
they speak their arrogant mouth.

Now they surround our tracks;
their eyes are alert, ready to throw to the ground.
They are like a lion, hungry to tear prey,
like a great lion crouching undercover.

Rise up, Adonai!
Confront and bring down their ways.
Rescue my self by your sword, Adonai,
by your hand from humans,
humans of the world whose reward is this life.

As for those who are cherished by you,
their belly is full, sons and daughters are plenty,
and they store up their wealth for their children.

In justice, I will see your faces
and be satisfied waking up to your likeness.

Glory...

Antiphon Lord, hold my steps to your paths.

PSALM 27

Antiphon The Lord is my light and my salvation;
Whom shall I fear?

Adonai is my light and my salvation.
Whom shall I fear?
Adonai is the stronghold of my life.
Of whom shall I be afraid?

When people acting evil advance
against me to devour my flesh,
when enmity and foes go against me,
they will stumble and fall.

Though an army besiege against me,
my heart will not fear.
Though war break out against me,
in this I will be confident.

One thing I ask of Adonai:
to seek and to dwell in Adonai's house,
to gaze on Adonai's beauty
all the days of my life
as a seeker in the temple.

I will be kept safely dwelling,
hidden in the shelter of the tabernacle,
on the day of trouble set high upon rock.

PSALM 27, continued

Then will my head be exalted above enmity,
and I will sacrifice at the tabernacle
the sacrifice of shouts of joy.

I will sing and make music to Adonai.
Hear, Adonai, my voice calling;
be merciful; answer me.
To you my heart says, "My face seeks you."

Your faces, Adonai, I will seek.
Hide not your faces from me;
turn not away from your servant in anger.

You are my help;
neither reject nor forsake me,
God of my salvation.
Even if my father and my mother forsake me,
you, Adonai, will receive me.

Teach me your way, Adonai,
and lead me through oppression to straight paths.
Do not give me over to the desire
of foes who rise with false witnesses
and breathers of violence.

Still I am confident: I will see
the goodness of Adonai in the land of the living.
Wait for Adonai!
Be strong and strengthen your heart.
And wait for Adonai!

Glory...

Antiphon The Lord is my light and my salvation;
Whom shall I fear?

PSALM 28:1-3,6-9

Antiphon My heart trusts in the Lord
and I am helped.

To you I call, my Rock Adonai,
turn not to me a deaf ear.
For if you remain silent, away from me,
then I will be like one going into the pit.

Hear the sound of my cries for mercy
calling to you for help as I lift my hands
toward the Holy Place of your Holiness.

Do not drag me away with those who do bad,
who speak cordiality with their neighbors
but with malice in their heart.

Praised be Adonai,
who heard the sound of my cries for mercy.
Adonai, my strength and my shield,
in whom my heart trusts,
I am helped and my heart leaps for joy
and in my song I will give thanks.

Adonai is the strength
and the saving fortress of the anointed.
Save your people! Bless your inheritance!
Be their shepherd and carry them to forever!

Glory...

Antiphon My heart trusts in the Lord
and I am helped.

COLOSSIANS 1:12-20

Antiphon He is the firstborn of all creation;
he is before all things
and in him all things hold together.

Give joyful thanks to the Father who made you fit
for your part of the lot of the saints in light,

who delivered us out of the authority of darkness
and transitioned us into the kingdom of the beloved Son,
in whom we have redemption, the forgiveness of our sins.

The Son is the image of the invisible God,
the firstborn of all creation.
In him all things were created,
in the heavens and on the earth,
the visible and the invisible,
whether thrones, lordships, rulers or authorities.

All things have been created through him and for him.
He is before all things,
and in him all things hold together.

He is the head of the body, the church,
and the beginning, the firstborn from the dead,
so that in all things he may hold the first place.

In him all the fullness was well pleased to dwell,
and through him reconciliation to himself of all things,
things on earth and things in the heavens,
making peace through the blood of his cross.

Glory...

Antiphon He is the firstborn of all creation;
he is before all things
and in him all things hold together.

WEEK I
THURSDAY MORNING

PSALM 18:31-51

Antiphon

Adonai is alive; may our Rock be exalted,
the God of our salvation,
alleluia.

The ways of God are perfect,
the word of Adonai is flawless,
a shield for all who need refuge.
For who is God besides Adonai?
And who is the Rock except our God?

God arms me with strength,
makes perfect my way,
makes my feet like the deer
and makes me to stand on my heights,
training my hands for the battle;
my arms can bend a bow of bronze.

You give to me your shield of victory,
your right hand sustains me,
and in stooping you make me great.
You broaden my path beneath me
so my ankles do not turn.

I pursued enemies and overtook them
and did not turn back until their defeat…
They fell beneath my feet.

You armed me with strength for the battle
and made the adversity bow at my feet.
You turned back enmity
and brought defeat to foes.

They cried for help, but no one saved them.
Adonai did not answer them.
I beat them as dust on surfaces of wind;
like mud in the streets I poured them out.

You delivered me from attacks of people,
you made me as a head of nations;
people I knew not are subject to me.

Hearing me in their ear they obey;
sons and daughters of foreigners cringe before me.
They lose heart
and they tremble from their strongholds.

Adonai is alive and praised;
may my Rock be exalted, the God of my salvation.
God gives victory to me
and subdues nations under me,

saving me from enmity,
exalting me above foes,
and rescuing me from violence.
For this I will praise Adonai among the nations,
and to your name I will sing praise.

You make great victories of your king
and show unfailing kindness to David your anointed
and his descendants to forever.

Glory... Repeat antiphon.

PSALM 57

Antiphon

Awake, my soul;
awake the harp and lyre;
I will awaken dawn.

Have mercy on me, God, have mercy on me,
for in you my soul takes refuge
and in the shade of your wings I take refuge
until disasters pass.

I cry out to God Most High,
to El who fulfills me,
who sends from the heavens and saves me
and rebukes the one pursuing me.

God sends love and fidelity to my self;
in the midst of ravenous lions I lie,
in the midst of human beings with teeth and spear
and arrows and tongues, their sharp swords.

Be exalted, God, above the heavens,
your glory over all the earth.

For my feet they spread a net
and my self was bowed down.
Before me they dug a pit
and fell inside it themselves.

My heart is steadfast, Elohim, my heart is steadfast;
I will sing and make music.
Awake, my liver! Wake up the harp and the lyre;
I will wake up the dawn.

I will praise you among the nations, Lord;
I will sing of you among the peoples,
for great to the heavens is your love
and to the skies is your fidelity.

Be exalted above the heavens, God,
your glory over all the earth.

Glory...

Antiphon

Awake, my soul;
awake the harp and lyre;
I will awaken dawn.

JEREMIAH 31:10-14

Antiphon My people will be filled with my bounty,
declares the Lord.

Hear, nations, the word of Adonai;
proclaim it to distant coastlands and say:
"The One who scattered Israel
will gather them and watch them
as one who is shepherd to a flock."

For Adonai will ransom and redeem Jacob
from the hand of those with more strength.

They will come and they will shout
up on the height of Zion
and they will rejoice in the bounty of Adonai,
the grain and new wine and oil,
and younglings of the flock and herd;
and they themselves like a well-watered garden
will sorrow no more, not again.

Then the maiden will be glad in dance,
and young men together with the old.
I will turn their mourning into gladness;
I will comfort them and give joy instead of sorrow.
I will satisfy with abundance the self of the priests
and my people will be filled with my bounty,
declares Adonai.

Glory...

Antiphon My people will be filled with my bounty,
declares the Lord.

PSALM 48

Antiphon Great is the Lord, greatly being praised
in the city of our God.

Great is Adonai, greatly being praised
in the city of our God, on the holy mountain,
beautiful loft, the joy of all the earth,

Mount Zion, the upmost heights,
sacred mountain, the city of the Great King.
God in the citadels is shown as a fortress when,
see, the kings join forces and advance together.

They saw, were astounded, and fled in terror;
trembling seized them, pain like a woman in labor.
By the east wind you destroyed ships of Tarshish;

just as we heard, so we saw in the city
of Adonai Sabaoth, in the city of our God.
God makes her secure to forever.

In your temple we meditate on your unfailing love.
Like your name, God, so your praise
goes to the ends of the earth;

your right hand is filled with justice.
Mount Zion rejoices because of your judgments;
the villages of Judah are glad.

Walk about Zion! Go around! Count her towers!
Consider at heart her ramparts! View her citadels!

So that you may tell to the next generation:
This God, our God, forever and ever
will guide us even to the end.

Glory…

Antiphon Great is the Lord, greatly being praised
in the city of our God.

WEEK I
THURSDAY EVENING

PSALM 25

Antiphon Turn to me, Lord,
and be gracious in my lonely affliction.

To you, Adonai, I lift up my soul;
in you, my God, I trust;
let me not be shamed
and let enmity not triumph over me.
Indeed all who hope in you will not be shamed;
shamed will be those doing defenseless treachery.

Show me your ways, Adonai; teach me your paths.
Guide me in your truth and teach me,
for you are my saving God;
you are my hope all the day.

Remember your mercies, Adonai,
and your loves, for they are from of old.
The sins of my youth and rebellious ways
you do not remember, as you are loving.

You do remember me, for you are good, Adonai.
Good and upright is Adonai,
who instructs sinners in the way,
guides humble ones in rightness,
and teaches the way to the humble.

All the ways of Adonai are loving and faithful
for those who keep the covenant demands.
For the sake of your name, Adonai,
now you forgive my iniquity, great as it is.

Who is the human who fears Adonai?
The one being instructed in the Lord's chosen way,
whose life will be days spent in prosperity,
whose descendants will inherit the land,
the confidence of Adonai is with those thus fearing;
the covenant is made known to them.

My eyes are ever on Adonai,
who will release my feet from the snare.
Turn to me! Be gracious to me!
For I am lonely and afflicted.

Troubles of my heart have multiplied;
free me from my anguish!
Look upon my affliction and distress!
Take away all of my sins!

PSALM 25, continued

See the enmity,
the increase of fierce hate!
Guard my life! Rescue me!
Let me not be shamed, for I take refuge in you.
May integrity and uprightness protect me
because I hope in you.

Redeem Israel, God, from all our troubles.

Glory…

Antiphon Turn to me, Lord,
and be gracious in my lonely affliction.

PSALM 30

Antiphon Lord my God,
I cried to you for help and you healed me.
I will thank you to forever.

I will exalt you, Adonai, for you lifted me
and did not let enmity gloat over me.

Adonai, my God, I cried to you for help
and you healed me.
Adonai, you brought my self up from Sheol;
you spared me from going into the pit.

Sing to Adonai, you saints!
Sing praise to the holy name!
One moment in anger: lifetimes in the Lord's favor;
in the night weeping remains,
but in the morning rejoicing

when I said in my security,
I will be unshaken to forever.
In your favor, Adonai,
you made my mountain stand firm;
you hid your faces and I was dismayed.

To you, Adonai, I called
and to you, Lord, I cried for mercy.
What would be the gain in my destruction?
What is gained if I go into the pit?

Will the dust praise you?
Will the dust proclaim your fidelity?
Hear, Adonai! Be merciful to me!
Be my one helper, Adonai!

You turned my wailing into dancing for me;
you removed my sackcloth and clothed me in joy
so that my heart may sing to you, and not be silent.
My God Adonai, I will thank you to forever.

Glory...

Antiphon

Lord my God,
I cried to you for help and you healed me.
I will thank you to forever.

PSALM 32

Antiphon

Blessed are human beings
whose sin the Lord counts not,
where transgressions are forgiven.

Blessed is the one forgiven of transgression,
who was covered with sin.
Blessed is the human
against whom Adonai does not count sin,
and in whose spirit there is no deceit.

When I kept silent, my bones wasted away
through my groaning all day.
For by day and night your hand was heavy upon me;
my strength was sapped as in summer heat.

I acknowledged my sin to you,
and did not cover up my iniquity;
I said I will confess my transgressions to Adonai
and you forgave the guilt of my sin.

For this let every godly one pray to you
at the time to find you.
Surely the rising of mighty waters
will not reach this one.
You are the hiding place for me;
you will protect me from trouble
and surround me with deliverance song.

I will instruct you and I will teach you
and counsel you in the way you should go;
My eye is over you.

Do not be like a horse,
like your mule with no understanding;
by bit and bridle and harness they are controlled
or else they will not even come to you.

Many woes have the bad doers,
but the truster in Adonai
is surrounded in unfailing love.

Rejoice in Adonai! Righteous ones, be glad!
And sing, all you upright of heart!

Glory...

Antiphon

Blessed are human beings
whose sin the Lord counts not,
where transgressions are forgiven.

REVELATION 11:17-18, 12:10-12a

Antiphon Now have come the salvation, the power,
and the kingdom of our God.

We thank you, Lord God Almighty,
the One who is and who was;
you have taken your great power and reign.

The nations raged and your anger came,
and the time to judge the dead
and to reward your slaves and prophets,
the saints, and those fearing your name,
the small and the great...

Now have come the salvation and power
and kingdom of our God
and the authority of Christ.
The accuser of our brothers and sisters was cast,
accusing them before our God day and night.

Their victory was because of the blood of the Lamb
and by the word of their witness.
They loved their life into their death,
and so be glad, you heavens,
and all you dwelling in them.

Glory...

Antiphon Now have come the salvation, the power,
and the kingdom of our God.

WEEK I
FRIDAY MORNING

PSALM 35:1-2c,3c,9-19,22-23,27-28

Antiphon
Awake, and rise to my defense;
my God and Lord, contend for me;
alleluia.

Contend, Adonai, with my contenders!
Restrain those who would attack!
Take up shield and buckler and arise to my aid!...
Say to my soul, "I am your salvation."...

Then my soul will rejoice in Adonai
and take delight in salvation.
All of my bones will exclaim, "Adonai!
Who, like you, rescues the poor from the strong?
Or the poor and the needy from the robbers?"

Ruthless witnesses come forward;
on things I do not know they question me.
They repay me evil for good; forlorn is my soul.

Yet when they were ill I clothed myself in sackcloth
and humbled myself with fasting
when my prayer had returned
to my breast unanswered.
As a friend and a sibling I went about weeping,
bowing down like a grieving mother.

PSALM 35, continued

But they took glee at my stumbling
and they gathered and gathered attackers
and did not cease to slander me unaware,
an ungodly circle of mockers
gnashing their teeth against me.

Until when, Lord? How long will you look on?
Rescue my life from the ravages,
my precious life from the lions.
I will give you thanks in the great assembly;
among people thronging I will praise you.

Let enmity neither gloat without cause or reason
nor wink the eye at me...

You have seen, Adonai; be not silent.
Be not far from me, Lord.
Awake!, my God and Lord,
and rise to contend to my defense.
Vindicate me in your righteousness, Adonai...

May those who delight in my vindication
shout and be glad and always say,
"May Adonai be exalted,
  who delights in the well being of the servant."
And my tongue will speak your righteousness
and praise of you all the day.

Glory...

Antiphon Awake, and rise to my defense;
my God and Lord, contend for me;
alleluia.

PSALM 51

Antiphon Lord, open my lips
and my mouth will declare your praise.

Have mercy on me, God,
in accord with your unfailing love;
in accord with the greatness of your compassion
blot out my transgressions.

Wash me of my many iniquities
and cleanse me from my sin,
for I know my transgressions
and my sin is before me always.

Against you yourself I sinned;
what I did is evil in your eyes.
You are proven right when you speak
and justified when you judge.
Surely we are sinners from birth,
from conception in a mother's womb.

Surely you desire truth in our inner parts;
in my inmost place you teach me wisdom.
You cleanse me with hyssop and I will be clean;
you wash me and I will be whiter than snow...

You let me hear joy and gladness;
let the bones you let be crushed now rejoice.
Hide your faces from my sins
and blot out all my iniquities.

PSALM 51, continued

A pure heart create in me, God!
Renew inside me a spirit to be steadfast.
Do not cast me from your presences,
nor take from me your Holy Spirit.

Restore to me the joy of your salvation
and sustain in me a willing spirit.
I will teach transgressors your ways
and sinners will turn back to you.

Save me from bloodguilt, God,
God of my salvation;
my tongue will sing of your righteousness.
Lord, open my lips
and my mouth will declare your praise.

Sacrifices give you no delight;
I could bring a burnt offering,
but it would give you no pleasure.
The sacrifices, God, you will not despise
are a broken spirit and a contrite heart.

Make Zion prosper in your pleasure,
and build up the walls of Jerusalem.
Then you will delight in the sacrifice of the just,
burnt offerings and whole offerings,
bulls offered on your altar.

Glory…

Antiphon Lord, open my lips
and my mouth will declare your praise.

ISAIAH 45:15-25

Antiphon: God fashioned and made
and formed the earth
creating it to be not an empty waste
but to be inhabited.

Truly, God, you hide yourself,
Saving God of Israel.
Makers of idols will know shame and disgrace,
all going off together in disgrace.

Israel will be saved by Adonai, salvation everlasting.
You will not know shame or disgrace to the ages.

For this says Adonai, the one creating the heavens,
God who fashioned and made
and formed the earth,
creating it to be not an empty waste,
but formed to be inhabited,

"I am Adonai, and there is no other.
Not in secret did I speak,
from some place in a dark land,
not saying to descendants of Jacob,
'seek me in vain.'
I, Adonai, speak truth and delare right things.

Gather together and come!
Assemble together, fugitives of the nations.
Those who carry idols of wood do not know:
they are praying to no-gods that cannot save.

ISAIAH 45:15-25, continued

Declare and present! Let them counsel together!
Who foretold this from long ago?
Who declared this from the distant past?
Not I, Adonai? There is no god apart from me,
God righteous and Saving; there is none but me.

Turn to me and be saved, all you ends of the earth,
for I am God and there is no other.

By myself I swore integrity out of my mouth,
the word that will not be revoked.

Indeed, in front of me every knee will bow,
and every tongue will swear, and say,
'In Adonai alone are justice and strength,'

to whom will come and be shamed
all who have raged otherwise."
In Adonai they will be found righteous
and all the descendants of Israel will exult.

Glory...

Antiphon: God fashioned and made
and formed the earth
creating it to be not an empty waste
but to be inhabited.

PSALM 100

Antiphon Come before the Lord
with joyful song.

Shout for joy to Adonai, all you earth!
Serve Adonai with gladness!
Come into the presence with joyful song.

Know that Adonai is God, who made us,
whose people we are,
in whose pasture we are the sheep.

Enter the gates with thanksgiving,
go into the courts with praise!
Give thanks and give praise to the Name!

Good is Adonai, and loving to forever,
and faithful through generations and generation.

Glory…

Antiphon Come before the Lord
with joyful song.

WEEK I
FRIDAY EVENING

PSALM 26

Antiphon I trust in the Lord;
I do not waver.

Vindicate me, Adonai,
for I have walked blameless in my life
and in Adonai I trusted without waver.

Test me, Adonai! And try me!
Examine my heart and my mind!
For your love is before my eyes
and I walk in your truth.

I do not sit with humans of deceit
nor consort with hypocrites.
I abhor the assembly of those who do evil
and do not sit with those who do wicked.

I wash my hands in innocence
and go about your altar, Adonai,
to proclaim a voice of praise
and to tell of all your wonderful deeds.

Adonai, I love the living place of your house,
the dwelling place of your glory.

Take not my soul away with sinners
nor my life with people doing bloody things,
those who scheme in their hands
with their right hand full of bribes.

But I walk blameless in my life.
Redeem me! Be merciful to me!
My foot stands on level ground;
in great assemblies I will praise Adonai.

Glory...

Antiphon I trust in the Lord;
I do not waver.

PSALM 41

Antiphon Lord, have mercy on me
and heal my being.

Blessed is the one who gives regard to the weak.
In the time of trouble Adonai will deliver.
Adonai will protect that one's life,
preserve it blessed in the land,
and give no surrender to the desire of foes.
Adonai will sustain on the sickbed,
and restore on that bed from all illness.

PSALM 41, continued

Adonai, have mercy on me!
Heal my self for I have sinned against you!
Enmity asks in malice:
"When will that one die and the name perish?"
When they come to see me,
they speak with false hearts, gather slander,
and then go out to the outside to speak.

Together against me they whisper,
imagining the worst for me:
"A vile disease has set in;
  that one will not recover."
Even my close friend has lifted the heel against me,
the human being I trusted, who ate my own bread.

But you, Adonai, have mercy on me
and raise me up that I may repay them.
In this I know that you are pleased with me,
for enmity does not triumph over me;
in my integrity you hold me up
and set me in your presences to forever.

Praised be Adonai, God of Israel,
from everlasting to the everlasting.
Amen and amen.

Glory...

Antiphon

Lord, have mercy on me
and heal my being.

PSALM 46

Antiphon The Lord of hosts is with us,
the God of Jacob a fortress to us.

God is our refuge and strength,
our help in troubles, ever present.
And so we will not fear,
even if earth were to give way,
even if mountains were to fall
into the heart of the sea,
even if sea waters foam
or mountains quake with that surging.

A river has streams that make glad God's city,
the holy dwelling place of the Most High.
God is inside her and she will not fall.
God will help her at the break of day.
Nations are in uproar, kingdoms fall;
the earth melts at the voice of God.

Adonai Sabaoth is with us;
the God of Jacob is our fortress.

Come and see the works of Adonai,
the desolations brought on the earth:
making wars to cease to the ends of the earth,
breaking the bow and shattering the spear
and burning with fire the chariot and shield.

"Be still! And know that I am God.
I will be exalted among the nations;
I will be exalted on the earth."

PSALM 46, continued

Adonai Sabaoth is with us;
the God of Jacob is our fortress.

Glory...

Antiphon The Lord of hosts is with us,
the God of Jacob a fortress to us.

REVELATION 15:3b-4

Antiphon All the nations will come
and worship before you,
Lord God Almighty.

Great and wonderful are your works,
Lord God Almighty.
Just and true are your ways,
King of the nations.

Who will not fear, O Lord,
or glorify your name?

Only you are holy.
All the nations will come and worship before you;
your ordinances are shown to all.

Glory...

Antiphon All the nations will come
and worship before you,
Lord God Almighty.

WEEK I
SATURDAY MORNING

PSALM 105

Antiphon

Look to the Lord,
the strength of the Lord;
seek always the faces of the Lord.

Hallelujah! Praise Adonai!
Give thanks to Adonai; call on the name.
Make known among the nations the Lord's deeds!

Glory be to the holy name;
let the heart of the seeker of Adonai rejoice.
Look to Adonai, to the strength;
seek always the faces of the Lord.

Remember the deeds of wonder done,
the miracles and the judgments mouthed,
you descendants and servants of Abraham,
you chosen ones of Jacob.

Adonai is our God, judge in all the earth,
remembering the covenant to forever
commanded for a thousand generations,
the word made with Abraham and the oath to Isaac

PSALM 105, continued

confirmed to Jacob as a decree,
to Israel as an everlasting covenant:
"I will give to you land of Canaan,
  a portion of your inheritance."

When they were few, few in numbers,
with strangers in their midst,
then they wandered from nation to nation,
from one kingdom to another people.

No one was allowed to oppress them
and for their sake kings were rebuked:
"Do not touch my anointed ones;
  do not harm my prophets."

Famine was allowed onto the land
and the king's food supply was destroyed.
A man Joseph was sent before them,
sold as a slave;
they bruised his foot with the shackle

and his neck entered the irons
till the time foretold of him came to pass.
The word of Adonai proved him true.
The king sent for him and released him;

the ruler of the peoples set him free
and made him master of his household
and ruler over all his possessions
to discipline the princes as was his pleasure
and to teach the elders.
Then Israel entered Egypt;
Jacob lived as an alien in the land of Ham.

This people became very numerous,
more fruitful than their foes.
The hearts of the rulers were turned to hate
and conspired against this servant people.

Moses was sent as servant of the Lord
and Aaron as chosen of the Lord.
They performed the deeds of the Lord,
signs and wonders in the land of Ham.

The Lord sent darkness and it was dark;
for they rebelled against the word.
Their waters were turned into blood
which caused their fish to die.

Their land was teemed with frogs,
even the bedrooms of their rulers.
Swarms of flies were sent at a word,
gnats through all of their country.

Their rains were turned into hail
and lightning flamed through their land.
Their vine and fig tree were struck down
and the trees of their country were shattered.

Locusts came at the word
and grasshoppers without number.
Every green thing in their land was eaten up,
eaten up with the produce of their soil.

PSALM 105, continued

Then their firstborn were struck down, all of them,
the firstfruit of their humanity in all of their land.
The Lord brought them out with silver and gold
and no one faltered among the tribes.
Egypt was glad when they left, glad with dread.

A cloud as a cover was spread out
and fire to give them light at night.
They asked for quail and the Lord brought it
and satisfied them with bread from heaven.

The rock was opened and waters gushed out
flowing in the desert as a river,
for the holy promise was remembered,
the promise made to servant Abraham,
and the people were brought out rejoicing,
the chosen ones with shouts of joy.

They received the lands of nations
and inherited the toil of peoples
so that they might keep the precepts
and observe the laws of the Lord.

Hallelujah! Praise Adonai!

Glory...

Antiphon

Look to the Lord,
the strength of the Lord;
seek always the faces of the Lord.

PSALM 119:145-152

Antiphon I rise before dawn and cry for help;
in your word I put my hope.

I call with all my heart: answer me, Adonai;
your decrees I will obey.
I call to you: save me,
and I will keep your statutes.

I rise before dawn and I cry for help;
in your word I put my hope.
My eyes stay open in the night watch
to meditate on your promise.

Hear my voice, as you are loving, Adonai,
as your law makes me alive.
Scheming devisers are near,
but they are far from your law.

You are near, Adonai,
and all your commands are true.
I learned long ago from your statutes
that you established them to forever.

Glory…

Antiphon I rise before dawn and cry for help;
in your word I put my hope.

EXODUS 15 :1b-4,8-13,17-18

Antiphon The Lord, my strength and my song,
has become to me salvation.

I will sing to Adonai, exalting exaltation,
who hurled horse and rider into the sea.

My strength and my song,
Yah has become to me salvation.
I will praise my God
and exalt the God of my ancestors.

Adonai the warrior, named Adonai,
hurled Pharaoh's army of chariots into the sea...
By the blast of your nostrils the waters piled up;
like a wall they stood firm in the heart of the sea,
raging deep waters congealed.

The enemy boasted, "I will pursue and overtake,
divide the spoils and gorge on them myself;
I will draw my sword;
my hand will destroy them."
You blew with your breath
and the sea covered them;
they sank like lead in the mighty waters.

Who is like you among "gods," Adonai?
Who like you is majestic and holy,
awesome in glory and working wonders?
You stretched your right hand
and the earth swallowed them.

You will lead in your love
the people you redeemed.
You will guide them in strength
to your holy dwelling…

You will bring them in and you will plant them
on the mountain of your inheritance,
the dwelling place you made, Adonai,
the sanctuary, Lord, that your hands established.
Adonai will reign forever and ever.

Glory…

Antiphon The Lord, my strength and my song,
has become to me salvation.

PSALM 117

Antiphon Praise the Lord, all you nations.

Hallelujah! Praise Adonai, all nations;
and extol, all peoples.

Great is this steadfast love toward us,
the fidelity of Adonai to forever.

Hallelujah! Praise Adonai!

Glory…

Antiphon Praise the Lord, all you nations.

WEEK II
VIGIL OF SUNDAY
(Saturday Evening)

PSALM 34

Antiphon Taste and see that the Lord is good;
seek and pursue peace.

I will extol Adonai at all times,
praise always on my lips.
My soul she will boast in Adonai,
let afflicted ones hear and let them rejoice.

Glorify Adonai with me!
Let us exalt the name together.
I sought Adonai, who answered me
and delivered me from all my fears.

They look to the name and are radiant;
their faces are never covered with shame.
This poor human called and Adonai heard,
and saved this one from all troubles.

An angel encamps around those who fear Adonai
and delivers them.
Taste and see that Adonai is good!
Blessed is the one who takes this refuge.

Fear Adonai, you saints;
for those who do so there is no lack.
Lions may grow weak and may grow hungry,
but seekers of Adonai lack no good thing.

PSALM 34, continued

Come, children! Listen to me!
I will teach you the fear of Adonai.
Who is the human who loves living?
Who desires days to see the good?

Keep your tongue from evil
and your lips from speaking the lie.
Turn from evil! And do good!
Seek and pursue peace!

The eyes of Adonai are on righteous ones
with ears open to their cry.
The faces of Adonai turn from those doing evil
to cut off from the earth their memory.

They cry and Adonai hears
and delivers them from all their troubles.
Close is Adonai to the brokenhearted,
saving those whose spirit is crushed.

Many are the troubles of the righteous
but Adonai delivers them from all of them,
protecting all of their bones;
not one of them will be broken.

Evil will slay the wicked and condemned will be
those who stay foes of the righteous.
The servants of Adonai are being redeemed
and the lives of any who take this refuge
will not be condemned.

Glory...

Antiphon Taste and see that the Lord is good;
seek and pursue peace.

PSALM 119:105-112

Antiphon New city of Zion,
let your heart sing for joy;
see how humbly
your King comes to save you.

Your word is the lamp to my foot
and the light for my path.
I have made an oath and confirmation
to follow your righteous laws.

I have suffered much, Adonai;
make me alive as is your word.
Accept the willing praise of my mouth!
And now, Adonai, teach me your laws!

My life is constantly in my hand,
but I will not forget your law.
Doers of badness set a snare for me,
but I did not stray from your precepts.

I have your statutes as a heritage to forever,
they are indeed the joy of my heart.
I set my heart to keep your decrees
to forever, the very end.

Glory...

Antiphon New city of Zion,
let your heart sing for joy;
see how humbly
your King comes to save you.

PSALM 16

Antiphon

Have courage,
all of you, lost and fearful;
take heart and say:
Our God will come to save us,
alleluia.

Keep me safe, El, for I take refuge in you.
I said to Adonai, "You are my Lord;
 I have no good apart from you."

As for saints who are in the land,
even glorious ones, all of my delight is in them.
Those who run after others
will increase their sorrows;
I will not pour out their blood libations,
nor take up their names on my lips.

Adonai, you assign my portion and my cup;
you make my lot secure.
Boundary lines fall for me in the pleasant places;
surely this inheritance is my delight.

I will praise Adonai who counsels me;
even the nights instruct my heart.
With Adonai before me, always at my right hand,
I will not be shaken.

And so my heart is glad and my tongue rejoices.
My body will rest in security
because you will not abandon my self to Sheol;
you will not let your holy one see decay.

You will make known to me the path of living,
fullness of joy in your presences,
eternal pleasures at your right hand.

Glory...

Antiphon

Have courage,
all of you, lost and fearful;
take heart and say:
Our God will come to save us,
alleluia.

PHILIPPIANS 2:6-11

Antiphon The law was given to Moses,
but grace and truth come
through Jesus Christ.

Christ Jesus, subsisting in the form of God,
did not deem equality with God something to grab,
but emptied himself, taking the form of a slave,
becoming in human likeness.

And being found in human fashion,
he humbled himself,
becoming obedient until death,
and death on a cross.

And so God highly exalted him,
and gave to him the name above every name,
that in the name of Jesus every knee should bend,
of heavenly beings and earthly beings,
and beings under the earth;

And every tongue acknowledge
to the glory of God the Father
that Jesus Christ is Lord.

Glory...

Antiphon The law was given to Moses,
but grace and truth come
through Jesus Christ.

WEEK II
RESURRECTION VIGIL

1 TIMOTHY 3 :16

Antiphon — In Christ who rose from the dead
our hope of resurrection dawned.

We confess that great
is the mystery of our fidelity:

Who was manifested in flesh,
justified in Spirit,
seen by angels,
proclaimed among nations,
believed in the world,
and taken up in glory.

We confess that great
is the mystery of our fidelity.

Glory...

Antiphon — In Christ who rose from the dead
our hope of resurrection dawned.

FOR SUNDAY OF WEEK 2

MARK 16:1-20

And when the sabbath was past, Mary the Magdalene,
and Mary the mother of James, and Salome
bought spices that they might come and anoint him.

MARK 16:1-20, continued

And very early on the first day of the week,
they came upon the tomb at the rising of the sun.
And they asked themselves,
"Who will roll away the stone
out of the door of the tomb for us?"
And looking up they beheld
that the stone had been rolled back,
for it was great exceedingly.
And entering into the tomb, they saw
a young man sitting on the right clothed in a white robe,
and they were greatly astonished. But he said to them,
"Be not greatly astonished. Jesus you seek,
the Nazarene who was crucified;
he was raised, he is not here.
Behold, the place where they put him.
But you go tell his disciples and Peter
that he goes before you to Galilee;
there you will see him, as he told you."
And going forth they fled from the tomb;
trembling and bewilderment had them,
and they told no one anything, for they were afraid.
And rising early on the first day of the week,
he appeared first to Mary the Magdalene,
from whom he had expelled seven demons.
She going reported to those who had been with him,
mourning and weeping.
And hearing that he lives and was seen by her,
they disbelieved.

And after these things,
to two of them walking he showed himself
in a different form, going into the country.
And those going reported to the rest,
and were not believed.
And later to the eleven as they reclined
he showed himself and reproached their disbelief
and their hardness of heart for not believing
the ones beholding him having been raised.
And he said to them, "Going into all the world,
you proclaim the gospel to all the creation.
The one believing and being baptized will be saved,
but the one disbelieving will be condemned.
And the ones believing will follow these signs:
In my name they will expel demons,
they will speak with new tongues,
they will take serpents
and if they drink anything deadly
by no means will it hurt them,
and they will place hands on the sick
who will recover."
And so the Lord Jesus after speaking to them
was taken up into heaven
and sat at the right hand of God.
But those going forth proclaimed everywhere,
while the Lord worked with them
and confirmed the word
through accompanying signs.

•

FOR SUNDAY OF WEEK 6

JOHN 20:1-18

Now on day one of the week, Mary the Magdalene
came in the early darkness to the tomb,
and saw the stone having been taken out of the tomb.
She ran therefore and came to Simon Peter
and to the other disciple whom Jesus loved,
and said to them, "They took the Lord out of the tomb,
and we do not know where they put him."
Peter and the other disciple
went forth and came to the tomb.
The two ran together,
and the other disciple ran before Peter more quickly
and came first to the tomb,
and stooping saw the linens lying,
but did not enter.
Simon Peter also came following him,
and entered into the tomb,
and behold, the linens lying,
and the cloth which had been on his head,
not lying with them, but apart in one place,
having been rolled up.
Then the other disciple also entered,
having come first to the tomb,
and he saw and believed,
for they did not yet know the scripture,
that he deemed it fitting to rise again from the dead.
And so the disciples went away again to themselves.

But Mary stood outside the tomb weeping.
And so as she was weeping,
she stooped into the tomb
and behold, two angels in white, sitting,
one at the head and one at the feet
where the body of Jesus lay.
And they said to her, "Woman, why do you weep?"
She said to them, "They took my Lord,
and I do not know where they put him."
Saying these things, she turned back,
and behold, Jesus standing.
She did not know it was Jesus. Jesus said to her,
"Woman, why do you weep? Whom do you seek?"
Thinking that it was the gardener, she said to him,
"Sir, if you did carry him, tell me where you put him,
and I will take him."
Jesus said to her, "Mary."
Turning, she said to him in Hebrew, "Raboni,"
which means "Teacher."
Jesus said to her, "Do not hold on to me,
for I have not yet ascended to the Father.
But you go to my brothers and sisters and tell them,
I ascend to my Father and your Father
and my God and your God.'"
Mary the Magdalene came announcing to the disciples,
"I have seen the Lord"
and these things he said to her.

•

WEEK II
SUNDAY MORNING

PSALM 104

Antiphon The Lord brings forth bread from the earth,
and wine to warm human hearts.

Soul of me, praise Adonai!
My God, Adonai, you are beyond measure.
Splendor and majesty clothe you,
wrapped in light as a garment,

stretching out over the heavens like the tent,
laying beams on the waters of the upper chambers.
You make a chariot of the clouds,
riding on wings of wind,
making messengers of the winds
and servants of flaming fire.

You have set foundations on earth,
unmoveable for ever and ever.
Deep is your garment, covering the earth;
above the mountains the waters stood.

At your rebuke, they then fled;
at the sound of your thunder they took flight.
They flowed over mountains
and went down into valleys
to the places you assigned for them.
You set a boundary they are not to cross;
never again are they to cover the earth.

You make springs of water pour into ravines;
between the mountains they flow.
They give water to all beasts of the field;
they quench the thirst of donkeys.
Birds of the air nest in branches beside them;
they give you their song.

You water mountains from your upper chambers;
by the fruit of your works the earth is satisfied.
You make grass grow for the cattle
and plants for human beings to cultivate

to bring forth food from the earth,
wine to make glad the human heart,
oil to make faces shine,
and bread to sustain the human heart.

They are all Adonai's well watered trees,
cedars of Lebanon planted
where birds make their nests,
and the pine tree where the stork makes a home,
mountains, the high ones, for wild goats,
and crags, a refuge for rock-badgers.

PSALM 104, continued

You mark off seasons by the moon,
and know the going down of the sun.
You bring darkness
and all beasts of the forest prowl in the night.
The lions roar for prey
seeking their food from God.

The sun rises, they steal away,
and into their dens they lie down.
Human beings go out to do their work
and labor until the evening.

How many are your works, Adonai!
All of them in wisdom you made.
The earth is full of your creatures.

There is the sea, vast and spacious;
living creatures countless there,
small ones and large ones.
There ships go about
and leviathan which you formed for frolic.

All of them look to you
to give them food at their time.
You give to them and they gather,
you open your hands
and they are goodly satisfied.

You hide your face and they are terrified,
you take away their breath and they die
and to their dust they return.
You breathe your Spirit, and they are created,
and you renew the faces of earth.

May the glory of Adonai endure to forever.
May Adonai rejoice in the works:
looking at the earth, she trembles,
touching the mountains, they smoke.

I will sing to Adonai during my life
and sing praise to my God while I still am.
May my meditation be found pleasing.
I rejoice in Adonai.
May sin vanish from the earth
and the wicked be so no more.

Praise, my soul, Adonai! Hallelujah!

Glory…

Antiphon The Lord brings forth bread from the earth,
and wine to warm human hearts.

PSALM 118

Antiphon

Zion is our mighty citadel,
our saving Lord its wall and its defense;
throw open the gates
for our God is here among us,
alleluia.

Give thanks to Adonai who is good,
whose love is to forever.

Let Israel now declare:
this love is to forever.
Let the house of Aaron declare:
this love is to forever.
Let those who fear Adonai declare:
this love is to forever.

In anguish I cried to Adonai
who answered me with freedom.
Adonai is with me, I will not be afraid.
What can any human do to me?
Before enmity I keep this in mind:
Adonai is with me, ready to help me.

Better to take refuge in Adonai
than to trust in the human;
Better to take refuge in Adonai
than to trust in a prince;

All of the nations surrounded me,
indeed did they surround me;
in the name of Adonai indeed I cut them.
They swarmed around me like bees,
they crackled like thorns in a fire;
in the name of Adonai indeed I cut them.

To push back they pushed me back to fall
but Adonai helped me.
Adonai became my strength and my song
and became to me salvation.
Shout joy and victory in your tents, you righteous.

Adonai's right hand does a mighty thing,
Adonai's right hand lifted high.
Adonai's right hand does a mighty thing.
I will not die; I will live
and proclaim these deeds indeed.
To chasten, Adonai let me be chastened,
but did not give me to death.

Open for me the gates of righteousness;
I will enter through them
and give thanks to Adonai.
This is Adonai's gate,
where righteous ones may enter.
I will give thanks to you for you answered me
and you became to me salvation.

PSALM 118, continued

The stone they rejected as builders
became the cornerstone.
With Adonai this happened
and it is marvelous in our eyes.
This is the day Adonai made;
let us rejoice and be glad.

Adonai, save now!
Adonai, grant success now!
Blessed is the one coming in the name of Adonai;
We bless you from Adonai's house.
Our El Adonai has shined light onto us.

Join with boughs the festal procession
up to the horns of the altar.
To you, my God, I will give thanks.
You, my God, I will exalt.
Give thanks to Adonai who is good,
whose love is to forever.

Glory...

Antiphon

Zion is our mighty citadel,
our saving Lord its wall and its defense;
throw open the gates
for our God is here among us,
alleluia.

DANIEL 3:52-57

Antiphon Come to the waters, all you who thirst;
seek the Lord while he can be found,
alleluia.

Blessed are you, O Lord, God of our ancestors,
praiseworthy and exalted above all forever.

Blessed is your glorious and holy name,
praiseworthy and exalted above all forever.

Blessed are you in the temple of your sacred glory,
praiseworthy and exalted above all forever.

Blessed are you who sit high on the cherubim
and look into the depths,
praiseworthy and exalted above all forever.

Blessed are you on your royal throne,
praiseworthy and exalted above all forever.

Blessed are you in the dome of heaven,
to be hymned and glorified forever.

Bless the Lord, all you works of the Lord,
sing praise and high exaltation forever.

Glory...

Antiphon Come to the waters, all you who thirst;
seek the Lord while he can be found,
alleluia.

PSALM 150

Antiphon Our God will come with great power
to enlighten the eyes of his servants,
alleluia.

Hallelujah! Praise Adonai!
To El in the sanctuary, give praise.
In the mighty heavens, give praise.
For the works of power, give praise.
For surpassing greatness, give praise.

With sounding of trumpet, give praise.
With harp and lyre, give praise.
With tambourine and dance, give praise.
With flute and string, give praise.

With cymbals clashing, give praise.
With cymbals resounding, give praise.
Let all that has breath praise Adonai!
Hallelujah! Praise Adonai!

Glory…

Antiphon Our God will come with great power
to enlighten the eyes of his servants,
alleluia.

WEEK II
SUNDAY EVENING

PSALM 23

Antiphon In pastures of greenness
the Lord makes me lie down.

Adonai is my shepherd; nothing do I lack.
My Lord lays me down in green pastures
and leads me beside still quiet waters,
restoring my soul and guiding me
in paths of justice for the Lord's own namesake.

So when I walk in the deep dark valley
I will not fear for you are with me,
your rod and staff a comfort to me.

A table you prepare before me
in the presence even of enmity.
My head you anoint with oil
and my cup is overflowing.

Surely goodness and love will follow me
all the days of my life
and I will dwell in the Lord's own house
for length of days.

Glory...

Antiphon In pastures of greenness
the Lord makes me lie down.

PSALM 110:1-6a,7

Antiphon The Lord will come on the clouds of heaven
with great power and might,
alleluia.

Adonai said to my Lord:
"Sit at my right hand
until I make enmity as a footstool for your feet."

A scepter of your might
Adonai will extend from Zion,
and rule in the midst of enmity!

Your troops are willing on the day of your battle.
In majesties of holiness from the womb of the dawn
to you is the dew of your youth.
Adonai swore and this mind will not change,
"You are a priest to forever
in the order of Melchizedek."

The Lord is at your right hand
and will crush kings on the day of wrath,
will judge the nations...,
and will drink from a brook on the way
with head lifted up because of all this.

Glory...

Antiphon The Lord will come on the clouds of heaven
with great power and might,
alleluia.

PSALM 115

Antiphon

The Lord will come; he is true to his word.
If he seems to delay, keep watch for him,
for he will surely come,
alleluia.

Not to us, Adonai, not to us,
but to your name give glory
because of your love, because of your fidelity.
Why say the nations, "Where now is their God?"

Our God now is in the heavens
and does all that God pleases.
Their idols are silver and gold,
made of human hands.

Made with a mouth, they cannot speak;
made with eyes, they cannot see;
made with ears, they cannot hear;
made with a nose, they cannot smell;

made with hands, they cannot feel;
made with feet, they cannot walk,
and they utter no sound with their throat.
Like them will become those who make them,
and all who trust in them.

Israel, trust Adonai, your help and your shield.
Aaron, trust Adonai, your help and your shield.
Ones fearing Adonai, trust Adonai,
your help and your shield.

PSALM 115, continued

Adonai remembers us and will bless us,
will bless the house of Israel,
will bless the house of Aaron,
will bless ones fearing Adonai,
the small ones with the great ones.

May Adonai make an increase to you,
to you and to your children.
You are blessed by Adonai,
Maker of heavens and earth.

Heavens, the heavens are to Adonai,
but earth is given to humanity.
The dead ones do not praise Adonai,
and not all those who go down in silence.

But we, we extol Adonai,
from now and to forevermore.
Hallelujah! Praise Adonai!

Glory...

Antiphon The Lord will come; he is true to his word.
If he seems to delay, keep watch for him,
for he will surely come,
alleluia.

REVELATION 19:1b,2a,5b,6b,7

Antiphon The Lord our king and lawgiver
will come to save us.

Alleluia! Praise the Lord!
Salvation and glory and power are to our God,
whose judgments are true and just.

Alleluia! Praise the Lord!
Praise our God, all you slaves of the Lord,
you small and you great, who hold God in awe.

Alleluia! Praise the Lord!
The Lord is reigning, our God, the Almighty.
Let us rejoice and let us exult,
and we will give the glory to the Lord.

Alleluia! Praise the Lord!
The day has come
for the marriage of the Lamb,
and the bride has prepared herself.

Glory...

Antiphon The Lord our king and lawgiver
will come to save us.

WEEK II
MONDAY MORNING

PSALM 31 :1-17,20-25

Antiphon Lord, shine your faces on your servant, alleluia.

In you, Adonai, I take refuge;
let me not be shamed to forever.
Deliver me in your righteousness.
Quickly turn to me your ear! Rescue me!

Be for me a rock of refuge,
a fortress house to save me.
Since you are my rock and my fortress,
for the sake of your name
you lead me and guide me.

You free me from the trap they set for me,
for you are my refuge.
Into your hand I commit my spirit;
you redeem me, Adonai God of truth.

I hate when folks cling to worthless idols,
and I trust in Adonai.
I will be glad and rejoice in your love
for you saw my affliction;
you knew the anguishes of my soul.

You do not put me into the hand of enmity;
you set my feet into the spacious place.

Be merciful to me, Adonai, in my distress;
my eyes and my soul and my body
grow weak with sorrow.

My life is consumed by anguish
and my years with groaning.
My strength fails because of my guilt
and my bones grow weak.

Because of enmity I am
the utter contempt of even my neighbors
and a dread to my friends
who see me on the street and flee.

I am forgotten as though dead;
my heart became like broken pottery,
for I hear the slander of many
and terror on every side
when they conspire together against me
and plot to take my life.

But I trust in you, Adonai;
I say you are my God;
my times are in your hand.
Deliver me from the hands
of enmity and pursuers.

Shine your faces on your servant!
Save me in your unfailing love!...

How great is the goodness
you store up for ones who fear you
and bestow on those taking refuge in you
in the sight of the children of humanity.

PSALM 31, continued

You hide them in the shelter of your presence;
from human intrigues you keep them
in a dwelling safe from the strife of tongues.

Adonai is praised for showing wonderful love
to me in the city besieged, and I said in my alarm,
"I am cut off from before your eyes."
Yet you heard the sound of my cries for mercy
when I called to you for help.

Love Adonai, all you saints,
Adonai faithful and preserving,
but paying back in full the arrogant.

Be strong and strengthen your heart,
all you hoping in Adonai!

Glory...

Antiphon Lord, shine your faces on your servant,
alleluia.

PSALM 42

Antiphon When can I go and meet the face of God?

As a deer breathes heavy for streams of water,
so my soul throbs for you, God.

My soul she thirsts for God, the living God.
When can I go and meet the faces of God?

My tears were food for me by day and by night,
while all day they said to me, "Where is your God?"

These things I remember
as my soul pours out before me:
How I would go with the multitude
to lead them to the house of God
sounding shouts of joy and thanksgiving,
a festive throng!

Why are you downcast, my soul,
and disturbed within me?
Put hope in God, whom I will yet praise,
the saving help and presence.

My God, within me my soul she is downcast.
For this I will remember you
from the land of Jordan and the heights of Hermon,
from the Mount of Mizar:

Deep calls to deep in the roar of your waterfalls.
All your waves and breakers are swept over me.

PSALM 42, continued

By day Adonai directs love
and at night the song within me
is a prayer to the God of my life.

I say to El my Rock, "why do you forget me?
  Why must I go about mourning,
  oppressed by enmity?"

With mortal agony in my bones,
taunted by foes,
while all day they say to me, "Where is your God?"

Why are you downcast, my soul?
Why are you disturbed within me?
Put hope in God, whom I will yet praise,
my saving help and God.

Glory…

Antiphon When can I go and meet the face of God?

SIRACH 36:1-6,13-22

Antiphon Show mercy, Lord,
to the people called by your name.

Come to our aid, God of all;
let all the nations be in fear of you.
Raise your hand to the foreign nations,
that they may see your might.

As you have used us to show them your holiness,
so now use them to show us your glory.
They will know as we know
that there is no God but you.

Give new signs and work new wonders;
show the splendor of your right hand and arm...

Gather all the tribes of Jacob,
that they may inherit the land as at the beginning.
Show mercy to the people called by your name:
Israel, whom you named your firstborn.

Have pity on your holy city, Jerusalem,
the foundation for your throne.
Fill Zion with your majesty,
and your temple with your glory.

Give witness of your deeds of old;
fulfill the prophecies spoken in your name.
Reward those who have hoped in you,
and let your prophets be proven true.

Hear the prayers of your servants,
as you are good to your people.
Thus all will know to the ends of the earth
that you are God eternal.

Glory...

Antiphon Show mercy, Lord,
to the people called by your name.

PSALM 19

Antiphon The heavens are declaring
the glory of God.

The heavens declare the glory of God,
and the sky proclaims the work of God's hands.
Day after day, speech pouring forth,
and knowledge on display night after night.

There is no speech, there is no language,
and no sound is heard.
Into all the earth their line goes out
and their words to the ends of the world.

There God has pitched a tent for the sun,
and like a bridegroom coming forth,
and like a champion running the course, rejoices.

At the end of the heavens is the rising,
to their furthest ends is the circuit,
and nothing is hidden from its heat.

The law of Adonai is perfect, reviving the soul;
statutes of Adonai are trustworthy,
making wise of the simple;
precepts of Adonai are right ones,
giving joy of heart;

the command of Adonai is radiant,
giving light to eyes;
the fear of Adonai is pure, enduring to forever;
ordinances of Adonai are sure and altogether just;

more precious than gold,
much more than pure gold,
more sweet than honey, the honey of honeycombs.

Your servant is being warned by them;
to keep them is a great reward.
Who can discern errors?
From those hidden from me, forgive me!

And keep your servant from willful sins!
May they not rule over me;
then will I be blameless
and innocent of great transgression.

May the words of my mouth be as pleasing
and the meditation of my heart be as pleasing
before you, Adonai,
my Rock and my Redeemer.

Glory...

Antiphon The heavens are declaring
the glory of God.

WEEK II
MONDAY EVENING

PSALM 12

Antiphon

Words of the Lord are flawless words,
like silver refined in a furnace of clay.

Help, Adonai, for the godly are no more;
the faithful vanish from humanity's children.
They speak the lie to each of their neighbors,
lips of flattering with heart and heart.

May Adonai close all flattering lips
and tongues speaking the boast that say:
"With our tongues we will triumph,
  our lips are with us; who is our master?"

But because of oppression of the weak,
because of groaning of needy ones,
now Adonai says, "I will arise and protect them."

Words of Adonai are flawless words,
like silver refined in the furnace of clay,
and being purified seven times over.

You, Adonai, you will keep them safe;
you are our protection to forever.
But doers of badness will still strut about
when vileness is honored among human beings.

Glory...

Repeat antiphon.

PSALM 40:2-14,17-18

Antiphon: My food is that I may do
the will of the one who sent me. John 4:34

Waiting, I waited for Adonai,
who turned to me and heard my cry,

who lifted me from the slime pit
and from the muddy mire,
and set my feet on rock,
making firm my standing place,

and put in my mouth a new song,
a hymn of praise to our God.
Many will see and fear and trust Adonai.

Blessed is the one who trusts in Adonai
and looks not to the proud
or those turning to false "gods."

Adonai, my God, many are your deeds of wonder
and your plans cannot be equaled.
Should I speak and tell of them
they would be too many to declare.

Sacrifice and offerings you did not desire,
but my ears you pierced open for me.
Burnt offering and sin offering you did not require.
Then I said, "Here, I have come;

PSALM 40:2-14,17-18, continued

in the scroll, in the book, it is written of me.
To do your will, my God, is my desire,
and your law is within my heart."

I proclaim righteousness in the great assembly.
See my lips unsealed. You, Adonai, you know!

Your righteousness I do not hide in my heart;
your faithfulness and your salvation I speak.
I do not conceal your love and your truth
from the great assembly.

Adonai, withhold not your mercies from me,
may your love and your truth protect me always
for countless troubles surround around me.

My sins overtook me and I cannot see.
They are more than the hairs of my head
and my heart fails me.

Be pleased, Adonai, to save me;
Adonai, come quickly to help me!...

May all who seek you rejoice in you and be glad
and may lovers of your salvation say always,
"Let God be exalted."

Yet I am poor and needy.
May the Lord think of me and not delay,
my help and my deliverer, my God.

Glory...

Antiphon: My food is that I may do
the will of the one who sent me. John 4:34

PSALM 45

Antiphon You, my king,
excel among humanity
with anointing of grace on your lips.

My heart is stirred, a noble theme;
I recite my verses for the king;
my tongue is a pen of a skillful scribe.

You were anointed with grace on your lips,
more excellent among children of humanity.
For thus has God blessed you to forever.

Gird your sword upon your side, mighty one,
your splendor and your majesty.
Your majesty, be victorious!
Ride forth on behalf of truth and humility
and let righteousness display
awesome deeds of your right hand.

Your arrows are sharp;
let nations fall beneath you into the heart
of ones who choose enmity with the royal one
on God's throne forever and ever.
A scepter of justice is the scepter of the kingdom.

PSALM 45, continued

You love righteousness
and hate when people do bad things;
for this your God anointed you
above your companions with oil of joy,
with myrrh and aloes and cassias on your robes,
and from ivory palaces strings make you glad.

Children of royalty are honored among you
and the queen bride stands at your right hand,
honored in gold of Ophir.

Listen, daughter, and consider!
Give your ear and forget your people
and the house of your parents.
The king is enthralled for your beauty;
he is your lord, so honor him!
With the gift of your face, daughter of Tyre,
wealthy people will seek you.

The all-glorious daughter of the king is within
with interweavings of gold in her gown.
In embroidered garments she is led to the king;

her virgin companions following her
are being brought to you.
They are led in with joy and gladness;
they enter the palace of the king.

In the place of your parents will your children be,
as princes and princesses through all the land.
I will make perpetual the memory of your name
through all generations and generation.
For this the nations will praise you
ever and to forever.

Glory…

Antiphon You, my king,
excel among humanity
with anointing of grace on your lips.

EPHESIANS 1:3-10

Antiphon

The mystery of God's will
in the fullness of time
is the heading up of all things in Christ.

Blessed be the God and Father
of our Lord Jesus Christ,
who has blessed us in Christ
with every spiritual blessing in the heavens.

God chose us in Christ
before the foundation of the world,
to be holy and free of blemish before him.

In love, God gave us a destiny:
as sons are adopted, through Jesus Christ himself,
in accord with the good pleasure of God's will
to the praise of the glory of grace
by which we are favored as God's beloved.

In Christ we have the redemption
through his blood, the forgiveness of sins,
in accord with the riches of his grace
which he made abound to us.

In all wisdom and intelligence
the mystery of God's will is made known to us
in accord with God's good pleasure and purpose:

A stewardship of the fullness of time,
heading up all things in Christ,
the things in the heavens and the things on earth.

Glory...

Repeat antiphon.

WEEK II
TUESDAY MORNING

PSALM 37

Antiphon Wait patiently for the Lord;
the meek will inherit the land,
alleluia.

Fret not over those who do badness;
envy not those who do wrong.
For like grass their efforts will soon wither,
and like the green plant they will die away.

Trust in Adonai and do good!
Dwell in the land and enjoy safe pasture!
Delight in Adonai
who will give the desires of your heart.

Commit your way and your trust
to Adonai who will do it:
making your righteousness shine like the dawn
and your justice like the noonday sun.

Be still before Adonai and wait with patience.
Fret not over the ways of the successful,
over schemes carried out by human beings.

Refrain from anger and turn from wrath!
Fret not; it brings only evil,
for humans doing badness will be cut off,
but those who hope in Adonai will inherit the land.

PSALM 37, continued

A little while and bad doings will be no more;
you will look and not find them in their places.
But the meek will inherit the land
and they will enjoy greatness of peace.

Plotters of bad things to do to the righteous
gnash their teeth at them.
But the Lord laughs at them,
knowing their day is coming.

They draw their sword and they bend their bow
to bring down the poor and the needy,
to slay those of the upright way.
Their sword will pierce into their own heart
and their bows will be broken.

Better the little bit of the righteous
than the wealth of many who do bad things,
for the powers of bad doers will be broken
while Adonai upholds the righteous.

Adonai knows the days of the blameless
and their inheritance will endure to forever.
They will not wither in times of disaster
and in days of famine they will enjoy plenty.

But wicked ways will perish
and those who choose enmity with Adonai
will vanish like the beauty of fields;
like smoke they will vanish.

A doer of badness borrows and does not repay,
but a righteous one is generous and giving.
The blessing on the righteous is to live in the land;
the curse of doing badness is to be cut off.

The steps of human beings are made firm
by Adonai who delights in their way.
Though we stumble, we will not fall
for Adonai upholds us by the hand.

I was young and now I am old,
yet never have I seen the righteous forsaken
or their children begging bread.
Generous and lending all the day,
their children are a blessing.

Turn from evil and do good! Then live to always!
For Adonai loves the just
and will not forsake the faithful.
They will be protected to forever…
Righteous ones will inherit the land
and they will dwell in her to forever.

The mouth of the righteous he utters wisdom
and the tongue she speaks justice.
The law of their God is in their heart
and their feet do not slip.

Wicked ways lie in wait for the righteous
seeking to kill them;
Adonai will not leave them under this power
nor let them be condemned when on trial.

PSALM 37, continued

Wait for Adonai and keep to the way
of the one who will exalt you to possess the land,
and you will see wicked ways cut off.

I saw a ruthless human flourishing
like a native green tree,
but passing away is seen no more;
though I looked he was not to be found.

Consider the blameless and observe the upright
for the future is for the person of peace.
But sinners sinning will be destroyed together;
the future of wicked ways will be cut off.

The salvation of the righteous is from Adonai,
their stronghold in times of trouble.
Their help and deliverance and salvation,
their deliverance from ways that are wicked,
is Adonai in whom they take refuge.

Glory…

Antiphon

Wait patiently for the Lord;
the meek will inherit the land,
alleluia.

PSALM 43

Antiphon Lord, send forth your light and your truth.

God, vindicate me;
plead my cause against a nation not godly;
rescue me from humans deceitful doing wicked.

God, my stronghold, why am I rejected?
Why must I go about mourning,
oppressed by enmity?

Send forth your light and your truth;
let them guide me to your dwellings
and bring me to your holy mountain.

Then I will go to the altar of God,
to El, my joy and delight,
and I will praise you with harp, God, my God.

Why are you downcast, my soul?
Why are you disturbed within me?
Put hope in God, whom I will yet praise,
the saving help of my face, my God.

Glory…

Antiphon Lord, send forth your light and your truth.

ISAIAH 38:10-14,17b-20

Antiphon Lord, save us all our days.

I asked, "Must I go in the prime of my days
through the gates of Sheol;
must I be robbed of the rest of my years?"

I said, "I will no longer see Adonai,
Adonai in the land of the living.
As a dweller of the place of cessation
I will look on humanity no longer."

My house was pulled down
and taken from me like the tent of my shepherd;
I rolled up my life,
as a weaver cuts off from a loom.

From day to night you made an end of me.
I waited till dawn;
all my bones are broken as by a lion.
From day to night you made an end of me.

Like a swift or thrush I cried;
I moaned like the dove.
My eyes to the heavens grew weak.
Lord, troubles are at me; come to my aid...

In your love you have kept my self
out of the pit of destruction;
indeed you put behind your back all my sins.

Sheol cannot praise you
and death cannot sing to you praise,
nor can those going down the pit
hope for your faithfulness.

The living alive praise you, as I do this day.
Fathers and mothers tell the children
all about your faithfulness.

Adonai saves us;
we will play our stringed instruments
and sing in the temple of Adonai
all the days of our lives.

Glory...

Antiphon Lord, save us all our days.

PSALM 65

Antiphon

For you, O God, silence,
and praise in Zion.

For you, O God, silence and praise in Zion,
and to you will our vow be fulfilled.

To you hearing our prayer all humanity will come.
Matters of sin overwhelmed over me;
you atoned for our transgressions.

Blessed are the ones you choose
and bring near to live in your courts.
We are filled with the goodness of your house
and the holiness of your temple.

Deeds awesome and righteous are your answer,
God of our salvation,
hope of all the ends of the earth and of the far seas.

You form mountains by your power,
arming yourself with strength.
You still the roar of the seas, the roar of their waves
and the turmoil of nations.

Those who live in far away places
fear your wonders;
in dawns of morning and in the evening
you call forth songs of joy.

You care for the land and water her;
with an abundance you enrich her.
God's stream is as you ordain the earth:
filled with waters, providing grain.
You drench its furrows and level its ridges;
you soften her with showers and bless the crops.

You crown the year with your bounty;
carts overflow with your abundance.
The desert grasslands are overflowing
and the hills are clothed with gladness.

The meadows are covered with the flock
and valleys are coated with grain.
They shout for joy; for joy they sing.

Glory...

Antiphon For you, O God, silence,
and praise in Zion.

WEEK II
TUESDAY EVENING

PSALM 53

Antiphon When God restores
the fortunes of the people of God,
let Jacob rejoice, let Israel be glad.

In the heart of a fool is said, "There is no God."
The evil way is vile and corrupt;
there is no one doing good.

God looks from the heavens
on children of humanity
to see if there is one who understands,
one who is seeking God.

All of them turned away together;
they became corrupt;
there is no one doing good, not even one.

Will the ones doing evil never learn?
Devouring my people, they eat bread;
they do not call on God.

There they dreaded and dread was not there,
for God scattered the bones of attackers
put to shame in God's rejection.

Who would be brought from Zion
for the salvation of Israel?
When God restores the fortunes of God's people,
let Jacob rejoice, let Israel be glad.

Glory...

Repeat antiphon.

PSALM 54:1-6,8-9

Antiphon See! God is helping me;
the Lord sustains my very self.

God, save me by your name
and by your might vindicate me.
God, hear my prayer!
Listen to the words of my mouth!

For strangers attack me
and ruthless people seek my life
without regard for God before them.
See, God is helping me!
The Lord is among those sustaining my self...

With a freewill offering I will sacrifice to you;
I will praise, Adonai, your good name,
for you delivered me from all trouble
and my eye has looked
on those who would be foes.

Glory...

Repeat antiphon.

PSALM 49

Antiphon

You cannot serve God and mammon.
Where your treasure is
there also will your heart be.

Matthew 6:24b,21

Hear this all peoples! Listen all alive in the world!
Men and women, all sons and daughters,
rich and poor alike:

My mouth will speak words of wisdom
and my heart utter understanding of things.
I will turn an ear to a proverb;
I will expound my riddle with a harp.

Why should I fear in days of evil
the badness of deceivers who surround me,
the trusters of wealth,
and the boasters of the greatness of their riches?

No human can redeem redemption of another,
nor for oneself give a ransom to God.
Ransom of a life is costly;
no ransom is ever enough
for one to live to forever
and not see the decay.

For we see that wise people die;
like the foolish and the senseless they perish,
and leave all their wealth to others.
Their thoughts are of their houses to forever
as their dwelling for generations and generation,
and so they call lands by their own names.

The human, despite riches, does not endure,
but perishes just like the beasts.

This is their fate who trust in themselves
and their followers who give them approval.
Like the sheep they are destined for Sheol,
and death will feed on them too.

Upright ones will rule over them in the morning
and their form will decay in Sheol, their mansion.
But God will redeem my soul
and take me from the hand of Sheol.

Be not overawed when human beings grow rich,
when they increase the splendor of their houses.
For in death they will take none of it;
with none of their splendor will they descend.

Though during their lives they blessed themselves,
and people do praise you when you prosper,
they will go to the generation of their ancestors
and never see light to forever.

Like the beast that must perish
so is a human with riches
but still poor in understanding.

Glory… Repeat antiphon.

REVELATION 4:8b,11; 5:9,10,12,13b

Antiphon

Worthy is the Lamb, slain to receive
the power and riches
and wisdom and strength
and honor and glory and blessing.

Worthy are you, our Lord and our God,
to receive the glory and honor and power,
because you have created all things,
and by your will all things were created and are.

Worthy are you to receive the scroll
and to open its seals,
because you were slain
and purchased for God by your blood
from every tribe and tongue and people and nation.

You made of them to our God
a kingdom and priests,
and they will reign over the earth.

Worthy is the Lamb, slain to receive
the power and riches and wisdom and strength
and honor and glory and blessing.

Glory...

Antiphon

Worthy is the Lamb, slain to receive
the power and riches
and wisdom and strength
and honor and glory and blessing.

WEEK II
WEDNESDAY MORNING

PSALM 39

Antiphon

We ourselves groan in ourselves
eagerly expecting adoption,
the redemption of our body,
alleluia.

I said, "I will watch my ways
  of sinning with my tongue;
  I will put on my mouth a muzzle
  as long as temptation is in my presence."
So in silent stillness I said nothing good,
and still my anguish increased.

My heart grew hot inside me;
in my meditation a fire burned.
I spoke with my tongue,
"Show me, Adonai, my end,
  what is the number of my days;
  let me know how fleeting I am.

  See the handbreadths you made!
  My days and my span are as nothing before you.
  Indeed, each of all humanity stands as a breath.
  Indeed, as a phantom the human goes out.
  Indeed, vainly bustling about, heaping up wealth
  without knowing who will get it."

PSALM 39, continued

But what am I looking for now, Lord?
My hope she is in you.
Save me from all my transgressions!
Make me not the scorn of fools.
I was silent and opened not my mouth,
for you, you have done it.

Remove your scourge from me;
from the blow of your hand I am overcome.
With a rebuke for sin you discipline the human
and you consume our wealth like a moth;
indeed we are each but a breath.

Hear my prayer, Adonai, and my cry for help;
listen, El, and be not deaf to my weeping.
For I am with you as an alien,
a stranger like all of my ancestors.
Look away from me that I may rejoice
before I depart and am no more.

Glory…

Antiphon

We ourselves groan in ourselves
eagerly expecting adoption,
the redemption of our body,
alleluia.

PSALM 77

Antiphon

God, in your holiness way,
what "god" is as great as God?

My cry is for God, indeed I cried for help.
My cry is for God to hear me.

In the day of my distress I sought the Lord,
my hand was stretched in the night without tiring;
my soul refused to be comforted.
I remembered God and I groaned;
I mused and my spirit grew faint.

You kept open the lids of my eyes;
I was troubled and could not speak.
I thought of former days and of years long ago.
I remembered my song in the night;
my heart mused and inquired of my spirit,

"Will the Lord reject to forever,
never to show favor again?
Is the unfailing love vanished to forever?
Has the promise failed for all generations?
Has God forgotten to be merciful
or withheld compassion in anger?"

Then I thought, "My appeal is this,
the years at the right hand of the Most High."
I will remember the deeds of Adonai;
yes, I will remember your long-ago miracles.
I will meditate on all of your works
and consider your mighty deeds.

PSALM 77, continued

God in your holiness way,
what "god" is as great as God?
You are the God who does miracles;
you display among the peoples your power.
You redeemed your people with your arm,
the descendants of Jacob and Joseph.

The waters saw you, God,
the waters saw you and writhed;
indeed the depths were convulsed.
Clouds poured down waters,
thunder resounded in the skies,
and your arrows flashed around.

Your thunder sounded in the whirlwind,
lightnings lit up the world;
the earth trembled and quaked.
Through the sea is your path,
and your way through mighty waters,
though your footprints were not seen.

You led your people like the flock
by the hand of Moses and Aaron.

Glory...

Antiphon God, in your holiness way,
what "god" is as great as God?

1 SAMUEL 2:1-10

Antiphon My heart rejoices in the Lord,
who humbles and exalts.

My heart rejoices in Adonai,
my horn is lifted high in Adonai.

My mouth boasts over enmity,
for I delight in being delivered.
There is no Holy One like Adonai,
indeed there is no one who compares;
there is no Rock like our God.

Arrogant pride is coming from their mouth.
Do not keep talking so proudly
or proudly let arrogance come from your mouth,
for Adonai is God who knows,
by whom all deeds are weighed.

Bows of warriors are broken
but those stumbling are armed with strength.
The full hire themselves out for more food,
but the hungry ones hunger no more.
She who was barren bore seven sons;
blessed with many sons, she is pining away.

Adonai allows death and is making alive,
brings down to Sheol and is raising up.
Adonai allows poverty and is sending wealth,
humbling and exalting,
raising the poor from the dust
and the needy from ash-heaps
to sit with princes and inherit thrones of honor.

For Adonai's are the foundations of the earth,
setting the world upon them.
The feet of the saints will be guarded
but doers of badness will be silenced in darkness.

For not by strength does the human prevail;
Adonai shatters opposition,
thundering from the heavens.
Adonai will judge the ends of the earth,
give strength, and exalt the horn
of the one chosen and Anointed.

Glory...

Antiphon My heart rejoices in the Lord,
who humbles and exalts.

PSALM 97

Antiphon The Lord reigns;
let the earth be glad.

PSALM 97

Adonai reigns; let the earth be glad.
Let all the distant shores rejoice.
Clouds and thick darkness surround the throne
founded on righteousness and justice.

Fire goes before, consuming foes on every side.
Lightnings light up the world;
the earth sees and trembles.

Mountains melt like wax before Adonai,
before the Lord of all the earth.
The heavens proclaim righteousness
and all peoples see the glory.

Let those who worship idols be shamed,
those boasting in their images.
Worship God, all you "gods."

Zion hears and rejoices
and the villages of Judah are glad
because of your judgments, Adonai.

For you, Adonai, are Most High over all the earth,
far exalted above all the "gods."

Evil is despised by lovers of Adonai,
who guards the lives of faithful ones
and delivers them from the hands of doers of bad.

Light is shed upon the righteous
and joy on the upright of heart.
Rejoice in Adonai, righteous ones,
and praise the holy name.

Glory... Repeat antiphon.

WEEK II
WEDNESDAY EVENING

PSALM 52

Antiphon I trust in God's unfailing love
forever and ever.

Why, mighty one, do you boast of evil
to the disgrace of El all the day?
Your tongue plots destruction
like a sharpened razor, practicing deceit.

You love evil rather than good,
falsehood rather than speaking truth.
Your tongue of deceit loves every harmful word.

Surely El will bring you down,
snatch you from your tent,
and uproot you from the land of the living.

Then the righteous will see and fear,
and they will laugh at you.
See the one who did not see God as the stronghold,
but grew strong by destruction
and trusted in the greatness of wealth.

But I am like an olive tree
flourishing in the house of God;
I trust in God's unfailing love forever and ever.

I will praise you to forever for what you have done,
and in the presence of your saints I will hope in you
for your name is good.

Glory...

Antiphon I trust in God's unfailing love
forever and ever.

PSALM 62

Antiphon Rest, my soul, in God alone;
from God is my salvation

My soul finds rest in God alone,
from whom is my salvation,
alone my salvation and my rock,
my fortress never to be shaken greatly.

Until when will you assault a human being,
will you throw down, all of you,
like a leaning wall or a tottering fence?

They fully intend to topple from the lofty place;
they delight in lies
and bless with their mouth and curse in their heart.

My soul finds rest in God alone,
from whom is my hope,
alone my salvation and my rock,
my fortress not to be shaken.

PSALM 62, continued

From God is my salvation and my honor;
my mighty rock and refuge.
Trust in God at all times, people;
pour out your heart to God our refuge.

Sons and daughters of humanity are but a breath;
the so-called great ones are an illusion.
On balanced scales they both rise;
together they are only a breath.

Trust not in extortion
and take no pride in stolen things;
even when riches increase
do not set your heart on them.

One thing God has spoken,
two things I have heard:
that to God is strength and to you, Lord, is love;
and surely you will reward to each
as are our deeds.

Glory...

Antiphon Rest, my soul, in God alone;
from God is my salvation

PSALM 67

Antiphon May God be gracious to us,
bless us,
and shine the holy face upon us.

May God be gracious to us and bless us,
may God's faces shine upon us.
How else can your ways be known on the earth
and your salvation among all the nations?

May the peoples praise you, God,
may the peoples praise you, all of them.

May the nations be glad and sing for joy
for you rule the peoples
and guide nations of the earth into justice.

May the peoples praise you, God,
may the peoples praise you, all of them.

The land will yield her harvest, God will bless us,
and all the ends of the earth will revere our God.

Glory...

Antiphon May God be gracious to us,
bless us,
and shine the holy face upon us.

COLOSSIANS 1:12-20

Antiphon All things have been created through him;
he is before all things
and in him all things hold together.

Give joyful thanks to the Father who made you fit
for your part of the lot of the saints in light,

who delivered us out of the authority of darkness
and transitioned us into the kingdom of the beloved Son,
in whom we have redemption, the forgiveness of our sins.

The Son is the image of the invisible God,
the firstborn of all creation.
In him all things were created,
in the heavens and on the earth,
the visible and the invisible,
whether thrones, lordships, rulers or authorities.

All things have been created through him and for him.
He is before all things,
and in him all things hold together.

He is the head of the body, the church,
and the beginning, the firstborn from the dead,
so that in all things he may hold the first place.

In him all the fullness was well pleased to dwell,
and through him reconciliation to himself of all things,
things on earth and things in the heavens,
making peace through the blood of his cross.

Glory...

Repeat antiphon.

WEEK II
THURSDAY MORNING

PSALM 44

Antiphon

For they won victory
not by their sword and their arm,
but by your right hand and arm
and the light of your faces,
alleluia.

With our ears, God, we have heard,
our fathers told us the deed
you did in their days, in days long ago.

You drove out nations by your hand
and you planted them;
you crushed peoples and made them flourish.
For they won victory not by their sword and arm,
but by your right hand and arm
and the light of your faces, for you loved them.

PSALM 44, continued

You are my King and my God;
decree the victories of Jacob.
Through you we push back enmity;
through your name we trample opposition.

Indeed I trust not in my bow
and my sword does not bring me victory,
but you give to us victory over enmity
and shame the adversity.
In God we boast all the day
and we will praise your name to forever.

But you let us be rejected and humbled
and you do not go out with our armies.
You turned us back before enmity
and adversaries plundered from us.

You gave us up like sheep devoured;
among the nations you scattered us.
You sold your people for no great price,
gaining nothing from their sale.

You made us a reproach to our neighbors,
scorn and derision to those around us.
You made us a byword among the nations,
a shaking of heads among the peoples.

All the day my disgrace is before me
and my shame covers my face
at taunts of reproachers and revilers
because of avenging enmity.

All of this happened though we did not forget you
and were not false to your covenant.
Our hearts did not turn back
and our feet did not stray from your path,
but you pushed us into haunts of jackals
and you covered us over with deep darkness.

If we forgot the name of our God,
if we spread out our hands to a foreign "god,"
would God not have discovered this,
the One knowing the secrets of the heart?
Yet for you we face death all the day;
we are considered as sheep for slaughter.

Wake up, Lord! Why do you sleep?
Rouse yourself! Do not reject us to forever.
Why do you hide your faces
and forget our misery and oppression?

Indeed our self is brought down to the dust;
our body clings to the ground.
Rise up as our help and redeem us!
because of your unfailing love.

Glory...

Antiphon

For they won victory
not by their sword and their arm,
but by your right hand and arm
and the light of your faces,
alleluia.

PSALM 80

Antiphon

Shepherd of Israel,
awaken your might;
bring us to salvation.

Hear us, One Shepherd of Israel,
you who lead Joseph like a flock.
From your throne on the cherubim, shine forth
before Ephraim, Benjamin and Manasseh!
Awaken your might! Come to our salvation!

O God, restore us!
Make your faces shine that we may be saved!

Until when, Adonai, God of Hosts,
will you smolder against the prayer of your people?
You fed them with bread of tears
and you made them drink tears by the bowlful.
You made us a contention to our neighbors,
and enmity mocks us.

God of Hosts, restore us!
Make your faces shine that we may be saved!

Out from Egypt, you brought a vine;
you drove out the nations and you planted it.
You cleared the ground before her;
her roots took root and she filled the land.

Mountains were covered by her shade
and the mighty cedars by her branches.
She sent out her branches to the Sea,
and her shoots as far as the River.

Why have you broken down her walls?
All who pass by the way pick at her.
The boar from the forest ravages her,
and creatures of the field feed on her.

God of Hosts, return now!
Look down from heaven!
See and watch over this vine,
this root that your right hand planted,
and the son you raised up for yourself.
Some would burn it or cut it down;
at the rebuke of your faces may those plans perish.

Let your hand be on the one at your right hand,
the descendent of Adam you raised up for yourself.
Then we will not turn away from you;
you revive us and we will call on your name.

Adonai, God of Hosts, restore us!
Make your faces shine that we may be saved!

Glory…

Antiphon Shepherd of Israel,
awaken your might;
bring us to salvation.

ISAIAH 12:1b-6

Antiphon Make known among the nations
the deeds of the Lord.

I will praise you, Adonai.
Though you were angry with me,
your anger turned away and you comforted me.

Surely God is my salvation!
I will trust and will not be afraid
for Yah is my strength and my song.

Adonai became for me salvation
and you will draw with joy
waters from wells of salvation...

Give thanks to Adonai! Call on the name!
Make the deeds known among the nations!
Proclaim that the name is exalted!

Sing to Adonai, who has done glory!
Let this be known to all the world.

Shout! And sing for joy, dwellers of Zion!
For great in your midst
is the Holy One of Israel.

Glory...

Antiphon Make known among the nations
the deeds of the Lord.

PSALM 81

Antiphon Sing for joy
to God our strength.

Sing for joy to God our strength!
Shout to the God of Jacob!

Begin the music! Strike the tambourine,
the melodious harp and the lyre!
Sound the ram horn at the new moon,
the full moon, the day of our feast!

For this is a decree for Israel,
an ordinance of the God of Jacob,
a statute established for Joseph
when time to go out from the land of Egypt
and the language we did not understand:

"I removed the burden from their shoulders,
their hands were freed from the basket.
In distress you called and I rescued you;

I answered from the thundercloud
and tested you at the waters of Meribah.
Hear, my people, and I will warn you, Israel,
if you will listen to me:

PSALM 81, continued

'No foreign "god" shall be among you;
you shall bow to no alien "god."
I am Adonai, your God,
who brought you out of the land of Egypt.
Open wide your mouth and I will fill it!'

But my people did not listen to my voice,
and Israel did not submit to me.
So I gave them to their stubborn heart
and they followed their devices.

If my people were listening to me,
if Israel would follow my ways,
as quickly would I subdue the enmity
and turn a firm hand to the foes.

Anyone hating Adonai would cringe
under punishment lasting to forever.
But I will feed my people with finest of wheat
and satisfy you with honey out of rock."

Glory...

Antiphon Sing for joy
to God our strength.

WEEK II
THURSDAY EVENING

PSALM 56:2-7,9-14

Antiphon
In God I trust,
I will not be afraid;
what can humanity do to me?

Be merciful to me, my God!
Human beings pursue me all the day,
attacking with oppression
and with slander all the day.

Indeed in their pride do the many attack me.
On the day I am afraid, in you I trust.
My praise is of God's word, in God I trust.
I will not be afraid; what can a mortal do to me?

All the day they twist my words against me;
all their plots are for harm.
They conspire, they lurk, they watch my steps;
they are eager for my life...

Record my lament, put my tears in your wineskin;
are they not in your record?
Enmity will turn back on the day I call;

PSALM 56:2-7,9-14, continued

I will know that God is for me.
In God whose word I praise,
in Adonai whose word I praise, in God I trust.
I will not be afraid; what can a human do to me?

Upon me, God, are my vows to you;
I will present thank offerings to you
for you delivered my soul from death
and my feet from stumbling,
to walk in God's presence
in the light of the living.

Glory...

Antiphon

In God I trust,
I will not be afraid;
what can humanity do to me?

PSALM 60:3-14a

Antiphon

O God,
you burst forth upon us;
you were angry,
now restore us.

God you rejected us and burst forth upon us;
you were angry, now restore us.

You shook the land and tore her open;
mend her fractures, for she quakes!
You showed your people a desperate time;
you made us drink wine to staggering.

For those who fear you, you raised a banner
to be unfurled against the bow,
that your beloved ones may be delivered.
Help us with your right hand and save us!

God spoke from the sanctuary:
"I will triumph and parcel out Shechem,
  and measure out the valley of Succoth;
  mine are Gilead and Manasseh,

  Ephraim my head helmet, Judah my scepter,
  and Moab my washbasin;
  On Edom I toss my sandal
  and over Philistia I shout in triumph"

Who will bring me to the Rock City?
Who will lead me to Edom?
Have you, God, not rejected us,
and not gone out, God, with our armies?

Against enmity give to us aid,
for worthless is human help.
In God will we gain the victory...

Glory...

Antiphon

O God,
you burst forth upon us;
you were angry,
now restore us.

PSALM 72

Antiphon

I will make you
a covenant of the people,
a light for the Gentiles.

Isaiah 42:6b

God, endow your justice to King Solomon
and your righteousness to the royal heir,
to judge your people in righteousness
and your afflicted with justice.

Mountains will bring prosperity to the people,
the hills too in righteousness.
He will defend people afflicted,
save the children of the needy,
and crush the oppressor.

They will fear you as long as the sun,
as long as the moon,
from generation to generations.
He will be like rain falling on a mown field,
like showers watering the earth.

In his days the righteous will flourish
in prosperous abundance til the moon is no more.
He will rule from sea to sea
and from the River to the ends of the earth.

Before him will desert tribes bow
and enmity will lick dust.
The kings of Tarshish and the distant shores
will bring tribute and present gifts,
with kings of Sheba and Seba.
They will bow down to him;
all the kings of all the nations will thus serve.

For he will deliver the needy one crying out
and the afflicted one when no one is helping.
He will take pity on the weak and the needy
and will save the lives of the needy ones;

he will rescue their lives
from oppression and violence,
for their lifeblood is precious in his eyes.

May he live and be given gold of Sheba,
and may all ever pray
that he be blessed all the day.

May grain be abundant throughout the land,
on tops of hills, swaying like the fruit of Lebanon,
and people flourish and thrive like grass in a field.

May his name endure to forever
and continue as long as the sun;
being thus blessed, may the nations bless him.

Praised is God, Adonai, God of Israel,
alone doing marvelous deeds.
Praised is the glory of the name to forever;
may the earth be filled with the glory of God.

Amen and amen. Glory... Repeat antiphon.

REVELATION 11:17-18, 12:10-12a

Antiphon

Our God
who is and who was
has taken great power to reign.

We thank you, Lord God Almighty,
the One who is and who was;
you have taken your great power and reign.

The nations raged and your anger came,
and the time to judge the dead
and to reward your slaves and prophets,
the saints, and those fearing your name,
the small and the great...

Now have come the salvation and power
and kingdom of our God
and the authority of Christ.
The accuser of our brothers and sisters was cast,
accusing them before our God day and night.

Their victory was because of the blood of the Lamb
and by the word of their witness.
They loved their life into their death,
and so be glad, you heavens,
and all you dwelling in them.

Glory...

Antiphon

Our God
who is and who was
has taken great power to reign.

WEEK II
FRIDAY MORNING

PSALM 38

Antiphon I confess my iniquity;
do not forsake me, Lord my salvation,
alleluia.

Adonai, rebuke me not in your anger
nor discipline me in your wrath,
for your arrows have pierced into me
and your hand has come down upon me.

There is no health in my body
because of your wrath;
my bones are unsound because of my sin.
Indeed my guilts overwhelm my head
like a heavy burden, too heavy for me.

I loathe them and they fester my wounds
because of my sinful folly.
I am bowed down and brought very low;
all the day I go about mourning.

Indeed my backside is filled with searing
and there is no health in my body.
Feeble and utterly crushed,
my heart groans in anguish.

PSALM 38, continued

Lord, before you is all of my longing;
my sighing is not hidden from you.
My heart pounds, my strength fails me,
and my eyes are without their light.

My friends and companions from the past
avoid being present to my woundedness,
and my neighbors stay far away.
People seeking my life set traps;
wanting to harm me, they talk of ruins
and plot deceptions all the day.

I am like a deaf man and cannot hear,
like a mute unable to open my mouth.
I became like one who does not hear,
like one whose mouth gives no reply.

Indeed, I wait for you, Adonai;
you will answer, Lord my God.
For I said, "let them not gloat over me;
  when my foot does slip, let them not exalt."

For my fall is ready for me
and my pain is ever with me.
Indeed I confess my iniquity;
I am troubled by my sin.

Vigorous ones seek enmity and for no reason,
many and numerous hating me.
Repaying the good with evil,
they slander me when I seek the good.

Forsake me not, Adonai;
my God, be not far from me.
Come quickly to my help,
Lord of my salvation.

Glory...

Antiphon I confess my iniquity;
do not forsake me, Lord my salvation,
alleluia.

PSALM 51

Antiphon A broken spirit and a contrite heart, O God,
you will not despise.

Have mercy on me, God,
in accord with your unfailing love;
in accord with the greatness of your compassion
blot out my transgressions.

Wash me of my many iniquities
and cleanse me from my sin,
for I know my transgressions
and my sin is before me always.

Against you yourself I sinned;
what I did is evil in your eyes.
You are proven right when you speak
and justified when you judge.
Surely we are sinners from birth,
from conception in a mother's womb.

Surely you desire truth in our inner parts;
in my inmost place you teach me wisdom.
You cleanse me with hyssop and I will be clean;
you wash me and I will be whiter than snow...

You let me hear joy and gladness;
let the bones you let be crushed now rejoice.
Hide your faces from my sins
and blot out all my iniquities.

A pure heart create in me, God!
Renew inside me a spirit to be steadfast.
Do not cast me from your presences,
nor take from me your Holy Spirit.

Restore to me the joy of your salvation
and sustain in me a willing spirit.
I will teach transgressors your ways
and sinners will turn back to you.

Save me from bloodguilt, God,
God of my salvation;
my tongue will sing of your righteousness.
Lord, open my lips
and my mouth will declare your praise.

Sacrifices give you no delight;
I could bring a burnt offering,
but it would give you no pleasure.
The sacrifices, God, you will not despise
are a broken spirit and a contrite heart.

Make Zion prosper in your pleasure,
and build up the walls of Jerusalem.
Then you will delight in the sacrifice of the just,
burnt offerings and whole offerings,
bulls offered on your altar.

Glory...

Antiphon A broken spirit and a contrite heart, O God,
you will not despise.

HABAKKUK 3:2-4,13a,15-19

Antiphon Even in wrath
you remember compassion.

Adonai, I heard your fame;
I stand in awe of your deeds, Adonai.
Now, in the midst of years, renew them!
In the midst of years, make them known!
Even in wrath you remember mercy.

Eloah came from Teman,
the Holy One from the Mount of Paran.
The heavens are covered with glory
and the earth is filled with praise

like the splendor of the rays of the sunrise
or the hand from a hiding place of power…
You came out to deliver your people,
to deliver your anointed one…

You trample on the sea,
your horses churning up the great waters.
I heard my heart and she trembled,
at the sound my lips quivered;

decay crept into my bones and my legs trembled.
Yet, I will wait patiently for the day,
calamity to come on the nation invading.

Though the fig tree does not bud
and there is no grape on the vine,
the crops of the olive fail
and fields produce no food,

the sheep cut themselves off from the pen
and there are no cattle in the stalls,
yet will I rejoice in Adonai
and be joyful in the God of my salvation.

Sovereign Adonai, my strength,
makes my feet like that of the deer,
makes me go to the heights.

Glory...

Antiphon Even in wrath
you remember compassion.

PSALM 147:1-11

Antiphon Extol the Lord, Jerusalem!

Hallelujah! Praise Adonai!
How good it is to sing praise to our God!
How pleasant and fitting to give praise!

PSALM 147:1-11, continued

Adonai builds up Jerusalem,
gathers Israel's exiles,
heals the ones with broken hearts
and binds up their wounds,
determines the number of the stars,
and calls to each of them by name.

Great and mighty in power is our Lord,
with unlimited understanding.
Adonai sustains the humble
and throws wickedness to the dust.
Sing to Adonai with thanksgiving!

Make music on the harp to our God,
who covers the skies with clouds
and supplies rain to the earth,
making grass to grow on the hills,
providing food for cattle
and young ravens when they call.

Adonai finds pleasure
not in the strength of the horse
nor delight in the legs of the human,
but is delighting in those who fear Adonai
who hope in this unfailing love.

Glory...

Antiphon Extol the Lord, Jerusalem!

WEEK II
FRIDAY EVENING

PSALM 59:2-5,10-11,17-18

Antiphon You protect me, my God.

Deliver me from enmity;
protect me, God,
from those who rise up against me.
Deliver me from those who do evil
and save me from people of bloody ways.

See, they lie in wait for my self;
fierce people conspire against me
for no offense of me nor sin, Adonai.
For no wrong they make ready to attack;
arise to help me and look!...

For you, my Strength, I watch,
for you God, my fortress, you God are my love.

God will go before me
and gloat over ones who slander...

But I will sing of your strength
and I will sing in the morning of your love,
for you are my fortress
and my refuge in times of trouble.

To you, my Strength, I sing praise
for you God, my fortress, you God are my love.

Glory... Repeat antiphon.

PSALM 116:1-9

Antiphon Lord, deliver my soul from death
and my feet from stumbling.

I love Adonai
who heard my voice and my cries for mercy
and turned an ear to me,
so all during my days I will call.

Cords of death entangled me
and anguishes of Sheol came upon me;
trouble and sorrow came over me.
Then I called on the name of Adonai:
"Oh, Adonai, save my self!"

Adonai is gracious and righteous,
our God the compassionate one.
Adonai protects the simple hearted;
I was in need and then I was saved.

Return, my soul, to your rest,
for good to you has been Adonai,
who delivered my soul from death,
my eyes from tears,
and my feet from stumbling,

that I may walk before Adonai
in the land of the living.

Glory…

Antiphon Lord, deliver my soul from death
and my feet from stumbling.

PSALM 121

Antiphon My help is from the Lord,
the Maker of heavens and earth.

I lift up my eyes to the hills.
From where does my help come?
My help is from and with Adonai,
Maker of heavens and earth,

who will not let your foot slip
nor slumber when watching over you.
Indeed the one watching over Israel
will not slumber and will not sleep.

Adonai watches over you,
the Most High at your right hand.
By day the sun will not harm you,
nor the moon by the night.

Adonai will keep you from all harm
and watch over your life.
Adonai will watch over your going and coming
from now and to forevermore.

Glory...

Antiphon My help is from the Lord,
the Maker of heavens and earth.

REVELATION 15:3b-4

Antiphon King of all nations,
just and true are your ways.

Great and wonderful are your works,
Lord God Almighty.
Just and true are your ways,
King of the nations.

Who will not fear, O Lord,
or glorify your name?

Only you are holy.
All the nations will come and worship before you;
your ordinances are shown to all.

Glory...

Antiphon King of all nations,
just and true are your ways.

WEEK II
SATURDAY MORNING

PSALM 106:1-16,19-48

Antiphon The Lord remembered the covenant for them
and relented,
alleluia.

Hallelujah! Praise Adonai!
Give thanks to Adonai who is good,
whose love is to forever.

Who can proclaim the mighty acts of Adonai?
Who can declare the fullness of praise?
Blessed are they who maintain justice,
doing the right at all times.

Remember me, Adonai, as you favor your people!
In your salvation, come with your aid for me
to enjoy the prosperity of your chosen ones,
to have joy in the joy of your nation,
and to give praise with your inheritance.

We have sinned as did our ancestors;
we have done wrong with wicked acts.
Our ancestors when in Egypt
gave no thought to your miracle deeds,
did not remember your many kindnesses,
and rebelled by *Yam Suf*, the Sea of Reeds.

PSALM 106, continued

Still you saved them for the sake of your name,
to make known your power.
You rebuked the Sea of Reeds; it dried up.
And you led them through the depths as the desert.

You saved them from the hands of foes
and redeemed them from the hand of enmity.

The waters covered the adversaries;
not one of them survived.
Then they believed in the promises made,
and sang out praise.

Soon did they forget those deeds
and would not wait for good counsel.
They craved cravings in the desert
and in the wasteland they tested their El,
who gave them their request
but sent a wasting disease on their life.

They envied Moses in the camp
and Aaron, the consecrated of Adonai…
They made a calf at Horeb
and gave worship to a cast idol.
They exchanged their Glory
for an image of a grass-eating bull.

They forgot El who had saved them,
doing great things in Egypt,
miracle deeds in the land of Ham
and awesome deeds by the Sea of Reeds.

By a word spoken they were to be destroyed,
except that Moses the chosen stood in the breach.
Then they despised the pleasant land
and did not believe the promise made.

They grumbled in their tents
and did not obey the voice of Adonai,
who lifted a hand to let them fall in the desert
and their descendents fall among the nations;
they were scattered through the lands.

They yoked themselves to Baal of Peor
and they ate of sacrifices to lifeless ones.
They provoked anger by their deeds
and a plague broke out among them.

Phinehas stood up and intervened
and the plague was checked;
this was credited to him as righteousness
for generation and generations to forever.

They angered by the waters of Meribah,
the cause of trouble for Moses,
who spoke rashly with his lips
when they rebelled against the Spirit.

They did not defeat the peoples
as Adonai commanded them,
but mingled with the nations
and adopted their customs.
They worshiped their idols
which became to them as a snare.

PSALM 106, continued

They sacrificed their sons and daughters.
They shed the innocent blood
of their own sons and daughters
whom they sacrificed to idols of Canaan,
desecrating the land by this blood.

They defiled themselves by their deeds
and prostituted themselves by their deeds.
Against the people burned the anger of Adonai,
abhorring the promised inheritance.

Into the hands of nations they were given,
ruled by their foes, oppressed by enmity,
and made subject to their power.
Many times were they delivered,
but they rebelled in their decisions
and wasted away in their sins.

On hearing their cry
the Lord took note of their distress
and remembered for them the covenant,
and relented in greatness of love.
They were made pitied by all of their captors.

Save us, Adonai our God!
Gather us from the nations
to give thanks to your holy name
and glory in your praise.

Praised be Adonai, God of Israel
from everlasting to everlasting
and let all the people say, "Amen!"
Hallelujah! Praise Adonai!

Glory...

Antiphon The Lord remembered the covenant for them
and relented,
alleluia.

PSALM 92 :1-9,11,13-16

Antiphon It is good to proclaim
your love in the morning
and your fidelity at night.

It is good to praise Adonai,
to make music to your name, Most High,
to proclaim in the morning your love
and at night your faithfulness,
on the ten-string and on the lyre,
and the melody of the harp.

PSALM 92 :1-9,11,13-16, continued

For you make me glad by your deeds, Adonai;
at the works of your hands I sing for joy.
How great are your works, Adonai;
very profound are your thoughts.
The senseless human does not know
and the fool does not understand.

Though wickedness springs up like grass
and doers of bad things seem to flourish,
their ways will be destroyed to forever.
But you, Adonai, are exalted to forever...

You gave me strength like a wild ox
and I was anointed with fine oil...
The just will flourish like the palm tree,
and grow like a cedar of Lebanon.

Planted in the house of Adonai,
in the courts of our God they will flourish.
In old age they will still bear fruit,
fresh and green they will stay,
to proclaim, "Adonai is upright,
in my Rock there is no wrong."

Glory...

Antiphon It is good to proclaim
your love in the morning
and your fidelity at night.

DEUTERONOMY 32:1-12

Antiphon Praise our God, beyond all measure.

Listen, heavens, and I will speak:
Hear, earth, the words of my mouth.
Let my teaching fall like the rain,
let my word descend like the dew,
like showers on grass, like abundant rains on plants.

The name of Adonai I will proclaim,
and praise the greatness of our God.
The work of the Rock is perfect indeed;
all the ways of our faithful God are just
and without wrong, upright and just.

The children acted corruptly with no shame,
a generation warped and crooked.
Foolish and unwise people,
you repay Adonai in this way?
Did not your Father create you
and make you and form you?

Remember the days of old!
Consider the years of generation and generation!
Ask your parents and they will tell you!
Ask your elders and they will explain to you

DEUTERONOMY 32 , continued

how the Most High gave inheritance to nations,
dividing sons and daughters of humanity
and setting up boundaries of peoples
by numbers of sons and daughters of Israel.

For the portion of Adonai is the people,
Jacob the allotment of inheritance,
found in desert land, a barren and howling waste,
shielded with care, guarded as the apple of the eye,

like an eagle stirring up the nest
and hovering over the young ones,
spreading wings to catch them
and carrying them on its flight feathers.

Led by Adonai alone,
no foreign "god" was with them.

Glory...

Antiphon Praise our God, beyond all measure.

PSALM 8

Antiphon Our Lord, how awesome,
how majestic is your name in all the earth.

Adonai, our Lord!
How majestic is your name in all the earth!

Your glory is set above the heavens!
From lips of children and infants
you ordained strength to bring to silence
enmity, opposition and vengeance.

When I consider your heavens,
the works of your fingers,
the moon and stars which you set in place,
what is a human that you would be mindful,
a child of Adam and Eve that you would care?

And you made us little lower than a "god"
crowning us with glory and honor,
making us to rule over works of your hands,
putting everything under our feet,

flocks and herds, all of them,
and also beasts of the field,
birds of the air and fishes of the sea,
swimming through the paths of the seas.

Adonai, our Lord!
How majestic is your name in all the earth!

Glory...

Repeat antiphon.

WEEK III
VIGIL OF SUNDAY
(Saturday Evening)

PSALM 61

Antiphon God, you are my refuge
and my tower of strength.

Hear, God, my cry! Listen to my prayer!
From the end of the earth I call to you
as my heart grows faint.

To the high rock you lead me
for you are my refuge and tower of strength
against the Foe (of death).

I would dwell in your tent for forevers
and take refuge in the shelter of your wings.
For you, God, hearing my vows,
gave inheritance to those fearing your name.

You increase the days upon days of the royal one,
and the years for generation and generation,
enthroned in God's presences forever,
appointed and protected in God's love and fidelity.

I will sing praise of your name forever
to fulfill my vows day by day.

Glory…

Repeat antiphon.

PSALM 113

Antiphon Rejoice, Jerusalem, let your joy overflow;
your Savior will come to you,
alleluia.

Hallelujah! Praise Adonai!
Praise, you who serve Adonai!
Praise the name Adonai!

Let Adonai be praised by name
from now and to forevermore.
From the rising of the sun to its setting
praised be the name Adonai.

Exalted over all the nations is Adonai,
the glory above the heavens.
Who is like our God Adonai,
sitting enthroned on high,
leaning to look down
on the heavens and the earth?

The One who raises the poor from dust
and lifts up the needy from ash heaps
to sit with princes, the princes of the people,
who settles the barren woman in a home,
a happy mother of children.

Hallelujah! Praise Adonai!

Glory…

Antiphon Rejoice, Jerusalem, let your joy overflow;
your Savior will come to you,
alleluia.

PSALM 116:10-19

Antiphon I, the Lord, am coming to save you;
already I am near;
soon I will free you from your sins.

I believed it and so said, "I am greatly afflicted."
I said when it dismayed me, "Everyone is a liar."

How can I repay to Adonai all the goodness to me?
I will lift the cup of salvation
and I will call on the name of Adonai.

My vows to Adonai I will now fulfill
in the presence of all the people.
Precious in the eyes of Adonai
are the saints to the death.

O, Adonai, I am truly your servant,
your servant and son of your maidservant;
you freed me from the chains.
I will offer to you the sacrifice of thanksgiving
and I will call on the name of Adonai.

My vows to Adonai I will now fulfill
in the presence of all the people,
in courts of the house of Adonai,
in your midst, Jerusalem.
Hallelujah! Praise Adonai!

Glory...

Antiphon I, the Lord, am coming to save you;
already I am near;
soon I will free you from your sins.

PHILIPPIANS 2:6-11

Antiphon Lord, send the Lamb,
the ruler of the earth,
from the rock in the desert
to the mountain of the daughter of Zion.

Christ Jesus, subsisting in the form of God,
did not deem equality with God something to grab,
but emptied himself, taking the form of a slave,
becoming in human likeness.

And being found in human fashion,
he humbled himself,
becoming obedient until death,
and death on a cross.

And so God highly exalted him,
and gave to him the name above every name,
that in the name of Jesus every knee should bend,
of heavenly beings and earthly beings,
and beings under the earth;

And every tongue acknowledge
to the glory of God the Father
that Jesus Christ is Lord.

Glory...

Antiphon Lord, send the Lamb,
the ruler of the earth,
from the rock in the desert
to the mountain of the daughter of Zion.

WEEK III
RESURRECTION VIGIL

HOSEA 6:1-6

Antiphon In Christ who rose from the dead
our hope of resurrection dawned.

Come and let us return to Adonai,
who let us be torn up but will heal us,
who let us be injured but will bind our wounds,

who will revive us after two days
and restore us on the third day
that we may live in the presence.

So let us know, let us press on to know Adonai,
who will appear coming as the sun rises,
who will come to us like the winter rain,
watering the earth like spring rain.

What can I do with you Ephraim?
What can I do with you Judah?
Your love indeed is like morning mist,
and like the early dew that disappears.

For this I cut to pieces with the prophets
and have slain with words of my mouth
and judgments of lightning flashes:
For it is mercy that I desire and not sacrifice,
knowledge of God rather than burnt offerings.

Glory... Repeat antiphon.

FOR SUNDAYS OF WEEK 3

LUKE 23:56b–24:12

And on the sabbath, indeed they rested
according to the commandment.
But on day one of the week, while still very early,
they came upon the tomb
carrying spices which they had prepared.
And they found the stone rolled away from the tomb,
and entering they did not find the body of the Lord Jesus.
As they were perplexed about this, behold,
two men stood by them in shining clothing.
And becoming terrified
and bending their faces to the earth, they said to them,
"Why do you seek the living one with the dead?
He is not here, but was raised.
Remember how he spoke to you while yet in Galilee,
saying, 'It is fitting that the Son of humanity be delivered
into the hands of sinful humans and be crucified,
and on the third day to rise again.'"
And they remembered his words,
and returning from the tomb
reported all these things to the eleven
and to all the rest.
Now they were Mary the Magdalene and Joanna
and Mary the mother of James, and the rest with them
told these things to the apostles.
And these words seemed to them as folly,
and they did not believe them.

•

FOR SUNDAYS OF WEEK 7

JOHN 20:19-31

When it was early evening on that day one of the week,
and the doors having been shut where the disciples were
because of fear of the Judeans,
Jesus came and stood in the midst and said to them,
"Peace to you."
And saying this
he showed to them both his hands and his side.
And so the disciples seeing the Lord rejoiced.
And so Jesus said to them again,
"Peace to you;
as the Father has sent me, I also send you."
And saying this he breathed in and onto them saying,
"Receive Holy Spirit.
Of whomever you forgive the sins,
they are forgiven of them;
of whomever you hold, they are held."

But Thomas, one of the twelve called Twin,
was not with them when Jesus came.
And so the other disciples said to him,
"We have seen the Lord."
But he said to them,
"Unless I see in his hands the mark of the nails
and put my finger into the place of the nails
and put my hand into his side,
by no means will I believe."

And after eight days,
again his disciples were within,
and Thomas was with them.
The doors having been shut,
Jesus came and stood in the midst and said,
"Peace to you."
Then he said to Thomas,
"Bring your finger here and see my hands,
and bring and put your hand into my side,
and be not faithless, but faithful."
Thomas answered and said to him,
"My Lord and my God."
Jesus said to him,
"Have you had faith because you have seen me?
Blessed are the ones not seeing and having faith."
And so
Jesus did many and other signs before the disciples,
which have not been written in this scroll.
But these have been written
that you may believe
that Jesus is the Christ, the Son of God,
and that believing
you may have life in his name.

•

WEEK III
SUNDAY MORNING

PSALM 2

Antiphon Here is a king of my own choosing
who will rule on Mount Zion.

Why do nations rage and peoples plot vanity?
Kings of the earth make their stand
and ruling ones gather together
against Adonai and Adonai's anointed one:
"Let us break their chains,
let us throw off their fetters."

The One enthroned in the heavens laughs,
the Lord scoffs and rebukes them.
In anger and in wrath the Lord terrifies them.
"I indeed installed my king
on my holy hill of Zion.

I will proclaim a decree of Adonai who said,
'You are my son, this day I am your father.
Ask of me and nations are your inheritance,
and your possession to the ends of earth.
You will rule them with a scepter of iron
and dash them to pieces of what potters make.'

Kings, now be wise!
Rulers of earth, be warned!
Serve Adonai with fear; rejoice with trembling!
Kiss my son, lest he be angry
and you be destroyed
for in a moment he can flare up in wrath.

Blessings on all who take refuge in him."

Glory...

Antiphon Here is a king of my own choosing
who will rule on Mount Zion.

PSALM 93

Antiphon The Lord is coming and without delay
and will reveal things kept hidden
and show himself to all humanity,
alleluia.

Adonai reigns, robed in majesty;
robed is Adonai and armed with strength.

The world is firmly established;
she cannot be moved.
Your throne was set up from long ago;
from eternity you are.

PSALM 93, continued

The seas lifted up, Adonai,
the seas lifted up their voice;
the seas lifted up their pounding.

More than thunders of great waters
or mighty breakers of the sea,
mighty in the height is Adonai.

Your statutes stand very firm;
your house, Adonai, is adorned in holiness
for length of days.

Glory...

Antiphon The Lord is coming and without delay
and will reveal things kept hidden
and show himself to all humanity,
alleluia.

DANIEL 3:57-90

Antiphon Mountains and hills shall be made level
crooked paths straight
and rough ways smooth.
Come, Lord, do not delay,
alleluia.

DANIEL 3:57-90

Bless the Lord, all you works of the Lord,
exalt and sing praise to forever.
Angels of the Lord, bless the Lord,
You heavens, bless the Lord,
All you waters above the heavens, bless the Lord,
All you powers, bless the Lord,
Sun and moon, bless the Lord,
Stars of heaven, bless the Lord.

All you rain and dew, bless the Lord,
All you winds, bless the Lord,
You fire and heat, bless the Lord,
You ice and cold, bless the Lord,
You dews and falling snows, bless the Lord,
You snows and frosts, bless the Lord,
You nights and days, bless the Lord,
You light and darkness, bless the Lord,
You lightning and clouds, bless the Lord.

Let the earth bless the Lord,
exalt and sing praise to forever.
You mountains and hills, bless the Lord,
All things growing in the ground, bless the Lord,
You seas and rivers, bless the Lord,
You springs and rain, bless the Lord,
You sea monsters and all swimmers, bless the Lord,
All you birds of the air, bless the Lord,
All you wild beasts and cattle, bless the Lord,
You sons and daughters, bless the Lord.

DANIEL 3:57-90, continued

O Israel, bless the Lord,
exalt and sing praise to forever.
You priests of the Lord, bless the Lord,
You servants of the Lord, bless the Lord,
You spirits and souls of the just, bless the Lord,
You holy and humble in heart, bless the Lord,
Hananiah, Azariah, and Mishael, bless the Lord,
exalt and sing praise to forever...

Give thanks to the Lord, who is good,
whose mercy endures to forever.
Bless the God of "gods"
all you who worship the Lord;
sing praise and give thanks to the One God
whose mercy endures to forever.

(*No doxology*)

Antiphon

Mountains and hills shall be made level
crooked paths straight
and rough ways smooth.
Come, Lord, do not delay,
alleluia.

PSALM 148

Antiphon I shall enfold Zion with my salvation
and shed my glory around Jerusalem,
alleluia.

Hallelujah! Praise Adonai!
Give praise from the heavens!
Give praise in the heights.
Give praise all you angels.
Give praise all you hosts.

Give praise sun and moon.
Give praise all stars shining.
Give praise, you heavens of the heavens
and waters above the skies.

Let them praise the name Adonai,
who commanded and they were created,
who set them in place forever,
to forever the decree Adonai gave,
not to pass away.

PSALM 148, continued

Praise Adonai, you earth,
give praise you sea creatures and all in the deep,
lightning and hail, snow and cloud,
wind of the storm, all who do Adonai's bidding,

the mountains and hills, fruit trees and cedars,
wild animals and all cattle,
small creatures and birds of flight,

kings of the earth and the nations,
princes and all people ruling on earth,
young men and also maidens,
old men and children:

Let them praise the name Adonai
whose name alone is exalted,
whose splendor is above earth and the heavens,

Who raised a horn for the people,
praise of all the saints,
of the sons and daughters of Israel,
of people close to the Lord.

Hallelujah! Praise Adonai!

Glory…

Antiphon I shall enfold Zion with my salvation
and shed my glory around Jerusalem,
alleluia.

WEEK III
SUNDAY EVENING

PSALM 64

Antiphon Let the righteous rejoice
and take refuge in the Lord.

Hear my voice, O God, in complaint;
threatened by an enemy, you protect my life.
You hide me from conspiracies,
from the noisy crowd of people doing bad things,

who sharpen their tongue like the sword,
aim their arrow of harmful words,
and shoot from ambush the innocent person;
they shoot suddenly and without fear.

They encourage those who plan harm,
and they talk of hidden snares,
saying, "who will see them?"
They plot injustices they call "the perfect plan!"
Surely the human mind and heart are cunning.

But God will shoot sudden arrows
striking down those plans.
Their ruin will be by their own tongues;
all who see them will shake heads at them.

PSALM 64, continued

They will fear all humanity,
then come to proclaim the work of God,
and ponder the deeds of God.
Let the righteous rejoice and take refuge in Adonai;
let all praise the upright of heart.

Glory…

Antiphon Let the righteous rejoice
and take refuge in the Lord.

PSALM 91

Antiphon Have no fear of terror at night;
in the shadow of the Almighty,
find rest.

One who dwells in the shelter of Elyon,
in the shadow of Shaddai, will find rest.
I will say of Adonai, my refuge, my fortress:
in my God do I trust.

Surely the Lord will save you
from fowler snare, from deadly pestilence.
With the feather of the Lord you will be covered,
and under those wings you will find refuge,
shield and rampart, the faithfulness of the Lord.

You will have no fear of terror at night
nor of arrows flying by day,
of pestilence stalking in the darkness,
nor of plague that destroys at midday.

A thousand may fall at your side,
and ten thousand at your right hand;
near to you they will not come.

Observe with your eyes, simply watch;
punishment of wicked ones you will see.
Make Adonai, who is my refuge,
make Elyon your dwelling.

Harm will not befall you,
nor will disaster come near your tent.
God's own Angels, the Lord will command
to guard you in all of your ways.

In their hands they will lift you up;
your foot will not strike against the stone.
Upon lion and cobra you will tread,
you will trample the great lion and serpent.

"Because you love me, I will rescue you,
I will protect all who acknowledge my Name.
You will call upon me and I will answer.
I am with you in trouble;
I will deliver you and honor you.

In length of days I will satisfy you,
and show you my salvation."

Glory...

Antiphon

Have no fear of terror at night;
in the shadow of the Almighty,
find rest.

PSALM 110 :1-6a,7

Antiphon Our Lord will come
to claim his glorious throne
in the assembly of the princes.

Adonai said to my Lord:
"Sit at my right hand
until I make enmity as a footstool for your feet."

A scepter of your might
Adonai will extend from Zion,
and rule in the midst of enmity!

Your troops are willing on the day of your battle.
In majesties of holiness from the womb of the dawn
to you is the dew of your youth.
Adonai swore and this mind will not change,
"You are a priest to forever
in the order of Melchizedek."

The Lord is at your right hand
and will crush kings on the day of wrath,
will judge the nations...,
and will drink from a brook on the way
with head lifted up because of all this.

Glory...

Antiphon Our Lord will come
to claim his glorious throne
in the assembly of the princes.

PSALM 111

Antiphon

Let the mountains break out with joy
and the hills answer with gladness,
for the world's true light, the Lord,
comes with power and might.

Praise Adonai!
I will extol Adonai with all my heart
in the council of the upright ones
and in the assembly.
Great are the works of Adonai,
pondered by all who delight in them.

Glorious and majestic are the deeds,
and this righteousness endures to forever.
Remembrance is caused of deeds of wonder
by gracious and compassionate Adonai,

providing food for ones fearing the One,
remembering the covenant to forever,
and having shown power at work,
giving the people the land of the nations.

Faithful and just is the handiwork of Adonai,
whose precepts are worthy of trust.
Steadfast are they forever to forever,
done in faithfulness and uprightness.

Redemption is provided for Adonai's people;
ordained to forever is the covenant.
Holy and awesome is the Name.

PSALM 111, continued

The beginning of wisdom is fear of Adonai,
good understanding for all who follow this.
Praise endures to eternity.

Glory...

Antiphon

Let the mountains break out with joy
and the hills answer with gladness,
for the world's true light, the Lord,
comes with power and might.

REVELATION 19:1b,2a,5b,6b,7

Antiphon Let us live in holiness and love
as we patiently await our blessed hope,
the coming of our Savior.

Alleluia! Praise the Lord!
Salvation and glory and power are to our God,
whose judgments are true and just.

Alleluia! Praise the Lord!
Praise our God, all you slaves of the Lord,
you small and you great, who hold God in awe.

Alleluia! Praise the Lord!
The Lord is reigning, our God, the Almighty.
Let us rejoice and let us exult,
and we will give the glory to the Lord.

Alleluia! Praise the Lord!
The day has come
for the marriage of the Lamb,
and the bride has prepared herself.

Glory... Repeat antiphon.

Antiphon Let us live in holiness and love
as we patiently await our blessed hope,
the coming of our Savior.

WEEK III
MONDAY MORNING

PSALM 50

Antiphon Our God will be shown and not in silence, alleluia.

El Elohim Adonai
speaks and summons earth
from the rising of the sun to its setting.
From Zion, perfect of beauty, God shines forth.

Our God comes and will not be silent,
before whom a fire devours,
around whom a storm is great.
The heavens at above are summoned,
and the earth to judge the people:

"Gather the ones consecrated to me,
  the ones making my covenant by sacrifice."
The heavens proclaim the righteousness of God,
the One who judges.

"Hear, my people, and I will speak, Israel,
  and I will testify against you;
  God, your God, am I.

  Not for your sacrifices do I rebuke you,
  or your burnt offerings ever before me.
  I do not need a bull from your stall
  or goats from your pen,

for every animal of the forest is mine,
cattle on the hills, the thousands.
I know every bird of the mountains,
and every creature of fields is mine.

Were I hungry, I would not tell it to you,
for the world is mine and all in her.
Do I eat the flesh of bulls?
Do I drink the blood of goats?

Sacrifice to God thank offerings!
And fulfill your vows to the Most High!
Call upon me in the day of trouble;
I will deliver you and you will honor me."

But God says to those who do the wicked,
"What to you to recite my laws
or to take my covenant on your lip?
For you hate instruction
and you cast my words behind you.

When you see a thief, you join in,
and cast your lot with doers of adultery.
You use your mouth for evil
and harness your tongue to deceit.

You sit and speak against your brother and sister
and give slander against your mother's children.
You did these, and I kept silent;
you thought me to be like you?

PSALM 50, continued

...Consider now this: ...there is no one to rescue
...those who insist on forgetting God.
One sacrificing a thank offering honors me
and prepares the way,
and I will show that one
to the salvation of God."

Glory...

Antiphon Our God will be shown and not in silence,
alleluia.

PSALM 84

Antiphon Blessed are the ones dwelling in your house,
my King and my God.

Dec. 17-23 The Lord,
the ruler over the kings of the earth,
will come;
blessed are they who are ready
to go and welcome him.

How lovely are your dwellings, Adonai Sabaoth!
My soul she yearns and even faints
for the courts of Adonai;
my heart and my flesh cry out for God alive.

Even the sparrow found a home
and the swallow a nest for her
where she may have her young ones
near your altar, Adonai Sabaoth,
my King and my God.

Blessed are the dwellers in your house,
ever they praise you.
Blessed are the ones whose strength is in you,
who make a pilgrimage in their hearts.

Passing through the Baca Valley, springs are made,
pools covered over with autumn rains.
They go from strength to strength
and appear before God in Zion.

Adonai, God Sabaoth, hear my prayer!
Listen, God of Jacob. God, our shield, look!
Look on the face of your anointed one!

Better is a day in your courts
than a thousand elsewhere.
I would rather be doorkeeper in my God's house
than to dwell in tents of those who do bad,

for God Adonai is sun and shield.
Adonai bestows favor and honor,
withholding no good thing from blameless walkers.

Adonai Sabaoth,
blessed is the one trusting in you.

Glory...

Repeat antiphon.

ISAIAH 2:2-5

Antiphon Come and let us go up
the mountain of the Lord.

Dec. 17-23 Sing a new song to the Lord;
proclaim his praises to the ends of the earth.

In the last of the days
the mountain of Adonai's temple will be established
as chief of the mountains,
raised above the hills.

All the nations will stream to it.
Many peoples will come and say,
"Come, let us go up to the mountain of Adonai,
to the house of the God of Jacob,
who will teach us the ways
so we may walk in the path."

Indeed, from Zion the law will go out
and from Jerusalem the word of Adonai,
who will judge between the nations
and settle disputes for many peoples.

They will beat their swords into plowshares
and their spears into pruning hooks.
Nations will not take up the sword against nations,
and they will train for war no more.

House of Jacob, come!
Let us walk in Adonai's light.

Glory...

Repeat antiphon.

PSALM 96

Antiphon Sing to the Lord and praise the name.

Dec. 17-23 When the Son of humanity comes
will he find faith in human hearts?

Sing to Adonai a new song!
Sing to Adonai, all the earth!
Sing to Adonai and praise the name!
Proclaim the salvation from day to day!

Declare among the nations the glory of the Lord!
Among all the peoples the marvelous deeds,
for great is Adonai, greatly being praised,
the one being feared above all so-called "gods."

For all "gods" of the nations are idols,
but Adonai made the heavens,
splendor and majesty and strength and glory
in the holy sanctuary.

Ascribe to Adonai, families of nations!
Ascribe to Adonai glory and strength!
Ascribe to Adonai the glory of the name!

Bring offerings and come into the courts!
Worship Adonai in holy splendor!
Tremble in the presence all the earth!

Say among the nations, "Adonai reigns!"
Firmly established, the world cannot be moved
and peoples will be judged with equity.

PSALM 96, continued

Let the heavens rejoice and the earth be glad.
Let the sea resound and all its fullness.
Let the fields and all that is in them be jubilant,
then all the trees of the forests will sing for joy

before Adonai who comes,
who comes to judge the earth,
who will judge the world and its peoples
in justice and in truth.

Glory...

Antiphon Sing to the Lord and praise the name.

Dec. 17-23 When the Son of humanity comes
will he find faith in human hearts?

WEEK III
MONDAY EVENING

PSALM 71

Antiphon

You are my hope,
Lord Adonai,
my confidence since my youth.

In you, Adonai, I take refuge;
let me not be shamed to forever.
In your righteousness you rescue and deliver me.
Turn your ear to me and save me!

Be to me as a rock, and a refuge to go to always.
Command that I be saved,
for you are my rock and my fortress.
My God, deliver me from the hands
and grasp of ones who do evil or the cruel,

for you are my hope, Lord Adonai,
my confidence since my youth.
I have relied on you from birth,
from my mother's womb you brought me forth;
my praise is ever to you.

PSALM 71, continued

To many I became like a portent
but you are my strong refuge.
My mouth is filled all the day
with praise of your splendor.
Cast me not away at my time of old age;
forsake me not when my strength is gone.

Enmity speaks against me;
waiting on my life, conspirers together say,
"God has forsaken that one! Pursue to seize,
 for no one is coming to the rescue!"
God, be not far from me.
God, come quickly to help me!

May accusations against me perish in shame.
May scorn and disgrace cover the desire to do harm.

But I will hope always and add to all your praise.
My mouth will tell of your righteousness,
all the day of your salvation,
though I know not its measure;

I will come in mighty acts of Lord Adonai;
I will proclaim the righteousness of you yourself.
You taught me, God, since my youth;
to this day I declare your marvelous deeds.

Even in my old age and gray hair
you do not forsake me, God,
till I delcare your power to this generation,
your might to all who will come,
and your righteousness to the sky,
you, God, who have done great things.
Who, God, is like you?

Though you let me see troubles, many and bitter,
you will again let me live.
And from the depths of the earth
you will again bring me up.
You will increase my honor
and you will again comfort me.

With the harp instrument I will praise you
and your faithfulness, my God;
I will sing praise to you with lyre,
Holy One of Israel.
My lips will shout for joy when I sing praise to you,
even my self whom you redeemed.

Also my tongue will tell all the day of your justice
for desires of some to harm me
are in shame and confusion.

Glory...

Antiphon

You are my hope,
Lord Adonai,
my confidence since my youth.

PSALM 123

Antiphon Our eyes are to our God
till the Lord shows to us mercy.

Dec. 17-23 The Lord,
the ruler over the kings of the earth,
will come;
blessed are they who are ready
to go and welcome him.

I lift up my eyes to you, sitting in the heavens.
As eyes of slaves are to the hand of their masters,
as the eyes of a maid are to the hand of her mistress,
see, our eyes are to Adonai
till our God shows to us mercy.

Have mercy on us, Adonai, have mercy on us,
for we have endured much contempt.

Much ridicule of the proud ones
and contempt of arrogant ones
have we ourselves endured.

Glory...

Antiphon Our eyes are to our God
till the Lord shows to us mercy.

Dec. 17-23 The Lord,
the ruler over the kings of the earth,
will come;
blessed are they who are ready
to go and welcome him.

PSALM 124

Antiphon Our help is in the name of the Lord,
the One Making heavens and earth.

Dec. 17-23 Sing a new song to the Lord;
proclaim his praises to the ends of the earth.

If Adonai was not for us, let Israel now say,
if Adonai was not for us
when human beings attacked against us,
then they would have swallowed us alive
when their anger flared against us.

Then the floods would have engulfed us,
the torrents would have swept over our selfs,
and the raging waters would have swept over us.

Praise be to Adonai,
who did not let us be torn by their teeth.
Our selfs, like a bird,
escaped from the snare of fowlers.

The snare being broken we escaped.
Our help is in the name of Adonai,
the Maker of heavens and earth.

Glory...

Antiphon Our help is in the name of the Lord,
the One Making heavens and earth.

Dec. 17-23 Sing a new song to the Lord;
proclaim his praises to the ends of the earth.

EPHESIANS 1:3-10

Antiphon God has given us a destiny as sons are adopted.

Dec. 17-23 When the Son of humanity comes
will he find faith in human hearts?

Blessed be the God and Father
of our Lord Jesus Christ,
who has blessed us in Christ
with every spiritual blessing in the heavens.

God chose us in Christ
before the foundation of the world,
to be holy and free of blemish before him.

In love, God gave us a destiny:
as sons are adopted, through Jesus Christ himself,
in accord with the good pleasure of God's will
to the praise of the glory of grace
by which we are favored as God's beloved.

In Christ we have the redemption
through his blood, the forgiveness of sins,
in accord with the riches of his grace
which he made abound to us.

In all wisdom and intelligence
the mystery of God's will is made known to us
in accord with God's good pleasure and purpose:

A stewardship of the fullness of time,
heading up all things in Christ,
the things in the heavens and the things on earth.

Glory... Repeat antiphon.

WEEK III
TUESDAY MORNING

PSALM 68

Antiphon Kingdoms of earth, sing to God;
sing praise to the Lord,
alleluia.

May God arise
and may foes in enmity flee and be scattered.
As smoke is blown, let it blow;
as wax melts before fire
may wicked ways perish from before God.

But may righteous ones be glad
and rejoice before God;
may they be happy with joy.
Sing to God! Sing praise to the name!
Extol the Rider of the Clouds,
and rejoice in the name Adonai,

Father of the fatherless
and defender of widows,
God dwelling in holiness.
God sets the lonely into a family
and leads prisoners forth with the songs,
but ones rebelling live on sun-scorched land.

PSALM 68, continued

When you went out before your people, God,
when you marched through the wasteland,
the earth shook and heavens poured rain
before the One God of Sinai,
before God, the God of Israel.

You gave a shower of abundances, God,
on your inheritance;
even the weary you refreshed.
Your people settled in her, God;
you provided for the poor from your bounty.

The Lord announced the word,
a great company of proclaimers.
Kings of armies flee, they flee,
and in camps of residence the plunder is divided.

While you sleep among campfires
wings of dove are sheathed with silver
and her feathers with the shine of gold.
When Shaddai scatters the kings,
the scattering is like snow on Zalmon.

A mountain of majesties, the mountain of Bashan,
a rugged mountain is the mountain of Bashan.
Why gaze in envy, you rugged mountains,
at the mountain God chooses for the reign?
Indeed Adonai will dwell to forever.

Chariots of God are tens of thousands,
thousands of the multitude into the Sinai sanctuary.
You ascended to the height and led captive;
you received gifts from human beings,
and even from those rebelling,
to your dwelling, God Adonai.

The Lord is being praised day to day,
bearing our burden is El our Savior.
Our El, the El of salvation,
the Lord Adonai is the escape from death.
Surely God will silence the plans of enmity,
in the crown of their hair where sins go on.

The Lord says, "From Bashan I will bring,
  I will bring from depths of the sea,
  that you may wash your foot in their defeat
  and the tongues of your dogs
  have their share from foes."

They view your processions, God,
processions into the sanctuary
of my God and my King.
Singers are in front, followed by music players
among maidens playing tambourines.

In great congregations, praise God;
praise Adonai in the assembly of Israel!
There little Benjamin leads the princes of Judah,
their throng the princes of Zebulun and Naphtali.

PSALM 68, continued

Your God summoned your power.
Show strength, God, as you did for us!
Because of your temple at Jerusalem,
to you the kings will bring gifts.

Rebuke the beast of the reeds,
the herd of bulls among calves of nations;
being humbled with bars of silver,
nations that delight in wars are scattered.
Envoys from Egypt will come;
Cush will submit their hands to God.

Kingdoms of the earth, sing to God!
Sing praise to the Lord!
To the Rider in the skies, the ancient skies, see!
The voice thunders, the voice of might.

Proclaim the power of God over Israel,
the majesty and power in the skies.
Awesome are you, God, in your sanctuary;
the God of Israel gives power and strengths
to the people praising God.

Glory...

Antiphon Kingdoms of earth, sing to God;
sing praise to the Lord,
alleluia.

PSALM 85

Antiphon Lord, you showed favor to your land;
you have forgiven the sins of your people.

Dec. 17-23 The Lord will come from his holy place
to save his people.

You showed favor, Adonai, to your land;
you restored the fortune of Jacob.
You forgave the iniquity of your people;
you covered all of their sin.
You set aside all of your wrath;
you turned from your fierce anger.

Restore us, God of our salvation!
And put away your displeasure toward us.
Will you be angry with us to forever?
Will you prolong your anger
to generation and generation?

Will you not revive us again
that your people may rejoice in you?
Show us, Adonai, your unfailing love
and grant us your salvation.

I will listen to what El Adonai will say,
promising peace to the people, even to the saints,
but not letting them return to folly.
Surely near to ones fearing is salvation,
the glory to dwell in our land.

PSALM 85, continued

Love and Faithfulness meet;
Justice and Peace kiss.
Faithfulness springs forth from the earth
and Justice looks down from the heavens.

Indeed Adonai will give the good
and our land will yield her harvest,
Justice going forward to prepare
the way for the steps of the Lord.

Glory...

Antiphon Lord, you showed favor to your land;
you have forgiven the sins of your people.

Dec. 17-23 The Lord will come from his holy place
to save his people.

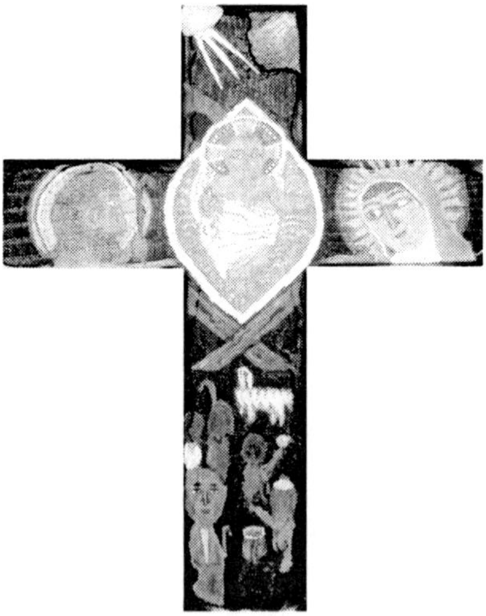

ISAIAH 26:1b-4,7-9,12

Antiphon My soul yearns for you in the night;
within me my spirit longs for you.

Dec. 17-23 Zion is our mighty citadel, our saving Lord its wall and its defense; throw open the gates, for our God is here among us, alleluia.

Our city is strong;
salvation makes walls and rampart.
Open gates, so the righteous nation may enter,
the one keeping faiths.

Your steadfast mind will keep peace,
peace because of trusting.
Trust in Adonai to forever,
for in Yah Adonai is the Rock of eternities…

The path of the righteous is level;
the Upright One smooths the way of the righteous.
Yes, in the way of your laws, Adonai, we wait,
for your name and your renown
are the desire of our heart.

My soul yearns for you in the night;
within me my spirit longs for you.
Just as your judgments are on the earth,
so people of the world learn justice…

Adonai, you establish for us peace;
indeed all we have accomplished you did for us.

Glory… Repeat antiphon.

PSALM 67

Antiphon

May God be gracious to us,
bless us,
and shine the holy face upon us.

Dec. 17-23

Lord,
make known your will throughout the earth;
proclaim your salvation to every nation.

May God be gracious to us and bless us,
may God's faces shine upon us.
How else can your ways be known on the earth
and your salvation among all the nations?

May the peoples praise you, God,
may the peoples praise you, all of them.

May the nations be glad and sing for joy
for you rule the peoples
and guide nations of the earth into justice.

May the peoples praise you, God,
may the peoples praise you, all of them.

The land will yield her harvest, God will bless us,
and all the ends of the earth will revere our God.

Glory...

Repeat antiphon.

WEEK III
TUESDAY EVENING

PSALM 74

Antiphon Remember, O God,
your people you purchased of old.

Why, God, do you reject us to forever?
Your anger smolders against sheep of your pasture.
Remember your people you purchased of old
and redeemed, your tribe of inheritance,
Mount Zion where you dwelt.

Lift high your steps through everlasting ruin,
the enmity destruction to the sanctuary.
All who would be foes roared,
and in your meeting place
set up their standard signs.

They behaved like ones wielding at above
axes through a thicket of trees,
and now her carved panels
they smashed with axe and hatchet.
They sent your sanctuary to the ground with fire
and defiled the dwelling place of your Name.

PSALM 74, continued

They said in their heart, "We will crush them."
Completely they burned in the land
all the places to worship God.
We see no miraculous signs;
there is no longer a prophet among us.
Until when? No one knows.

Until when, God, will foes in enmity
mock and revile your name?
To forever?
Why do you hold back your hand,
even your right hand from the fold of your bosom?

But God, my King from of old,
bringing salvation onto the midst of the earth,
you split open the sea by your power,
you break the heads of monsters in the waters.

You crushed the heads of Leviathan,
giving him as food to people and desert creatures.
You opened up streams and springs
and dried up everflowing rivers.

To you is the day and to you is the night,
and you established the moon and the sun.
You set all the boundaries of the earth;
summer and winter were made by you.

Remember those who in enmity mock Adonai
and the foolish people who revile your name.
Do not hand the life of your dove to the wild beast;
remember to forever the life of your afflicted ones.

Dark places of the land are filled with them
and haunts of violence.
Have regard for the covenant.
Let not the oppressed retreat, nor the disgraced;
may the poor and the needy praise your name.

Rise up, God! Defend your cause!
Remember the all-day mockery of fools.
Ignore not the clamor of foes,
nor those in enmity and continual uproar.

Glory...

Antiphon Remember, O God,
your people you purchased of old.

PSALM 125

Antiphon The Lord surrounds the people of God
from now and to forevermore.

Dec. 17-23 The Lord will come
from the holy place
to save his people.

Ones trusting in Adonai are like Mount Zion;
not to be shaken, they endure to forever.

As mountains surround around Jerusalem,
so Adonai surrounds around the people
from now and to forevermore.

Indeed the sceptor of badness will not remain
over the lot of the righteous
lest the hands of the righteous be used for bad.

Do good, Adonai, to the good,
even to those upright in their hearts!
But those who turn to evil ways
Adonai will banish with those who do evil.

Peace be upon Israel!

Glory…

Antiphon The Lord surrounds the people of God
from now and to forevermore.

Dec. 17-23 The Lord will come
from the holy place
to save his people.

PSALM 131

Antiphon Unless you turn and become as a child,
by no means may you enter the kingdom.
see Mark 10:15

Dec. 17-23 Zion is our mighty citadel, our saving Lord its wall and its defense; throw open the gates, for our God is here among us, alleluia.

Adonai, my heart is not proud
and my eyes are not haughty
and I am unconcerned with the great matters,
with things so wonderful as to be beyond me.

But indeed I have become still and quiet in my soul
like a child with a mother, being weaned.
Like one being weaned is my soul within me.

Israel, put your hope in Adonai
from now and to forevermore.

Glory...

Antiphon Unless you turn and become as a child,
by no means may you enter the kingdom.
see Mark 10:15

Dec. 17-23 Zion is our mighty citadel, our saving Lord its wall and its defense; throw open the gates, for our God is here among us, alleluia.

REVELATION 4:8b,11; 5:9,10,12,13b

Antiphon Lord, out of every tribe and tongue
and people and nation,
you made to our God a kingdom and priests.

Dec. 17-23 Lord,
make known your will throughout the earth;
proclaim your salvation to every nation.

Worthy are you, our Lord and our God,
to receive the glory and honor and power,
because you have created all things,
and by your will all things were created and are.

Worthy are you to receive the scroll
and to open its seals,
because you were slain
and purchased for God by your blood
from every tribe and tongue and people and nation.

You made of them to our God
a kingdom and priests,
and they will reign over the earth.

Worthy is the Lamb, slain to receive
the power and riches and wisdom and strength
and honor and glory and blessing.

Glory...

Repeat antiphon.

WEEK III
WEDNESDAY MORNING

PSALM 89:2-38

Antiphon Wherever you are, Lord,
there is mercy, there is truth,
alleluia.

Forever will I sing the great love of Adonai;
with my mouth I will make known
your faithfulness to generation and generation.
Indeed I will declare forever love standing firm,
your faithfulness established in the heavens.

"I made a covenant with my chosen ones,
sworn to my servant David.
I will establish your line to forever,
and to generation and generation
I will make firm your throne."

The heavens praise your wonder, Adonai,
and your faithfulness in the holy assembly.
For who in the sky can compare to Adonai;
who is like Adonai among heavenly beings?

God is greatly feared in the council of holy ones
and is awesome over all who surround around.
Adonai Sabaoth, who is like you?
Mighty Adonai, your faithfulness is around you.

PSALM 89:2-38, continued

You rule over the surging of the sea;
when waves mount up you still them.
You crushed Rahab like the slain
and scattered enmity
with the arm of your strength.

To you are the heavens and to you is the earth;
the world and her fullness you founded.
North and South you created;
Tabor and Hermon sing for joy at your name.

To you is the arm strong with power;
your hand is exalted, your right hand.
Righteousness and Justice
are the foundation of your throne;
Hesed-Love and Faithfulness go before your faces.

Blessed are people who learn to acclaim Adonai;
they walk in the light of your presences.
In your name they rejoice all the day
and in your righteousness they exult,

for you are the glory of their strength
and by your favor you exalt our horn.
Indeed Adonai is our shield
and the Holy One of Israel is our king.

Once in a vision you spoke to your faithful ones:
"I bestowed strength on a warrior;
I exalted from the people a young man.

I found David my servant,
I anointed him with my sacred oil,
and my hand will sustain him;
surely my arm will strengthen him.

No enemy will subject him to tribute
and no wicked people will oppress him.
Before him I will crush foes
and strike down adversity,

and my faithfulness and my love are with him,
and through my hands will the horn be exalted.
And I will set his hand over the sea
and his right hand over the rivers.

He will call me out: 'You are my Father,
  my God and Rock of my salvation.'
I will also appoint him firstborn
and most exalted among kings of the earth.

I will maintain my love for him to forever
and my unfailing covenant with him.
I will establish his line to forever
and his throne as days of the heavens.

If his sons and daughters forsake my law
and do not follow my statutes,
if they violate my decrees
and keep not my commands,

then I will punish their sins with the rod
and their iniquity with floggings.
But I will not take my love from them,
nor will I ever betray my faithfulness.

PSALM 89:2-38, continued

I will not violate my covenant
nor will I alter the utterance of my lips.
Once I swore by my holiness;
I will not lie to David:

His line will continue to forever
and his throne like the sun before me.
Like the moon it is established forever,
a faithful witness in the sky."

Glory...

Antiphon Wherever you are, Lord,
there is mercy, there is truth,
alleluia.

PSALM 86

Antiphon Bring joy to me, your servant,
for to you, Lord, I lift up my soul.

Dec. 17-23 The Lord, the mighty God,
will come forth from Zion
to set the people free.

Hear in your ear, Adonai;
answer me for I am poor and needy.
Guard my life for I am devoted;
save your servant, my God,
the one trusting in you.

Have mercy on me, Lord,
for to you I call all the day.
Bring joy to me, your servant,
for to you, Lord, I lift up my soul.

Indeed, Lord, you are kind and forgiving
and abundant in love for all who call to you.
Hear my prayer, Adonai;
listen to the sound of my cries for mercy.

In the day of my trouble I will call to you
for you will answer me...
There is none like you among so-called "gods"
and there are no deeds like yours, Lord.

All the nations you made will come
and they will worship before you, Lord,
and they will bring glory to your name
for you are great and do marvelous deeds,
you, God, by yourself.

Teach me, Adonai, your way
and I will walk in your truth.
Make my heart undivided
that I may fear your name.

I will praise you, Lord my God, with all my heart
and I will glorify your name to forever
for great is your love of me
and you deliver my soul from the depth of Sheol.

Arrogant ones attack against me, God;
a band of ruthless people seek my life
and do not regard you before them.

PSALM 86, continued

But you, Lord El, Compassionate and Gracious,
are slow of anger and abundant in love and fidelity.
Turn to me! And have mercy on me!

Grant your strength to your servant
and save the child of your maidservant!
Give to me a sign of goodness
that enmity may see and find shame,
for you, Adonai, help me and comfort me.

Glory...

Antiphon

Bring joy to me, your servant,
for to you, Lord, I lift up my soul.

Dec. 17-23

The Lord, the mighty God,
will come forth from Zion
to set the people free.

ISAIAH 33:13-16

Antiphon Blessed is the one walking rightly
and speaking right things.

Dec. 17-23 I shall not cease to plead with God for Zion
until the Holy One is sent in radiant beauty.

Hear what I did, you who are far away!
And acknowledge my power, you who are near.

Sinners are terrified in Zion
and trembling grips the godless.
Who of us can dwell in fire that consumes?
Who of us can dwell in everlasting burning?

One walking rightly and speaking right things,
rejecting the gain of extortions,
keeping hands from accepting the bribe,
stopping ears from hearing of blood,
shutting eyes against contemplation of evil:

That one will dwell on the heights
in a mountain fortress refuge,
supplied with bread and waters unfailing.

Glory...

Antiphon Blessed is the one walking rightly
and speaking right things.

Dec. 17-23 I shall not cease to plead with God for Zion
until the Holy One is sent in radiant beauty.

PSALM 98

Antiphon Shout for joy before the Lord, the King!

Dec. 17-23 The Spirit of the Lord rests upon me
and has sent me
to preach good news to the poor.

Sing to Adonai a new song
who has done marvelous things,
working salvation at the right hand and holy arm.

Adonai made known salvation,
righteousness revealed for the eyes of the nations.
Love is remembered and faithfulness
to the house of Israel

and all the ends of the earth see
the salvation of our God.
Shout for joy to Adonai, all you earth!
Burst forth, and sing, and make music!

Make music to Adonai with harp,
with harp and the sound of singing,
with trumpets and blast of ram horn:
Shout for joy before the King Adonai!

Let the sea resound, the fullness of the world,
and those living in her.
Let the rivers clap hands,
let the mountains sing together for joy

before Adonai who comes to judge the earth,
who will judge the world in righteousness
and peoples with equity.

Glory...

Repeat antiphon.

WEEK III
WEDNESDAY EVENING

PSALM 70

Antiphon To my poverty and need God came quickly.

God, save me; Adonai hasten to help me!
May plans to seek my life be shamed and confused;

may the desire for my ruin turn back in disgrace
and ones saying "aha!, aha!" turn back in shame.

May all who seek you rejoice in you and be glad
and may lovers of salvation say always,
"Let God be exalted."

Yet I am poor and needy, God,
come quickly to me and do not delay,
Adonai, my help and deliverer.

Glory...

Repeat antiphon.

PSALM 126

Antiphon Those who sow in tears
will reap a song of joy.

Dec. 17-23 The Lord, the mighty God,
will come forth from Zion
to set the people free.

When Adonai returned Zion from captivity
we felt like people in a dream.
Then our mouth was filled with laughter,
and our tongue with a song of joy.

Then they said among the nations
"Their Adonai did greatness for them."
Adonai did greatness for us;
we were full of joy.

Restore our good fortune, Adonai,
like streams in the Negev desert.
Sowers are now in tears;
they will reap with a song of joy.

Going out, the sower goes out weeping,
carrying seeds for the sowing.
Returning, the sower will return
carrying sheaves with a song of joy.

Glory...

Repeat antiphon.

PSALM 127

Antiphon Lord, build the house;
Lord, watch over the city.

Dec. 17-23 I shall not cease to plead with God for Zion
until the Holy One is sent in radiant beauty.

If Adonai does not build the house,
the builders labor in vanity.
If Adonai does not watch over the city,
the watcher stands guard in vain.

It is vanity to rise early or stay up late,
or to eat the bread of hard toil;
the Lord provides as the beloved get their sleep.
See, heritage of Adonai!

Sons are a reward, and daughters of the womb.
Like arrows in the hand of a warrior,
so are children of one's youth.

Blessed is the one whose quiver is full of them;
they will not be shamed
when they contend at the gate with enmity.

Glory...

Antiphon Lord, build the house;
Lord, watch over the city.

Dec. 17-23 I shall not cease to plead with God for Zion
until the Holy One is sent in radiant beauty.

COLOSSIANS 1:12-20

Antiphon He is the firstborn of all creation;
he is before all things
and in him all things hold together.

Dec. 17-23 The Spirit of the Lord rests upon me
and has sent me
to preach good news to the poor.

Give joyful thanks to the Father who made you fit
for your part of the lot of the saints in light,

who delivered us out of the authority of darkness
and transitioned us into the kingdom of the beloved Son,
in whom we have redemption, the forgiveness of our sins.

The Son is the image of the invisible God,
the firstborn of all creation.
In him all things were created,
in the heavens and on the earth,
the visible and the invisible,
whether thrones, lordships, rulers or authorities.

All things have been created through him and for him.
He is before all things,
and in him all things hold together.

He is the head of the body, the church,
and the beginning, the firstborn from the dead,
so that in all things he may hold the first place.

In him all the fullness was well pleased to dwell,
and through him reconciliation to himself of all things,
things on earth and things in the heavens,
making peace through the blood of his cross.

Glory...

Repeat antiphon.

WEEK III
THURSDAY MORNING

PSALM 89:39-53

Antiphon I am the root and stock of David;
I am the morning star,
alleluia.

Lord, you have rejected and spurned,
you were angry with your anointed one.
You renounced the covenant of your servant,
the crown you defiled in the dust.

You broke through all of the walls
and reduced the strongholds to ruin.
Those passing on the way plundered
and the neighbors were full of scorn.

PSALM 89:39-53, continued

You exalted the right hand of foes
and made all the enemies rejoice.
You turned back the edge of our sword
and did not support us in the battle.

You put an end to the splendor
and cast the throne to the ground.
You cut short the days of youth
and covered us over with shame.

Until when, Adonai?
Will you hide yourself to forever?
Will your wrath burn like fire?
Remember how fleeting am I!
For what futility you created
sons and daughters of Adam and Eve!
What human can live and not see death,
or save the self from the power of Sheol?

Where, Lord, are your former great loves
sworn to David in your faithfulness?
Remember, Lord, the mocking of your servants!
I bear this in my heart from many nations, Adonai:
the mockery of enmity,
the mockery of the steps of your anointed one.

Praised be Adonai to forever. Amen and amen.

Glory…

Antiphon

I am the root and stock of David;
I am the morning star,
alleluia.

PSALM 87

Antiphon Glorious things are being said of you,
city of God.

Dec. 17-23 To you, O Lord, I lift up my soul;
come and rescue me,
my refuge and my strength.

On the holy mountain is the foundation of Adonai,
who loves the gates of Zion
more than all of Jacob's dwellings.
Glorious things are being said of you, city of God.

"I will record Rahab and Babylon
among those who know me;
see Philistia and Tyre with Cush:
this one was born there!"

Indeed of Zion it will be said,
"One and another were born in her,
and the Most High will establish her."
Adonai will write when registering peoples,
"This one was born there."
And making music the ones will sing,
"All of my fountains are in you."

Glory...

Repeat antiphon.

ISAIAH 40:10-17

Antiphon

See the Sovereign Lord come with power:
with ruling arm, reward, and recompense.

Dec. 17-23

Bless those, O Lord,
who have waited for your coming;
let your prophets be proven true.

See! Sovereign Adonai comes with power,
and with a ruling arm.
See! And with reward
and accompanied with recompense.

Like a shepherd tending the flock
and gathering lambs in the arms,
carrying them in the heart
and leading gently those with young.

Who can measure the waters in a hand's hollow?
Or mark off the heavens with handbreadths?
Or hold the dust of the earth in a basket?
Or weigh mountains on a scale
or hills in a balance?

Who has understood the mind of Adonai?
What human has given counsel or instruction,
or whom was consulted for enlightenment
and teaching about what is right
and teaching knowledge?
Who can show the path of understanding?

Surely nations are like drops in a bucket
and are regarded as dust on a scale.
Surely islands are weighed like fine dust.

Even Lebanon is not sufficient to make fire,
nor their animals sufficient for burnt-offering.
Before God, all the nations are as nothing,
regarded as worthless and less than nothing.

Glory...

Repeat antiphon.

PSALM 99

Antiphon Exalt the Lord, our God; and worship
at the mountain of the Lord's holiness.

Dec. 17-23 Turn to us, O Lord,
make haste to help your people.

Adonai reigns; let the nations tremble.
The One sits enthroned on the cherubim;
let the earth shake.

Great in Zion is Adonai,
and exalted over all of the nations.
Let them praise your great and awesome name,
"Holy are you, and mighty."

PSALM 99, continued

The King of justice loves you
and establishes equity and justice,
having done what is right in Jacob.

Exalt Adonai our God!
And worship at the feet on the footstool,
"Holy are you, and mighty."

Moses and Aaron are among the priests,
and Samuel among those calling the name,
calling on El Adonai, who answered them,
who spoke to them from the pillar of cloud.
They kept the statutes and decrees given to them.

Adonai, our God, you answered them.
You were the one Forgiving El to them,
though punishing their misdeeds.

Exalt Adonai our God!
And worship at the holy mountain,
for holy is our God Adonai!

Glory...

Antiphon Exalt the Lord, our God; and worship
at the mountain of the Lord's holiness.

Dec. 17-23 Turn to us, O Lord,
make haste to help your people.

WEEK III
THURSDAY EVENING

PSALM 79:1-5,9-11,13

Antiphon Help us, God of our salvation;
deliver us and atone for our sins
for the sake of your name.

God, the nations invaded into your inheritance,
they defiled your holy temple,
they reduced Jerusalem to rubbles.
They gave the bodies of your servants
as food to birds of the air,
the flesh of your saints to beasts of earth.

They poured out their blood
like the waters around Jerusalem
and no one is there burying.
We are a reproach to our neighbors,
scorn and derision to those around us.
Until when, Adonai, will you be angry?
Will the fire of your jealousy burn to forever?...

PSALM 79:1-5,9-11,13, continued

Hold not against us the sins of our ancestors;
may your mercies be quick to meet us
for we are in desperate need.
Help us, God of our salvation,
for the glory of your name,
and deliver us and atone for our sins
for the sake of your name.

Why should the nations say, "Where is their God?"
Let vengeance be known among the nations
before our eyes for your servants,
for their blood being poured out.
May the groan of prisoners come before you;
and by your strong arm preserve the condemned...

We your people, the sheep of your pasture,
will praise you to forever.
Generation to generation
will recount your praise.

Glory...

Antiphon

Help us, God of our salvation;
deliver us and atone for our sins
for the sake of your name.

PSALM 86:1-7,11

Antiphon Bring joy to me, your servant,
for to you, Lord, I lift up my soul.

Hear in your ear, Adonai,
answer me for I am poor and needy.
Guard my life for I am devoted;
save your servant, my God,
the one trusting in you.

Have mercy on me, Lord,
for to you I call all the day.

Bring joy to me, your servant,
for to you, Lord, I lift up my soul.
Indeed, Lord, you are kind and forgiving
and abundant in love for all who call to you.

Hear my prayer, Adonai;
listen to the sound of my cries for mercy.
In the day of my trouble I will call to you
for you will answer me...

Teach me, Adonai, your way
and I will walk in your truth.
Make my heart undivided
that I may fear your name.

Glory...

Antiphon Bring joy to me, your servant,
for to you, Lord, I lift up my soul.

PSALM 132

Antiphon: Let us go to dwellings of the Lord;
may your saints sing for joy.

Dec. 17-23 To you, O Lord, I lift up my soul;
come and rescue me,
my refuge and my strength.

Adonai, remember David
and all the hardships he endured,
the oath he swore to Adonai,
the vow he made to the Mighty One of Jacob.

I will not enter into the structure of my house;
I will not go to the mats of my bed;
I will not allow my eyes to sleep
nor let slumber come to my eyelids,
till I find a place for Adonai,
a dwelling for the Mighty One of Jacob.

See, we heard her in Ephrathah;
we came upon her in fields of Jaar.
"Let us go to the dwellings;
let us worship at the feet on the footstool."

Arise, Adonai, to your rest,
you and the ark of your might.
May your priests be clothed in righteousness
and may your saints sing for joy.
For the sake of your servant David
reject not the face of your anointed one.

Adonai swore an oath to David,
sure and not to be revoked.
"From the descendants of your body
  I will place on your throne.

  If your sons and daughters keep my covenant
  and my statutes that I teach them
  then their children to forever
  will sit on your throne."

For Adonai chose Zion
and desired her as a dwelling:
"This is my resting place to forever;
  here I will sit, for I desired her.

  To bless I will bless her provisions;
  her poor ones I will satisfy with food,
  her priests I will clothe in salvation,
  and her saints will sing; they will sing for joy.

  Here I will make grow a horn for David;
  I will set up a lamp for my anointed one.
  Enmity will be clothed with shame.
  The crown on David will be resplendent."

Glory...

Antiphon: Let us go to dwellings of the Lord;
may your saints sing for joy.

Dec. 17-23 To you, O Lord, I lift up my soul;
come and rescue me,
my refuge and my strength.

REVELATION 11:17-18, 12:10-12a

Antiphon Now have come the salvation, the power,
and the kingdom of our God.

Dec. 17-23 Turn to us, O Lord;
make haste to help your people.

We thank you, Lord God Almighty,
the One who is and who was;
you have taken your great power and reign.

The nations raged and your anger came,
and the time to judge the dead
and to reward your slaves and prophets,
the saints, and those fearing your name,
the small and the great…

Now have come the salvation and power
and kingdom of our God
and the authority of Christ.
The accuser of our brothers and sisters was cast,
accusing them before our God day and night.

Their victory was because of the blood of the Lamb
and by the word of their witness.
They loved their life into their death,
and so be glad, you heavens,
and all you dwelling in them.

Glory…

Repeat antiphon.

WEEK III
FRIDAY MORNING

PSALM 69:2-22,30-37

Antiphon I am worn out from my calling out;
my throat is parched and my eyes fail,
looking for my God.

Save me, Adonai,
for waters have come to my neck.

I sink into the deep mire; there is no foothold.
I have come into deep waters; floods engulf me.

I am worn out from calling out;
my throat is parched and my eyes fail,
looking for my God.

Those hating me for no reason
are more numerous than the hairs of my head.
Many are the ones destroying me
in enmity for no reason.

What I did not steal then I must restore.
You, God, you know my folly
and my guilts are not hidden from you.

PSALM 69, continued

May those who hope in you, God of Israel,
not be disgraced because of me.
For your sake I endure scorn
and shame covers my face.

I am a stranger to my brothers and sisters,
an alien to the children of my mother.
Zeal for your house consumes me
and insults of your insulters fall on me.

When I weep and fast, my self is a scorn to me.
When I put on my clothing of sackcloth
then I am as sport to them.
Those sitting at the gate mock at me
and drinkers of strong drink in their songs.

But I pray to you, Adonai, in the time of favor;
in the greatness of your love, God,
answer me with your sure salvation.

Rescue me from the mire and let me not sink;
let me be delivered from those who hate
and from the depths of the waters.
Let not the flood of waters engulf me,
nor the depth swallow me
nor the pit close its mouth over me.

Answer me, Adonai, for good is your love!
In the greatness of your mercies, turn to me!
Hide not your faces from your servant;
to my trouble, be quick! Answer me!
Come near because of the foes;
rescue my self and redeem me!

You know my scorn and shame and disgrace;
all in enmity are before you.
Scorn broke my heart and I became helpless
and I looked to have sympathy but there was none,
and for comforters, but found none.

They put gall in my food
and for my thirst gave me vinegar to drink...
I am in pain and suffering;
may your salvation protect me, God.

I will praise God's name in song and glory
with a thanksgiving more pleasing to Adonai
than ox or bull with horn and hoof.

The poor ones will see and be glad;
may your hearts now live, you seekers of God,
for Adonai hears the needy ones
and despises not the captives.

Let heaven and earth give praise
with the seas and all moving in them.
For God will save Zion
and rebuild the cities of Judah;

then they will settle there and possess her
and the children of the servants will inherit her
and lovers of the Name will dwell in her.

Glory...

Antiphon I am worn out from my calling out;
my throat is parched and my eyes fail,
looking for my God.

PSALM 51

Antiphon Restore to me, Lord,
the joy of your salvation
and sustain in me a willing spirit.

Dec. 17-23 Our King will come from Zion;
the Lord, God-is-with-us,
is his mighty name.

Have mercy on me, God,
in accord with your unfailing love;
in accord with the greatness of your compassion
blot out my transgressions.

Wash me of my many iniquities
and cleanse me from my sin,
for I know my transgressions
and my sin is before me always.

Against you yourself I sinned;
what I did is evil in your eyes.
You are proven right when you speak
and justified when you judge.
Surely we are sinners from birth,
from conception in a mother's womb.

Surely you desire truth in our inner parts;
in my inmost place you teach me wisdom.
You cleanse me with hyssop and I will be clean;
you wash me and I will be whiter than snow…

You let me hear joy and gladness;
let the bones you let be crushed now rejoice.
Hide your faces from my sins
and blot out all my iniquities.

A pure heart create in me, God!
Renew inside me a spirit to be steadfast.
Do not cast me from your presences,
nor take from me your Holy Spirit.

Restore to me the joy of your salvation
and sustain in me a willing spirit.
I will teach transgressors your ways
and sinners will turn back to you.

Save me from bloodguilt, God,
God of my salvation;
my tongue will sing of your righteousness.
Lord, open my lips
and my mouth will declare your praise.

Sacrifices give you no delight;
I could bring a burnt offering,
but it would give you no pleasure.
The sacrifices, God, you will not despise
are a broken spirit and a contrite heart.

Make Zion prosper in your pleasure,
and build up the walls of Jerusalem.
Then you will delight in the sacrifice of the just,
burnt offerings and whole offerings,
bulls offered on your altar.

Glory… Repeat antiphon.

JEREMIAH 14:17b-22

Antiphon Lord, we admit our no-good ways;
indeed we sinned against you.

Dec. 17-23 Wait for the Lord
who will come with saving power.

Let my eyes overflow with tears by night, by day,
without cease, for the grievous wounds suffered
by the virgin daughter of my people,
a very crushing blow.

If I go out in the country, see: ones slain by sword!
If I go in the city, see: the ravages of famine!
Indeed, both prophet and priest
have gone to a land they do not know.

To reject you rejected Judah?
Is Zion despised by your self?
Why have you afflicted us so we have no healing?

Our hope is for peace, but no good happens;
for a time of healing, but see: the terror!
We are aware, Adonai, of our no-good ways
and the guilt of our ancestors;
indeed we ourselves sin against you.

For the sake of your Name, neither despise us
nor dishonor the throne of your glory.
Remember, and break not your covenant with us!

Is there one among the worthless nations
that can bring rain or send showers from the skies?
Is that One not you, our God Adonai?
And so we hope in you,
for you do all these things.

Glory...

Repeat antiphon.

PSALM 95

Antiphon The Lord is our God,
and we are the people
of the pasture and flock
and care of our God.

Dec. 17-23 Eagerly I watch for the Lord;
I wait in joyful hope
for the coming of God my Savior.

Come, let us sing to Adonai;
let us shout to our saving Rock.
Come, let us extol Adonai
with thanksgiving and with song.

Adonai is the great El,
the great King above all those little "g" gods,
holding in hand the depths of earth
and peaks of mountains,
the sea and dry land formed in this hand.

PSALM 95, continued

Come, let us worship and bow and kneel
before Adonai who made us.
For God is our God, and we are the people
of the pasture and flock and care of our God.

"If today you hear this voice
do not harden your heart,
as at Meribah and the desert day at Massah
where your ancestors tested me;
they tried me though they saw my deeds.

For forty years was my anger on that generation,
the people straying in their heart;
and so they did not know my ways,
and so were unable to enter my rest."

Glory...

Antiphon The Lord is our God,
and we are the people
of the pasture and flock
and care of our God.

Dec. 17-23 Eagerly I watch for the Lord;
I wait in joyful hope
for the coming of God my Savior.

WEEK III
FRIDAY EVENING

PSALM 22

Antiphon

My God did not despise, disdain,
nor hide from
the suffering of the afflicted.

My God, my God, why have you forsaken me?
Far from my salvation are the words of my groan.
My God, I cry out by day, but you do not answer;
nor is silent my night.

Yet you Holy One are enthroned, praises Israel.
In you our ancestors trusted and were delivered.
To you they cried and they were saved.
In you they trusted and were not disappointed.

But I am a worm and not human,
the scorn of humanity and despised by people.
All those seeing me mock at me;
they shake their heads in insult:
"In the one you trust, let your Adonai rescue you;
let the one who 'delights' in you deliver you!"

PSALM 22, continued

You brought me out from the womb,
to trust in you at the breasts of my mother.
From the womb I was cast upon you;
from the womb of my mother, you are my God.
Be not far from me,
for trouble is near with no one to help.

Many bulls surround me;
the strong of Bashan encircle me.
They open wide their mouths against me,
lions tearing up prey and roaring.

Like the waters I am poured out
and my bones are all out of joint.
My heart like wax melts away within my insides.

Like a broken clay pot, my strength is dried up,
and my tongue is stuck in the roof of my mouth;
you lay me in the dust of death.
Dogs indeed surround around me,
a band of bad doers encircles me as a lion
ready to tear into my hands and my feet.

I can count all of my bones;
they stare and they gloat over me.
They divide my garments among them
and for my clothing they cast lots.

But you, Adonai, be not far off;
come quickly to help me, my Strength!
Deliver my precious life from the sword
and from the power of the dog.
Rescue me from the mouth of the lion
and from the horns of wild oxen.

I will declare your name to my brothers and sisters
and praise you within the assembly.

You fearing Adonai, give praise!
All you descendants of Jacob, give honor!
All you descendants of Israel, give reverence
before Adonai, who despised not, nor disdained,
nor hid the holy face from those suffering affliction,
but heard their cry for help.

From you is my praise within the great assembly;
my vows will I fulfill before those who fear you.
The poor ones will eat to satisfaction,
and the seekers will praise Adonai;
may your heart live to forever.

All the ends of the earth will remember
and turn to Adonai,
and all the families of nations will bow down,
for to Adonai is the dominion, ruling over nations.
All those rich on the earth will feast and worship
and kneel, all who go down to the dust,
all who cannot keep their own self alive.

Those to come will be served by being told,
and in the same way serve generations to come.
They will come and they will proclaim
the deeds of the faithfulness of the Lord,
the story, to people yet to be born.

Glory...

Antiphon My God did not despise, disdain,
nor hide from
the suffering of the afflicted.

PSALM 88

Antiphon Day and night I cry out before you;
may my prayer come before you.

Adonai, Elohay, my Savior,
I cry out day and night before you.
May my prayer come before you;
turn your ear to my cry.

My soul is full of troubles
and my life draws near to Sheol.
I am counted among those going down to the pit,
like a human with no strength,

set apart with the dead ones
like slain ones lying in the grave,
whom you no longer remember,
whom are cut off from your care.

You put me in the pit of the lowest,
in the darkest deep.
Your anger lies heavy upon me
and all your waves overwhelm.

You took away my friends
and made me repulsive to them;
in confinement I cannot escape.
My eye is dim from grief;
I call to you, Adonai,
and in every day spread my hands to you.

Is it to the dead ones you show wonder?
Do the dead rise up and praise you?
Is your love declared in the grave
or your fidelity in the no-more?
Is your wonder known in the darkness
or your righteous deeds in the land of oblivion?

But to you, Adonai, I cry for help
and in the morning my prayer comes before you.
Why do you reject my self, Adonai?
Why hide your faces from me?

Afflicted and coming close to death and despairing,
from youth I have suffered your terrors.
Your anger has swept over me
and your terrors have destroyed me.

They surround me all the day like the floods,
engulfing over me completely.
You took far away my loving companion;
my one friend is darkness.

Glory…

Antiphon Day and night I cry out before you;
may my prayer come before you.

PSALM 135

Antiphon I know that our God is great,
greater than all "gods."

Dec. 17-23 Our King will come from Zion;
the Lord, God-is-with-us, is his mighty name.

Hallelujah! Praise Adonai!
Praise the name of Adonai!
Servants of Adonai, give praise!
You who minister in the house of Adonai,
in the courts of the house of our God,

praise Adonai, for good is Adonai!
Sing praise to the Name, for it is pleasant!
Adonai has chosen Jacob, Israel the chosen treasure.

For I know that great is our Lord;
greater than all the "gods" is Adonai,
who does as Adonai pleases
in the heavens and on earth and in the deep sea,

making clouds rise from the ends of the earth,
sending lightning with the rain,
and bringing wind from the storehouses,

who struck down the firstborn of Egypt,
from human to animals,
sending signs and wonders to the midst of Egypt
against Pharaoh and against all of his servants,

having struck down many nations and mighty kings:
Sihon, king of the Amorites, and Og of Bashan,
and all the kingdoms of Canaan,
who gave their land as an inheritance,
an inheritance to Israel, the people of Adonai.

Your name, Adonai, is to forever,
your renown to generation and generation,
for you, Adonai, will vindicate your people
and will have compassion on your servants.

Idols of the nations are silver and gold,
the making of human hands.
A mouth to them but they cannot speak.
Eyes to them but they cannot see.

Ears to them but they cannot hear,
and there is no breath in their mouth.
Like them will be their makers
and all who trust in them.

House of Israel, praise Adonai!
House of Aaron, praise Adonai!
House of Levi, praise Adonai!
You who fear Adonai, praise Adonai!

Praised be Adonai from Zion,
dwelling in Jerusalem.
Hallelujah! Praise Adonai!

Glory…

Repeat antiphon.

REVELATION 15:3b-4

Antiphon All the nations will come
and worship before you,
Lord God Almighty.

Dec. 17-23 Eagerly I watch for the Lord;
I wait in joyful hope
for the coming of God my Savior.

Great and wonderful are your works,
Lord God Almighty.
Just and true are your ways,
King of the nations.

Who will not fear, O Lord,
or glorify your name?

Only you are holy.
All the nations will come and worship before you;
your ordinances are shown to all.

Glory…

Antiphon All the nations will come
and worship before you,
Lord God Almighty.

Dec. 17-23 Eagerly I watch for the Lord;
I wait in joyful hope
for the coming of God my Savior.

WEEK III
SATURDAY MORNING

PSALM 107

Antiphon Give thanks to the Lord for unfailing love
and deeds of wonder for all human beings,
alleluia.

"Give thanks to Adonai, who is good,
whose love is to forever."

Let this be said by the redeemed of Adonai,
who redeemed them from the hand of the foe
and gathered them from the lands,
from east and west, from north and the south sea.

Some wandered in the desert wasteland,
finding no way to a city for settling.
Hungry and thirsty, their life ebbed away in them.

Then they cried out to Adonai in their trouble,
who delivered them from their distresses,
who led them by a direct way
to go to a city for settling.

Let them give thanks to Adonai for unfailing love,
for deeds of wonder done
for sons and daughters of Adam and Eve,
for satisfying the throats of the thirsty
and filling the hungry with goodness.

PSALM 107, continued

Some sit in the dark and deep gloom,
prisoners of suffering and iron,
for they rebelled against the word of El
and despised the counsel of the Most High
who subjected their heart to the bitter labor,
and no one was there to help.

Then they cried in their trouble to Adonai,
who saved them from their distress,
brought them out from the dark and deep gloom,
and broke away their chains.

Let them give thanks to Adonai for unfailing love,
for deeds of wonder done
for sons and daughters of Adam and Eve,
for breaking down gates of bronze
and cutting through bars of iron.

Some were fools through their rebellious ways,
afflicted because of their iniquities.
Loathing all food,
they drew themselves near to the gates of death.

Then they cried in their trouble to Adonai,
who saved them from their distress,
sending forth the word to heal them
and rescue them from their graves.

Let them give thanks to Adonai for unfailing love,
for deeds of wonder done
for sons and daughters of Adam and Eve,
and let them sacrifice offerings of thanksgiving
and tell of the works with songs of joy.

Some went to the sea in ships
to do trade on the mighty waters.
They saw the works in the deep,
the wonderful deeds of Adonai,
who spoke and stirred up the tempest wind
and lifted up the waves.

They mounted up to the heavens
and went down to the deep;
in peril their courage melted away.
They reeled and staggered like drunkards,
all of them at their wits end.

Then they cried in their trouble to Adonai,
who brought them out from their distress,
stilling the storm to a whisper
and hushing the waves.
They were glad when it grew calm
and they were guided to the haven they desired.

Let them give thanks to Adonai for unfailing love,
for deeds of wonder done
for sons and daughters of Adam and Eve,
and let them exalt in the assembly of the people,
and in the council of elders give praise.

PSALM 107, continued

Adonai turned rivers into desert,
springs of waters into thirsty ground,
and land of fruit into a salt waste
because of wicked ways of those living there.

Adonai then turned desert into pools of waters,
parched ground into springs of waters,
and brought hungry ones to live there.

They founded and settled a city,
sowed fields and planted vineyards,
and yielded the fruit of harvest.
They were blessed and they increased greatly,
and their herds were not allowed to diminish.

Then they decreased and were humbled
by oppression, calamity and sorrow.
With contempt poured on them,
nobles were made to wander in a trackless waste.

But the needy were lifted from affliction
and their families increased like a flock.
They see the upright and they rejoice,
but doers of badness shut their mouth.

Whoever is wise, heed these things
and consider the great love of Adonai.

Glory…

Antiphon Give thanks to the Lord for unfailing love
and deeds of wonder for all human beings,
alleluia.

PSALM 119:145-152

Antiphon You are near, Adonai,
and all your commands are true.

Dec. 17-23 Our God will come from Lebanon,
and as brilliant as the sun.

I call with all my heart: answer me, Adonai;
your decrees I will obey.
I call to you: save me,
and I will keep your statutes.

I rise before dawn and I cry for help;
in your word I put my hope.
My eyes stay open in the night watch
to meditate on your promise.

Hear my voice, as you are loving, Adonai,
as your law makes me alive.
Scheming devisers are near,
but they are far from your law.

You are near, Adonai,
and all your commands are true.
I learned long ago from your statutes
that you established them to forever.

Glory...

Repeat antiphon.

WISDOM 9:1-6,9-11

Antiphon

Wisdom of God,
come forth beside me
that I may learn what is pleasing to you.

Dec. 17-23

May the Holy One from heaven
come down like gentle rain;
may the earth burst into blossom
and bear the tender Savior.

God of my ancestors, Lord of mercy,
who made all things by your word
and through your wisdom framed humanity
to be master of the creatures you have created,
and to govern the world in holiness and justice
and judge justly and with an upright heart,

Give me Wisdom, your companion at your throne,
and do not reject me from among your children,
for I am your servant, born of your handmaid,
a feeble human with a short life
and a weak understanding of justice and laws.

Though a human be ever so perfect in human eyes,
without your Wisdom that same one
will be of no account...

With you is Wisdom, who knows your works
and was present when you created the world,
who knows what is pleasing in your eyes
and what is right in accord with your ordinances.

Send her forth from the holy heavens
and dispatch her from your majestic throne,
that she may labor beside me
and I may learn what pleases you.

For she knows and understands all things
and will guide me to prudence in my actions
and guard me in her magnificence.

Glory...

Repeat antiphon.

PSALM 117

Antiphon The fidelity of the Lord is to forever.

Dec. 17-23 Israel, prepare yourself to meet the Lord,
who is coming.

Hallelujah! Praise Adonai, all nations;
and extol, all peoples.

Great is this steadfast love toward us,
the fidelity of Adonai to forever.

Hallelujah! Praise Adonai!

Glory...

Repeat antiphon.

WEEK IV
VIGIL OF SUNDAY
(Saturday Evening)

PSALM 134

Antiphon Praise the Lord
all servants and ministers at night.

See Adonai and give praise,
all you servants of Adonai,
and ministers at night in the house of Adonai.

Lift up your hands in the sanctuary
and praise Adonai!

May you be blessed from Zion by Adonai,
the One Making heavens and earth.

Glory…

Antiphon Praise the Lord
all servants and ministers at night.

PSALM 122

Antiphon
He comes, the desire of all human hearts;
his dwelling place shall be
resplendent with glory, alleluia.

I rejoiced with those saying to me,
"Let us go to Adonai's house."
Our feet stand in your gates, Jerusalem.

Jerusalem is built like a city
formed together, a compact.
There the tribes go up, the tribes of Adonai.

Make it in Israel a statute
to praise the name of Adonai,
for there the thrones stand for judgment,
thrones of the house of David.

Pray for the peace of Jerusalem!
May those who love you be secure.
May peace be within your walls,
security within your citadels.

For the sake of my sisters and brothers and friends
I will say, "Now, peace be within you."
For the sake of the house of our God Adonai
I will seek your prosperity.

Glory...

Antiphon
He comes, the desire of all human hearts;
his dwelling place shall be
resplendent with glory, alleluia.

PSALM 130

Antiphon Come, Lord, do not delay;
free your people from all sin.

From the depths I cry to you, Adonai.
Lord, hear my voice.
Let your ears be attentive to my cries for mercy.

If you kept a record of sins, Adonai,
Lord, who could stand?
But with you is the forgiveness,
and so you are revered in awe.

I wait, my soul waits for Adonai,
in whose word I put hope.
My soul waits for the Lord
more than watchers for the morning,
even watchers for the morning.

Put hope, Israel, in Adonai!
For unfailing love is from Adonai,
in whom is full redemption,
who will redeem Israel from all their sins.

Glory...

Antiphon Come, Lord, do not delay;
free your people from all sin.

PHILIPPIANS 2:6-11

Antiphon The fullness of time has come upon us at last:
God sends his Son into the world.

Christ Jesus, subsisting in the form of God,
did not deem equality with God something to grab,
but emptied himself, taking the form of a slave,
becoming in human likeness.

And being found in human fashion,
he humbled himself,
becoming obedient until death,
and death on a cross.

And so God highly exalted him,
and gave to him the name above every name,
that in the name of Jesus every knee should bend,
of heavenly beings and earthly beings,
and beings under the earth;

And every tongue acknowledge
to the glory of God the Father
that Jesus Christ is Lord.

Glory...

Antiphon The fullness of time has come upon us at last:
God sends his Son into the world.

WEEK IV
RESURRECTION VIGIL

JEREMIAH 7:3b-7

Antiphon In Christ who rose from the dead
our hope of resurrection dawned.

This says Adonai Sabaoth, God of Israel:
"Reform your ways and your actions
and I will let you live in this place!

Trust you not in words of deception to say,
'Temple of Adonai, Temple of Adonai,
Temple of Adonai are these.'

If indeed to change you change
your ways and your actions,
if to deal you deal with each other with justice,
you oppress no alien, orphan or widow,
you shed no innocent blood in this place,
you follow no other "gods" to your own harm,
then I will let you live in this place
in the land I gave to your ancestors
from ever and to ever."

Glory...

Antiphon In Christ who rose from the dead
our hope of resurrection dawned.

FOR SUNDAYS OF WEEK 4 **LUKE 24:13-35**

And, behold, two of them on the same day
were journeying to a village named Emmaus,
sixty stadia *(7 miles)* distant from Jerusalem,
and they were talking to each other
about all these things having occurred.
And it came to pass as they talked and discussed:
Jesus himself drawing near journeyed with them,
but their eyes were held to not recognize him.
And he said to them, "What are these words
which you exchange with each other walking?"
And they stood with sad faces.
And the one named Cleopas answering said,
"You are only a stranger in Jerusalem and do not know
the things happening there in these days?"
And he said to them, "What things?"
And they said to him,
"The things about Jesus the Nazarene,
who was a prophet-man, powerful in work and word
before God and all the people,
how both the chief priests and our rulers
delivered him to judgment of death and crucified him.
But we were hoping
that he was the one about to redeem Israel.
But also with all these things,
this is the third day since these things happened.
But also some of our women astonished us.

LUKE 24:13-35, continued

Being at the tomb early and not finding his body,
they came saying they had seen
a vision of angels who say that he lives.
And some of the ones with us went to the tomb,
and found as indeed the women said,
but him they did not see."
And he said to them,
"O foolish ones and slow in heart to believe
in all things which the prophets spoke.
Did the Christ not deem it fitting to suffer these things
and to enter into his glory?"
And beginning from Moses and from all the prophets,
he explained to them in all the scriptures
the things concerning himself.
And as they drew near to the village
to which they were journeying,
he pretended to journey farther.
And they urged him saying, "Remain with us,
because it is toward evening and the day has declined."
And he went in to remain with them.
And it came to pass as he reclined with them,
taking the bread, he blessed,
and having broken he handed it to them.
And their eyes were opened and they recognized him;
and he became invisible to them.
And they said to each other,
"Was not our heart burning in us
as he spoke to us on the way,
as he opened up to us the scriptures?"

And rising up in the same hour,
they returned to Jerusalem and found
the eleven collected and the ones with them saying,
"Truly the Lord was raised and appeared to Simon."
And they related the things on the way,
and how he was known by them
in the breaking of the bread.

•

FOR SUNDAYS OF WEEK 8 **JOHN 21:1-19**

After these things Jesus again
showed himself to the disciples on the sea of Tiberias,
and this is how he showed himself:
There were together Simon Peter and Thomas,
called Twin, and Nathanael from Cana of Galilee, and
the sons of Zebedee, and two others of the disciples.
Simon Peter said to them, "I am going to fish."
They said to him, "We also are coming with you."
They went forth and embarked in the boat,
and in that night they caught nothing.
But when it became morning, Jesus stood on the shore;
however, the disciples did not know that it was Jesus.
And so Jesus said to them,
"Children, have you not any fish?"
They answered him, "No."
So he said to them,

JOHN 21:1-19, continued

"Throw the net on the right side of the boat,
and you will find."
And so they threw,
and they were no longer able to drag
from the multitude of the fishes.
And so the disciple whom Jesus loved said to Peter,
"It is the Lord."
Simon therefore Peter, hearing that it was the Lord,
girded himself with his garment, for he was naked,
and threw himself into the sea.
But the other disciples in the little boat came,
for they were not far from the land
but about two hundred cubits *(100 yards)*,
dragging the net of the fishes.
When they disembarked onto the land,
they saw a coal fire and a fish lying and bread lying.
Jesus said to them,
"Bring from the fishes you caught now."
Simon Peter went up and dragged the net to the land,
full of a hundred fifty-three great fish,
and being so many the net was not torn.
Jesus said to them, "Come, you; break the fast."
Not one of the disciples dared to question him,
"who are you," knowing that it was the Lord.
Jesus came and took the bread and gave it to them,
and the fish likewise.
This was now the third time that Jesus
showed himself to the disciples raised from the dead.

When they had breakfasted, Jesus said to Simon Peter,
"Simon of John,
do you agape-love me more than these?
He said to him,
"Yes, Lord, you know that I philia-love you."
He said to him, "Feed my lambs."
He says to him again secondly,
"Simon of John, do you agape-love me?"
He said to him,
"Yes, Lord, you know that I philia-love you."
He said to him, "Shepherd my sheep."
He says to him the third,
"Simon of John, do you philia-love me?"
Peter is grieved that he said to him the third
'do you love me?' and said to him,
"Lord, you know all things,
you know that I love philia-you."
Jesus said to him, "Feed my sheep:
Amen amen I tell you, when you were younger,
you girded yourself and walked where you wished;
but when you grow old, you will stretch out your hands
and another will gird you and will carry you
where you do not wish."
And this he said signifying by what death
he would glorify God.
And saying this he told him,
"Follow me."

•

WEEK IV
SUNDAY MORNING

PSALM 66

Antiphon Let all the earth shout to God,
who has given us life.

Shout to God all the earth!
Sing the glory of the name!
Offer glory and praise to God!
Say to God, "How awesome are you;
how great are your deeds."

Before you and your power
those in enmity cringe.
All of the earth bow down to you,
they sing praise to you,
they sing praise to your name.

Come and see the deeds of God who is awesome,
the works on behalf of all sons and daughters.
God turned the sea into dry land;
through the river they passed on foot.

Let us rejoice in God.
God rules forever with power,
with eyes watching the nations.
Let not rebels rise up.

Peoples, praise our God! Make heard the praise!
God preserves our life among the living,
and lets not our foot to slip.

God, you tested us, refined us as silver is refined.
You let us be brought into prison,
you let burdens be put on our backs,
you let human beings ride over our head.

We went through the fire and through the waters
and you brought us to the place of abundance.

I will come to your temple with burnt offerings,
I will fulfill to you my vows, promised on my lips,
spoken in a time of trouble.

Sacrifices of fat animals I will sacrifice to you;
with offerings of rams I will offer bull and goats.

Come! Listen! Let me tell all who fear God
what God has done for my very self.
To God my mouth cried out
with praise on my tongue.

If I cherished sin in my heart
the Lord would not have listened.
Surely God listened and heard my voice of prayer.

God, be praised, who rejected not my prayer
nor took from within me
the Lord's own *hesed* love.

Glory...

Antiphon Let all the earth shout to God,
who has given us life.

PSALM 118

Antiphon

Sound the trumpet in Zion;
the day of the Lord is near;
he comes to save us,
alleluia.

Give thanks to Adonai who is good,
whose love is to forever.

Let Israel now declare:
this love is to forever.
Let the house of Aaron declare:
this love is to forever.
Let those who fear Adonai declare:
this love is to forever.

In anguish I cried to Adonai
who answered me with freedom.
Adonai is with me, I will not be afraid.
What can any human do to me?
Before enmity I keep this in mind:
Adonai is with me, ready to help me.

Better to take refuge in Adonai
than to trust in the human;
Better to take refuge in Adonai
than to trust in a prince;

All of the nations surrounded me,
indeed did they surround me;
in the name of Adonai indeed I cut them.
They swarmed around me like bees,
they crackled like thorns in a fire;
in the name of Adonai indeed I cut them.

To push back they pushed me back to fall
but Adonai helped me.
Adonai became my strength and my song
and became to me salvation.
Shout joy and victory in your tents, you righteous.

Adonai's right hand does a mighty thing,
Adonai's right hand lifted high.
Adonai's right hand does a mighty thing.
I will not die; I will live
and proclaim these deeds indeed.
To chasten, Adonai let me be chastened,
but did not give me to death.

PSALM 118, continued

Open for me the gates of righteousness;
I will enter through them
and give thanks to Adonai.
This is Adonai's gate,
where righteous ones may enter.
I will give thanks to you for you answered me
and you became to me salvation.

The stone they rejected as builders
became the cornerstone.
With Adonai this happened
and it is marvelous in our eyes.
This is the day Adonai made;
let us rejoice and be glad.

Adonai, save now!
Adonai, grant success now!
Blessed is the one coming in the name of Adonai;
We bless you from Adonai's house.
Our El Adonai has shined light onto us.

Join with boughs the festal procession
up to the horns of the altar.
To you, my God, I will give thanks.
You, my God, I will exalt.
Give thanks to Adonai who is good,
whose love is to forever.

Glory…

Antiphon

Sound the trumpet in Zion;
the day of the Lord is near;
he comes to save us,
alleluia.

DANIEL 3:52-57

Antiphon The Lord is here; go out to meet him, saying:
Great his birth, eternal his kingdom,
strong God, Ruler of all, Prince of Peace,
alleluia.

Blessed are you, O Lord, God of our ancestors,
praiseworthy and exalted above all forever.

Blessed is your glorious and holy name,
praiseworthy and exalted above all forever.

Blessed are you in the temple of your sacred glory,
praiseworthy and exalted above all forever.

Blessed are you who sit high on the cherubim
and look into the depths,
praiseworthy and exalted above all forever.

Blessed are you on your royal throne,
praiseworthy and exalted above all forever.

Blessed are you in the dome of heaven,
to be hymned and glorified forever.

Bless the Lord, all you works of the Lord,
sing praise and high exaltation forever.

Glory…

Antiphon The Lord is here; go out to meet him, saying:
Great his birth, eternal his kingdom,
strong God, Ruler of all, Prince of Peace,
alleluia.

PSALM 150

Antiphon Your all-powerful Word, O Lord,
will come to earth from the throne of glory,
alleluia.

Hallelujah! Praise Adonai!
To El in the sanctuary, give praise.
In the mighty heavens, give praise.
For the works of power, give praise.
For surpassing greatness, give praise.

With sounding of trumpet, give praise.
With harp and lyre, give praise.
With tambourine and dance, give praise.
With flute and string, give praise.

With cymbals clashing, give praise.
With cymbals resounding, give praise.
Let all that has breath praise Adonai!
Hallelujah! Praise Adonai!

Glory...

Antiphon Your all-powerful Word, O Lord,
will come to earth from the throne of glory,
alleluia.

WEEK IV
SUNDAY EVENING

PSALM 23

Antiphon In pastures of greenness
the Lord makes me lie down.

Adonai is my shepherd; nothing do I lack.
My Lord lays me down in green pastures
and leads me beside still quiet waters,
restoring my soul and guiding me
in paths of justice for the Lord's own namesake.

So when I walk in the deep dark valley
I will not fear for you are with me,
your rod and staff a comfort to me.

A table you prepare before me
in the presence even of enmity.
My head you anoint with oil
and my cup is overflowing.

Surely goodness and love will follow me
all the days of my life
and I will dwell in the Lord's own house
for length of days.

Glory…

Antiphon In pastures of greenness
the Lord makes me lie down.

PSALM 76

Antiphon Giving light, you are more majestic
than mountains of game.

God is known in Judah; great in Israel is the Name.
In Salem is God's tent, in Zion the dwelling place.
There flashes broke the arrow,
shield and sword, and weapons of war.

Giver of Light, you are,
more majestic than mountains of game.
Human beings of valiant heart lie plundered;
they sleep their sleep
and warriors can no more lift up their hands.
At your rebuke, God of Jacob,
both chariot and horse lie still.

You are feared, you.
Who can stand before you when you are angry?
From the heavens you pronounced judgment;
when God rose for the judgment
to save all the afflicted of the land,
the land feared and she was quiet.

Even the wrath of humanity comes to praise you,
and you hold close the survivor of wrath.
Make vows! Fulfill vows to your God Adonai!
Let all the neighbors of God bring their gift
to the One rightly feared,
who breaks the spirit of rulers of the earth,
the One rightly feared by the kings and the queens.

Glory... Repeat antiphon.

PSALM 112

Antiphon

Crooked paths will be straightened
and rough ways made smooth.
Come, O Lord, do not delay,
alleluia.

Praise Adonai!
Blessed are the ones who fear Adonai,
and delight greatly in the commandments.
Mighty in the land will that one be,
and blessed with generations of upright children,

wealth and richness in their houses,
and righteousness enduring to forever.
Light dawns in the darkness
for the upright, gracious,
compassionate and righteous.

The good human, generous and lending,
conducts affairs with justice.
Surely to forever the good one will not be shaken;
remembered forever will the righteous one be.

The good will have no fear of bad news,
being steadfast of heart and trusting Adonai
with heart secure, no fear to the end,
when face to face with enmity.

The good one scatters, giving to the poor,
with righteousness enduring to forever;
the dignity of the good one will be lifted in honor.

The doers of bad things will see this and be vexed
with gnashing of teeth and a wasting away,
wicked longings coming to nothing.

Glory…

Antiphon

Crooked paths will be straightened
and rough ways made smooth.
Come, O Lord, do not delay,
alleluia.

REVELATION 19:1b,2a,5b,6b,7

Antiphon Ever wider will his kingdom spread,
eternally at peace,
alleluia.

Alleluia! Praise the Lord!
Salvation and glory and power are to our God,
whose judgments are true and just.

Alleluia! Praise the Lord!
Praise our God, all you slaves of the Lord,
you small and you great, who hold God in awe.

Alleluia! Praise the Lord!
The Lord is reigning, our God, the Almighty.
Let us rejoice and let us exult,
and we will give the glory to the Lord.

Alleluia! Praise the Lord!
The day has come
for the marriage of the Lamb,
and the bride has prepared herself.

Glory…

Antiphon Ever wider will his kingdom spread,
eternally at peace,
alleluia.

WEEK IV
MONDAY MORNING

PSALM 73

Antiphon Surely, the God of Israel
is good to the pure of heart!
Alleluia.

Surely good to Israel is El, to those pure of heart.
But my feet almost slipped,
as nearly lost were my footholds,
for I envied the arrogant
and the prosperity I have seen of the wicked.

None of them struggle with death
and healthy are their bodies.
Human burdens are not theirs, nor human plagues.

And so pride wraps them as a necklace
clothing violence on them.
Their eyes bulge with fat;
their conceits pass the limits of the mind.

They scoff and they speak with malice
and threaten arrogant oppression.
Their mouths lay claim to the heavens,
and their tongues to possession of the earth.

And so their people turn to here for themselves
and they drink up waters of abundance.
They say, "How does El know?"
and, "Is there knowledge of this to the Most High?"
See these bad doers:
even carefree of Always they increase their wealth.

Surely in vain have I kept my heart pure
and washed my hands in innocence.
But I am plagued all the day
and punished in the mornings.

If I said that I would speak as they do,
see the generation of your children I would betray!

My efforts to understand this
are oppressive to my eyes.
Until! I entered into sanctuaries of God
and understood about their final destiny.

Surely you place them on slippery ground
and cast them down to ruins.
How sudden is their destruction,
swept away complete by terrors.
As with a dream when waking up, Lord,
their fantasy you will despise when you arise.

PSALM 73, continued

When my heart was grieved, and my spirits bitter,
and senseless, and unknowing,
I was but a brute beast before you.

Yet I am always with you;
you hold me by my right hand.
With your counsel you guide me
and will take me after the glory.

Who in the heavens is to me?
And with you, nothing on earth do I desire.
My flesh and my heart may fail,
but the strength of my heart is Elohim
and my portion to forever.

For see! Those far from you will perish...
But the nearness of Elohim is my good.
I have made you my refuge, Lord Adonai,
to tell of all your deeds.

Glory...

Antiphon

Surely, the God of Israel
is good to the pure of heart!
Alleluia.

PSALM 90

Antiphon
Dec. 17-23

The Lord,
the ruler over the kings of the earth,
will come;
blessed are they who are ready
to go and welcome him.

PSALM 90

You, Lord, you are our dwelling place
from generation to generation.
Before the mountains were born,
before you brought forth earth,
from eternity to eternity, you are God.

You turn humans back to dust and say,
"Return, sons and daughters of humanity."
A thousand years in your eyes
are like the day yesterday that went by,
like one watch of the night.

You sweep humans into the sleep
like new grass in the morning that sprouts.
In the morning the human springs up and sprouts,
and then by the evening is withered and dry.

Indeed we can be consumed in your anger
and terrified by your indignation.
You set our iniquities before you,
our secrets in the light of your presences.

Indeed all our days pass away under your anger;
we finish our years like a sigh.
Our days last for seventy years
or eighty if given the strength.

The best part of them are trouble and sorrow,
passing quickly, and we fly away.
Who knows the power of your anger,
who fears your wrath?

PSALM 90, continued

Number our days aright;
teach, that we may gain hearts of wisdom.
How long, Adonai, until you relent?
Have compassion on your servants.

Satisfy our morning hunger with your unfailing love
that we may sing for joy and be glad all our days.
Make us glad, equal to our affliction,
the years of trouble we have seen.

May your deeds be shown to your servants
and your splendor to their children.
May the favor of the Lord our God rest upon us
and the work of our hands be made good;
yes, make good the work of our hands.

Glory...

Antiphon Dec. 17-23
The Lord,
the ruler over the kings of the earth,
will come;
blessed are they who are ready
to go and welcome him.

ISAIAH 42:10-16

Antiphon Dec. 17-23
Sing a new song to the Lord;
proclaim praises to the ends of the earth.

Sing to Adonai a new song,
praise from the ends of the earth!

Ones going down to the sea and all in it,
and the islands, the ones living in them,
and the desert and its towns
and settlements where Kedar lives,
let them arise, let them sing for joy,

and the people of Sela
let them shout from the top of mountains.
Let them give to Adonai the glory
and proclaim praise in the islands.

Adonai will march out like the mighty human
and stir up zeal like a warrior,
and shouting and raising a cry
will triumph over enmity.

I was silent for a long time
and held back in quiet;
like a woman bearing a child,
I cry out and gasp and pant.

I will lay waste mountains and hills
letting all their vegetation dry up;
I will turn rivers into islands and dry up pools.

I will lead blind ones by ways they did not know;
along paths they did not know I will guide them.
I will turn what is dark before them into light
and rough places into smooth.

These things I will do
and I will not forsake them.

Glory...

Repeat antiphon.

PSALM 135

Antiphon Dec. 17-23

When the Son of humanity comes to earth
will he find faith in human hearts?

Hallelujah! Praise Adonai!
Praise the name of Adonai!
Servants of Adonai, give praise!
You who minister in the house of Adonai,
in the courts of the house of our God,

praise Adonai, for good is Adonai!
Sing praise to the Name, for it is pleasant!
Adonai has chosen Jacob, Israel the chosen treasure.

For I know that great is our Lord;
greater than all the "gods" is Adonai,
who does as Adonai pleases
in the heavens and on earth and in the deep sea,

making clouds rise from the ends of the earth,
sending lightning with the rain,
and bringing wind from the storehouses,

who struck down the firstborn of Egypt,
from human to animals,
sending signs and wonders into the midst of Egypt
against Pharaoh and against all of his servants,

having struck down many nations and mighty kings:
Sihon, king of the Amorites, and Og of Bashan,
and all the kingdoms of Canaan,
who gave their land as an inheritance,
an inheritance to Israel, the people of Adonai.

Your name, Adonai, is to forever,
your renown to generation and generation,
for you, Adonai, will vindicate your people
and will have compassion on your servants.

Idols of the nations are silver and gold,
the making of human hands.
A mouth to them but they cannot speak.
Eyes to them but they cannot see.

Ears to them but they cannot hear,
and there is no breath in their mouth.
Like them will be their makers
and all who trust in them.

House of Israel, praise Adonai!
House of Aaron, praise Adonai!
House of Levi, praise Adonai!
You who fear Adonai, praise Adonai!

Praised be Adonai from Zion,
dwelling in Jerusalem.
Hallelujah! Praise Adonai!

Glory...

Antiphon Dec. 17-23 When the Son of humanity comes to earth
will he find faith in human hearts?

WEEK IV
MONDAY EVENING

PSALM 82

Antiphon

One is the lawgiver and judge,
the one able to save and destroy;
who are you
to be judging your neighbor? James 4:12

God Elohim is presiding in the assembly of El,
giving judgment among little "g" gods:

"Until when will you defend the unjust
and show partiality to the faces of bad doers?
Defend the weak and the orphans!
Maintain the rights of the poor and oppressed!
Rescue the weak and the needy!
Deliver them from the hands of bad doers!"

They know nothing and they understand nothing.
They walk in darkness
and all the foundations of earth are shaken.

"I said, 'you are gods, all of you,
sons and daughters of Elyon Most High,'
but like all humans you too will die
and like other rulers you too will fall."

Rise up, Elohim, and judge the earth!
For you inherit all of the nations!

Glory... Repeat antiphon.

PSALM 120

Antiphon I call on the Lord in my distress
and the Lord answers me.

In my distress I call on Adonai who answers me.
Adonai, save my self from lips of the lie
and from the deceitful tongue.

What will be done to you and what more
will be done to you, deceiful tongue?
Sharp arrows of war,
with coals of broom trees.

Woe to me that I dwell in Meshech
and live among tents of Kedar.

Too long has my self lived
among haters of peace.
I am of peace,
but when I speak they are for war.

Glory...

Antiphon I call on the Lord in my distress
and the Lord answers me.

PSALM 136

Antiphon
Dec. 17-23

The Lord,
the ruler over the kings of the earth,
will come;
blessed are they who are ready
to go and welcome him.

Give thanks for Adonai who is good
  and is loving to forever.
Give thanks to the One who is El of the "els"
  and is loving to forever.
Give thanks to the One who is Lord of the lords
  and is loving to forever,

to the One who has done great wonders alone
  and is loving to forever,
who made the heavens by understanding
  and is loving to forever,
who spread out the earth upon the waters
  and is loving to forever,

who made the great lights
  and is loving to forever,
the sun as governor over the day,
  and is loving to forever,
the moon and stars as governors over the night,
  and is loving to forever,

who struck down Egypt in their firstborn
  and is loving to forever,
who brought Israel out from among them
  and is loving to forever,
with mighty hand and outstretched arm,
  and is loving to forever,

who divided the Reed Sea into halves
  and is loving to forever,
and brought Israel through its midst,
  and is loving to forever,
but swept Pharoah and his army into the Reed Sea,
  and is loving to forever,

who then led the people through the desert
  and is loving to forever,
who struck down great kings
  and is loving to forever,
and killed mighty kings,
  and is loving to forever,

Sihon, king of the Amorites,
  and is loving to forever,
and Og, the king of Bashan,
  and is loving to forever,

who gave the land as an inheritance
  and is loving to forever,
an inheritance to servant Israel,
  and is loving to forever,
who remembered us in our low estate
  and is loving to forever,

PSALM 136, continued

and freed us from enmity,
  and is loving to forever,
who gives food to every creature
  and is loving to forever.
Give thanks to El of the heavens,
  who indeed is loving to forever!

Glory...

Antiphon
Dec. 17-23

The Lord,
the ruler over the kings of the earth,
will come;
blessed are they who are ready
to go and welcome him.

EPHESIANS 1:3-10

Antiphon Dec. 17-23 When the Son of humanity comes to earth
will he find faith in human hearts?

Blessed be the God and Father
of our Lord Jesus Christ,
who has blessed us in Christ
with every spiritual blessing in the heavens.

God chose us in Christ
before the foundation of the world,
to be holy and free of blemish before him.

In love, God gave us a destiny:
as sons are adopted, through Jesus Christ himself,
in accord with the good pleasure of God's will
to the praise of the glory of grace
by which we are favored as God's beloved.

In Christ we have the redemption
through his blood, the forgiveness of sins,
in accord with the riches of his grace
which he made abound to us.

In all wisdom and intelligence
the mystery of God's will is made known to us
in accord with God's good pleasure and purpose:

A stewardship of the fullness of time,
heading up all things in Christ,
the things in the heavens and the things on earth.

Glory... Repeat antiphon.

WEEK IV
TUESDAY MORNING

PSALM 102

Antiphon

Lord, let my cry for help come to you;
hide not your face,
alleluia.

Adonai, hear my prayer
and let my cry for help come to you.
Hide not your faces from me
on the day of my distress.
Turn your ear to me on the day I call!
Quickly! Answer me!

My days vanish like smoke
and my bones burn like a glowing ember.
My heart is blighted like the grass
and so withered that I forget to eat my food.
Because of my loud groaning
my bones cling to my skin.

I am like a desert owl;
like an owl of the ruins lying awake,
I became like a bird alone on the housetop.
Enmity taunts me all the day,
railing against me, cursing by me.

I eat ash as food and mingle my drink with tears
because of your anger and your wrath,
for you took me up and threw me aside.
My days are like the long shadow,
and like the grass I wither away.

But you, Adonai, sit enthroned to forever,
and your renown is to generation and generation.
You will arise.
You will have compassion on Zion,
for the time to show favor to her,
the appointed time, has come,
for her stones are dear to your servants
and her dust moves them to pity.

The nations will fear the name of Adonai
and all the kings of the earth your glory,
for Adonai will rebuild Zion and appear in glory
and respond to the prayers of the destitute
and not despise their plea.

Let this be written for future generations
that people yet to be created may praise Yah.
Adonai looked down from the high sanctuary place
viewing from heavens to earth,
to hear the groans of prisoners
and release those to be put to death
to declare in Zion the name of Adonai
and give praise in Jerusalem
when peoples assemble together,
and kingdoms, to give worship.

PSALM 102, continued

Adonai broke my strength in mid-course
and cut short my days, and I said,
"My El,
  take me not away in the midst of my days.
  Your years are through generation of generations.

  In the beginning you founded the earth
  and the heavens, the work of your hands.
  They will perish, but you remain
  and they will all wear out like the garment;
  like clothing you will change them
  and they will be discarded.

  But you: the same; your years will never end.
  Children of your servants will live
  and their descendants
  will be established before you."

Glory...

Antiphon — Lord, let my cry for help come to you;
hide not your face,
alleluia.

PSALM 101

Antiphon Dec. 17-23 — The Lord will come from the holy place
to save the people.

PSALM 101

I will sing of *hesed* love and justice;
to you, Adonai, I will sing praise.
I will take care to be blameless in life.
When will you come to me?

I will walk with a blameless heart
in the midst of my house.
I hate and will not set before my eyes
vile things that faithless people do;
they will not cling to me.

The perverse heart will be far from me;
I do not know evil.
I will silence the secret slandering of a neighbor;
haughty eyes and proud hearts I will not endure.

My eyes are on the faithful of the land,
to dwell with me;
one walking in a blameless way
will minister to me.

Anyone practicing deceit
will not dwell in the midst of my house;
nor will one speaking falsehoods
stand before my eyes.

Each morning I will silence bad doers in the land
to cut off doings of bad things
from the city of Adonai.

Glory...

Antiphon Dec. 17-23 — The Lord will come from the holy place
to save the people.

DANIEL 3:26-27,29,34-41b

Antiphon
Dec. 17-23

Zion is our mighty citadel,
our saving Lord its wall and its defense;
throw open the gates,
for our God is here among us,
alleluia.

Blessed be you, Lord, God of our ancestors,
your name worthy of praise and glory forever.

For you are just in all you do;
all your deeds are true and your ways right,
and all your judgments are true...

We have sinned and broken your law
in turning from you;
in all ways possible we have sinned...

For the sake of your name,
do not give us up to forever
and do not void your covenant.

Do not take your mercy from us
for the sake of Abraham your beloved,
for the sake of your servant Isaac,
and Israel, your holy one,

to whom you promised to multiply
descendants like the stars of heaven
and like the sand on the shore of the sea.

For we, Lord, have become
least of the other nations
and are brought low in the world this day
because of our sins.

We have in our day no ruler, prophet, or leader,
no burnt offering, sacrifice, oblation or incense,
no place to make an offering before you
and so find your favor.

But with a contrite heart and a humble spirit
may we be accepted
as if they were burnt offerings of rams and bulls
or thousands of fat lambs.
As such may our sacrifice be seen by you today
and may we follow you without reserve,
for no shame will come to those who trust you.

And so we follow you with all our heart;
we fear you and seek your face.

Glory…

Antiphon Dec. 17-23

Zion is our mighty citadel,
our saving Lord its wall and its defense;
throw open the gates,
for our God is here among us,
alleluia.

PSALM 144:1-10

Antiphon
Dec. 17-23

Lord, make known your will
throughout the earth;
proclaim your salvation to every nation.

Praised be Adonai, my Rock,
who trains my hands for war, my fingers for battle,

my love and fortress, my stronghold and deliverer,
my shield in whom I take refuge,
who subdues peoples under me.

What, Adonai, is a human that you care for us?
Children of humanity, that you think of them?
Like a breath is the human,
whose days like a shadow are fleeting.

Adonai, part your heavens and come down!
Touch the mountains so they smoke!
Send lightning, lightning, and you scatter them!
Shoot your arrows and you rout them!

Reach your hands from on high!
Deliver me! Rescue me from the mighty waters
and from the hand of foreign peoples speaking lies,
whose right hands are the right hand of deceit.

I will sing a new song to you, God,
and on the lyre of ten make music to you,
the One giving victory to the kings,
the One delivering from the deadly sword
your servant David.

Glory… Repeat antiphon.

WEEK IV
TUESDAY EVENING

PSALM 13

Antiphon My heart rejoices, Lord,
in your salvation.

Until when, Adonai? Will you forget me forever?
Until when will you hide your faces from me?
Until when must I wrestle with thoughts of my soul
and sorrow in my heart by day?
Until when will an enemy triumph over me?

Look! Answer me, my God Adonai!
Give light to my eyes, or I will sleep the death!
Or enmity will say, "I overcame that one,"
and foes will rejoice when I fall.

But my trust is in your unfailing love;
my heart rejoices in your salvation.
I will sing to Adonai, who is good to me.

Glory...

Antiphon My heart rejoices, Lord,
in your salvation.

PSALM 137:1-6

Antiphon Dec. 17-23
The Lord will come from the holy place
to save the people.

By rivers of Babylon, there we sat and wept
as we remembered Zion;
On the poplars in their midst we hung our harps,

for there our captors asked us for words of song,
our tormentors for joy:
"Sing for us from the songs of Zion!"

How can we sing in a foreign land
a song of Adonai?
If I forget you, Jerusalem,
may my right hand forget its skill.

May my tongue cling to the roof of my mouth
if I remember you not,
if I consider any but Jerusalem
as the height of my joy.

Glory...

Antiphon Dec. 17-23
The Lord will come from the holy place
to save the people.

PSALM 138

Antiphon Dec. 17-23

Zion is a mighty citadel,
our saving Lord its wall and its defense;
throw open the gates,
for our God is here among us,
alleluia.

I will praise you with all my heart.
Before those who would be "gods"
I will sing praise of you.
I will bow toward your holy temple
and I will praise your name
for your love and your faithfulness.

You are exalted above all,
your name and your word.
On the day I called, then you answered me.
You made me bold and stout in my heart.

May all the kings of the earth praise you, Adonai,
when they hear the words of your mouth.
May they sing of the ways of Adonai,
for great is the glory of Adonai.

Though on high, Adonai looks upon the lowly
and knows the proud from afar.
Though I walk in the midst of trouble,
you keep me alive
against the anger of ones being foes.

PSALM 138, continued

You stretch out your hand, your right hand,
and you save me.
Adonai will fulfill me.
Your love, Adonai, is to forever.
Abandon not the works of your hands.

Glory…

Antiphon Dec. 17-23

Zion is a mighty citadel,
our saving Lord its wall and its defense;
throw open the gates,
for our God is here among us,
alleluia.

REVELATION 4:8b,11; 5:9,10,12,13b

Antiphon Dec. 17-23

Lord,
make known your will throughout the earth;
proclaim your salvation to every nation.

Worthy are you, our Lord and our God,
to receive the glory and honor and power,
because you have created all things,
and by your will all things were created and are.

Worthy are you to receive the scroll
and to open its seals,
because you were slain
and purchased for God by your blood
from every tribe and tongue and people and nation.

You made of them to our God
a kingdom and priests,
and they will reign over the earth.

Worthy is the Lamb, slain to receive
the power and riches and wisdom and strength
and honor and glory and blessing.

Glory...

Antiphon Dec. 17-23

Lord,
make known your will throughout the earth;
proclaim your salvation to every nation.

WEEK IV
WEDNESDAY MORNING

PSALM 103

Antiphon Praise the Lord, my soul,
and remember the blessings of the Lord,
alleluia.

My soul, praise Adonai!
All my inmost being, praise the holy Name!
My soul, praise Adonai,
whose benefits are not to be forgotten:

forgiveness of all of your sins,
healing of all your diseases,
redemption of your life from the pit,
crowning you with love and compassion,
satisfying your desire with good,
renewing your youths like the eagle,
working righteousness and justice
for all who are oppressed.

Adonai's ways are made known to Moses
and the deeds to peoples of Israel.

Compassionate and gracious is Adonai,
slow to anger and abundant in love,
neither accusing to always
nor harboring anger to forever,
neither treating us in accord with our sins
nor repaying us in accord with our iniquities.

As high as the heavens are above the earth
so great is the love for ones who fear Adonai.
As far as the east is from the west
so far from us are our transgressions removed.

As a father has compassion on his children,
so has Adonai compassion on ones fearing,
knowing our form and remembering we are dust.

The days of a human are like the grass
flourishing like flowers of the field,
for wind blows over and it is no more
and the place remembers it no more.

But the love for those who fear Adonai
is from everlasting to everlasting.
The righteousness is for children of the children
of those keeping the covenant
and those remembering to obey the precepts.

Adonai established a throne in the heavens
and rules over all the kingdoms.
Praise Adonai, you angels,
you strong and mighty ones doing the bidding,
obeying the voice of the word.

Praise Adonai, you hosts,
you serving and doing the will.
Praise Adonai, all you works,
in all places of the dominion.
My soul, praise Adonai!

Glory...

Repeat antiphon.

PSALM 108

Antiphon
Dec. 17-23

The Lord, the mighty God,
will come forth from Zion
to set the people free.

My heart is steadfast, God; I will sing
and even my soul will make music.
Awake the harp and lyre; I will wake up the dawn!

I will praise you among the nations, Adonai,
and I will sing of you among the peoples,
for greater than above the heavens is your love
and to the skies your faithfulness.

Be exalted above the heavens, God,
your glory over all the earth
that your loved ones may be delivered.
Save your right hand, and help me!

God spoke from the sanctuary:
"I will triumph and parcel out Shechem,
and measure the valley of Succoth;

mine are Gilead and Manasseh,
Ephraim my head helmet, Judah my scepter,
and Moab my washbasin;
On Edom I toss my sandals
and over Philistia I shout in triumph."

Who will bring me to the Fortress City?
Who will lead me into Edom?
Have you, God, not rejected us,
and not gone out, God, with our armies?

Against enmity give to us aid,
for worthless is human help.
In God will we gain victory...

Glory...

Antiphon Dec. 17-23 The Lord, the mighty God,
will come forth from Zion
to set the people free.

ISAIAH 61:10-62:5

Antiphon Dec. 17-23 I shall not cease
to plead with God for Zion
until the Holy One is sent
in all radiant beauty.

To delight, I delight in Adonai,
my soul rejoices in my God,
who clothed me in garments of salvation
and arrayed me in a robe of righteousness,
as a bridegroom dresses his head like a priest
and a bride adorns herself with her jewels,

ISAIAH 61:10-62:5, continued

for as the soil makes the sprout come up
and as a garden makes seeds to grow
so will Sovereign Adonai
make righteousness spring up
and praise before all the nations.

For the sake of Zion, I will not keep silent;
for the sake of Jerusalem I will not remain quiet,
till righteousness comes out like the dawn
and salvation blazes like a torch.

The nations will see your righteousness
and all the kings your glory
and you will be called by a new name
that the mouth of Adonai will bestow.
You will be a crown of splendor
in the hand of Adonai
and a royal diadem in the hand of your God.

No longer will you be called One Being Deserted,
nor will your name be called Desolation,
but you will be called "my delight is in her"
and your land "espoused."
Adonai will delight in you
and your land will be married.

As a young man marries a maiden,
your Builder will marry you;
and as a bridegroom rejoices over a bride,
so will your God rejoice over you.

Glory…

Antiphon
Dec. 17-23

I shall not cease
to plead with God for Zion
until the Holy One is sent
in all radiant beauty.

PSALM 146

Antiphon
Dec. 17-23

The Spirit of the Lord rests upon me
and has sent me
to preach good news to the poor.

Hallelujah! Praise Adonai, my soul!
I will praise Adonai during my life;
I will sing praise to my God while I still am.

Put your trust not in princes
nor in human beings in whom there is no salvation.
Their spirits depart,
and they return to the ground.
On that day their plans come to nothing.

Blessed are they whose help is the God of Jacob,
whose hope and God are Adonai,
the maker of heaven and earth
and the sea and all that is in them.

The one staying faithful to forever
defends the cause of the oppressed
and gives food to the hungry.

PSALM 146, continued

Adonai sets prisoners free;
Adonai gives sight to the blind;
Adonai lifts those who are bowed down;
Adonai loves the righteous.

Adonai watches over alien strangers,
and sustains the orphan and the widow,
but frustrates the ways that are wicked.
Adonai reigns to forever,
your God, Zion, from generation to generation.

Hallelujah! Praise Adonai!

Glory…

Antiphon Dec. 17-23

The Spirit of the Lord rests upon me
and has sent me
to preach good news to the poor.

WEEK IV
WEDNESDAY EVENING

PSALM 75

Antiphon God is the judge,
only God.

We give thanks to you, God;
we give thanks for your name is Near,
and they tell of your wonderful deeds.

You choose and appoint the time
to be the upright judge.
The earth quakes, and all its people,
and you hold her pillars firm.

I say to the arrogant, "boast not,"
and to the bad doers, "lift not your horn;
lift not your horns against the heavens
nor speak with neck outstretched."

For there is no one from east or from west
and no one from the desert to exalt.
But God is the one judge,
bringing down this one and exalting another.

A cup is full in the hand of Adonai,
and wine foams and mixed spice pours out.
Indeed from this they drink to her dregs,
all the bad doers of the earth.

PSALM 75, continued

And I will declare to forever,
and sing praise to the God of Jacob.
All the horns of bad doers will be cut off,
and the horns of the righteous will be lifted up.

Glory…

Antiphon God is the judge,
only God.

PSALM 94

Antiphon The Lord knows human thoughts.

God of vindication,
Adonai, God of vindication, shine forth!
Rise up, One Judge of the earth!
Pay back desserts to the proud!

Until when, bad doers?
Until when, Adonai, will bad doers be jubilant?
They pour out and speak arrogance;
all the bad doers boast.

They crush your people, Adonai,
and they oppress your inheritance.
They slay the widow and alien;
they murder the orphan.

They say Adonai does not see
and the God of Jacob pays no heed.
Take heed, senseless ones among the people;
fools, when will you become wise?

Does the one who implants the ear not hear?
Does the one who forms the eye not see?
Will the one who disciplines nations not punish?
Will the one who teaches have no knowledge?

Adonai knows the thoughts of humans,
that they are futile.

Blessed is the one whom you discipline, Adonai,
the one you teach from your law
to grant relief from days of trouble
till a pit is dug for bad doers,

for the people of Adonai will not be rejected,
the inheritance never forsaken.
Judgment will again be on righteousness,
after which will go all the upright of heart.

Who will rise up for me against people being bad?
Who will take a stand for me against bad doers?
Unless Adonai helps me,
I would as soon dwell in the silence of my self.

When I said, "My foot slips,"
your love, Adonai, supported me.
When my anxieties were great inside me
your consolations brought joy to my soul.

PSALM 94, continued

Can a throne of corruptions be allied with you,
one that brings misery by decree?
They band together against the life of the righteous
and condemn the innocent to blood.

But Adonai became to me as a fortress,
and my God as a rock of refuge.
A rock of refuge is my God,
who will repay their sin to them
and destroy them for their wicked ways.
Our God, Adonai, will destroy them.

Glory…

Antiphon The Lord knows human thoughts.

PSALM 139:1-18,23-24

Antiphon
Dec. 17-23

The Lord, the mighty God,
will come forth from Zion
to set the people free.

Adonai, you search me and you know me.
You know my sitting and my rising;
you perceive my thoughts from afar.
You discern my going and my lying down,
and you are familiar with all of my ways.

When a word is not yet on my tongue
you see it, Adonai; you know them all.
Behind and before you hem me in
and you lay your hand upon me.
Too wonderful for me is this knowledge,
more lofty than what I can attain.

Where can I go that is away from your Spirit?
Where could I flee from your presences?
If I go up to the heavens, you are there;
if I make a bed in Sheol, you I see!

If I rise on the wings of dawn,
if I settle on the far side of the sea,
even there your hand will guide me
and your right hand will hold me...

PSALM 139:1-18,23-24, continued

If I say, "Surely darkness will hide me
and the night will light around me,"
even darkness will not be dark to you
and night will shine as the day;
as the darkness, so the light.

For you created my inmost beings;
you knit me together in my mother's womb.
I praise you because I am full of fear and wonder;
my self knows well how wonderful are your works.

My frame was not hidden from you
when I was made in the secret place,
woven together in the depths of earth.

Your eyes saw my body
and in your book were written and ordained
all the days before the first day was.

How precious to me, El, are your thoughts,
how vast are they, the sums of them;
if countable they number more than the sand.
Awake and still, I am with you.

Search me, El, and know my heart!
Test me, and know my anxious thoughts!
See if there is in me an offensive way,
then lead me in the way everlasting!

Glory...

Antiphon Dec. 17-23

The Lord, the mighty God,
will come forth from Zion
to set the people free.

COLOSSIANS 1:12-20

Antiphon
Dec. 17-23

The Spirit of the Lord rests upon me,
sending me
to preach good news to the poor.

Give joyful thanks to the Father who made you fit
for your part of the lot of the saints in light,

who delivered us out of the authority of darkness
and transitioned us into the kingdom of the beloved Son,
in whom we have redemption, the forgiveness of our sins.

The Son is the image of the invisible God,
the firstborn of all creation.
In him all things were created,
in the heavens and on the earth,
the visible and the invisible,
whether thrones, lordships, rulers or authorities.

All things have been created through him and for him.
He is before all things,
and in him all things hold together.

He is the head of the body, the church,
and the beginning, the firstborn from the dead,
so that in all things he may hold the first place.

In him all the fullness was well pleased to dwell,
and through him reconciliation to himself of all things,
things on earth and things in the heavens,
making peace through the blood of his cross.

Glory...

Repeat antiphon.

WEEK IV
THURSDAY MORNING

PSALM 3

Antiphon

You, Lord, shield around me,
my glorious One,
you lift my head,
alleluia.

How many, Adonai, are the foes,
many rising against me, many saying of me,
"No deliverance by God for this self!"

But you, Adonai, shield around me,
my glorious One, you lift my head.
My voice cries to Adonai
who answers me from the holy hill.

I lie down and I sleep;
and I wake because Adonai sustains me.
I will have no fear of tens of thousands of people
who are drawn up on every side against me.

Arise, Adonai! Deliver me, my God!
You struck the jaw of enmity
and broke the teeth of badness.
From Adonai is the deliverance.
May your blessing be on your people.

Glory... Repeat antiphon.

PSALM 6

Antiphon Be merciful to me, Lord, and heal me, alleluia.

Adonai, do not rebuke me in your anger
nor discipline me in your wrath.
Be merciful to me, Adonai, for I am faint!
Heal me, Adonai, for my bones are in agony
and my soul is in great anguish.

But you, Adonai, how long?
Turn, Adonai, and deliver my soul!
Save me because of your unfailing love!
Not from death are you remembered.
Who can praise you from Sheol?

I am worn out from my groaning;
through all the night I flood my bed with tears,
I drench my couch.
My eye grows weak with sorrow;
she fails because of all foes.

Away from me, all doers of badness,
for Adonai has heard the sound of my weeping.
Adonai has heard my cry for mercy.
Adonai accepts my prayer.
May enmity be ashamed and greatly dismayed,
and turn back in humble confusion.

Glory…

Antiphon Be merciful to me, Lord, and heal me, alleluia.

PSALM 143:1-11

Antiphon
Dec. 17-23

To you, O Lord, I lift up my soul;
come and rescue me,
my refuge and my strength.

Adonai, hear my prayer!
Listen in your faithfulness to my cries for mercy!
Relieve me in your righteousness!
Bring not your servant into judgment
for not anyone alive is righteous before you.

Indeed enmity pursues my self
and crushes my life to the ground
and makes me dwell in dark places
like dead ones of long ago.
My spirit grows faint within me;
within me my heart is dismayed.

I remember days of long ago
and meditate on all of your work
and consider the deed of your hands.
I spread out my hands to you;
like land parched is my soul for you.

Be quick! Answer me, Adonai! My spirit faints!
Hide not your faces from me
or I will be like and with ones going down the pit.

Bring in the morning your word of unfailing love,
for in you I put trust.
Show me the way I should go
for to you I lift up my soul!

Rescue me, Adonai, from enmity; in you I hide.
Teach me to do your will, for you are my El.
May your good Spirit lead me on level ground.

For the sake of your Name, Adonai,
you keep me alive in your righteousness;
you bring my self out from trouble.

Glory...

Antiphon Dec. 17-23 To you, O Lord, I lift up my soul;
come and rescue me,
my refuge and my strength.

ISAIAH 66:7-14a

Antiphon Dec. 17-23 Bless those, O Lord,
who have waited for your coming;
let your prophets be proven true.

"Before she goes into labor she gives birth;
before pain comes upon her, she delivers a son.
Who has heard of such as this?
Who has seen such as these?

Can a country be born in one day
or a nation be brought forth in one moment?
Yet she is in labor,
then Zion gives birth to her children.

ISAIAH 66:7-14a, continued

Do I bring to the moment of birth
and not give delivery?"
asks your God Adonai;
"Do I bring one to delivery and then close up?

Rejoice with Jerusalem and be glad for her!
All who love her, rejoice with her!
Rejoice, all who mourn over her,

for you will nurse and you will be satisfied
at the breast of her comforts,
for you will drink deeply and you will delight
in the overflow of her abundance."

For this says Adonai:
"See, I extend peace to her like a river,
and wealth of nations like a flooding stream,
and you will nurse, being carried at her side,
and you will be playdanced on her knees.

As a child is comforted by a mother,
so will I comfort you
and over Jerusalem you will be comforted.

When you see, your heart will rejoice
and your bones will flourish like the grass."

Glory...

Antiphon Dec. 17-23

Bless those, O Lord,
who have waited for your coming;
let your prophets be proven true.

WEEK IV
THURSDAY EVENING

PSALM 128

Antiphon May the Lord bless you from Zion
and see to the prosperity of Jerusalem
all the days of your life.

Blessed are all who fear Adonai
and walk in the way.

Indeed you will eat from the labor of your hands.
To you will be blessings and prosperity,
and your spouse like a fruitful vine
inside and outside your house,
sons and daughters around your table
like shoots of the olives.

See: one who fears Adonai is blessed;
may Adonai bless you from Zion.
See and enjoy the prosperity of Jerusalem
all the days of your life,
and the joy of the children of your children.

Peace be upon Israel.

Glory…

Repeat antiphon.

PSALM 129

Antiphon The Lord gains victory over me.

"From my youths they oppressed me greatly,"
let Israel now say.
"From my youths they oppressed me greatly,
but gained no victory over me.

On my back the plowers plowed;
their furrows they made long.
Righteous Adonai cut free the cords of bad doers."

May all haters of Zion be shamed and turned back;
May they be like grass on housetops,
which withers before it grows,

which cannot fill one hand of the reaper
nor an arm of the gatherer,
and passers-by will not say,
"Blessing of Adonai upon you!"

"We bless you in the name of Adonai!"

Glory...

Antiphon The Lord gains victory over me.

PSALM 144

Antiphon
Dec. 17-23

To you, O Lord, I lift up my soul;
come and rescue me,
my refuge and my strength.

Praised be Adonai, my Rock,
who trains my hands for war, my fingers for battle,

my love and fortress, my stronghold and deliverer,
my shield in whom I take refuge,
who subdues peoples under me.

What, Adonai, is a human that you care for us?
Children of humanity, that you think of them?
Like a breath is the human,
whose days like a shadow are fleeting.

Adonai, part your heavens and come down!
Touch the mountains so they smoke!
You send lightning, lightning, and scatter them!
Shoot your arrows and you rout them!

Reach your hands from on high!
Deliver me! Rescue me from the mighty waters
and from the hand of foreign peoples speaking lies,
whose right hands are the right hand of deceit.

PSALM 144, continued

I will sing a new song to you, God,
and on the lyre of ten make music to you,
the One giving victory to the kings,
the One delivering from the deadly sword
your servant David.

Deliver me! Rescue me from foreigners' hands,
whose mouths speak the lie,
whose right hands are the right hand of deceit.

Our sons in their youth
are like well nurtured plants,
our daughters like carved pillars adorning a palace,

our barns filled with provisions from kind to kind,
our sheep becoming thousands
and tens of thousands in our fields,
and our oxen drawing loads,

no break in the walls and no exile
nor a cry of distress in the streets:
Blessed are the people of whom all this is true;
blessed are the people whose God is Adonai.

Glory...

Antiphon Dec. 17-23

To you, O Lord, I lift up my soul;
come and rescue me,
my refuge and my strength.

REVELATION 11:17-18, 12:10-12a

Antiphon Dec. 17-23 Turn to us, O Lord;
make haste to help your people.

We thank you, Lord God Almighty,
the One who is and who was;
you have taken your great power and reign.

The nations raged and your anger came,
and the time to judge the dead
and to reward your slaves and prophets,
the saints, and those fearing your name,
the small and the great...

Now have come the salvation and power
and kingdom of our God
and the authority of Christ.
The accuser of our brothers and sisters was cast,
accusing them before our God day and night.

Their victory was because of the blood of the Lamb
and by the word of their witness.
They loved their life into their death,
and so be glad, you heavens,
and all you dwelling in them.

Glory...

Antiphon Dec. 17-23 Turn to us, O Lord;
make haste to help your people.

WEEK IV
FRIDAY MORNING

PSALM 55:2-15,17-24

Antiphon

Cast your cares on the Lord
who will sustain you,
alleluia.

Listen, Elohim, to my prayer!
Ignore not my plea, but hear me and answer me,
as I am troubled by my thoughts
and distraught at the voice of enmity,
at the stares of the faces of bad doers,
for they bring suffering down upon me
and revile me in anger.

My heart is in anguish within me
and the terrors of death assail me.
Fear and trembling harass me
and horror has overwhelmed me.

And I said, "Would that I had wings like the dove;
I would fly away and rest.
See! I would flee far and stay in the desert.
I would hurry to my place of shelter
from the storm of the tempetuous wind."

Confuse them, Lord; confound their speech,
for I see violence and strife in the city.
By day and by night they prowl about on her walls;
within her are malice and abuse.

Destructive forces are within her
and threats and lies never leave her streets.
It is not an enemy insulting me,
nor a foe rising against me
that I endure, from whom I hide;

but it is you, ordered as a human like me,
my companion and my friend with whom
together we shared close companionship
walking with the throng at the house of Elohim...

To Elohim I call and am saved by Adonai
who hears my voice when I cry out in distress
in evening and in morning and at noon,
who ransoms my self in wholeness from the battle
though many are opposite me.

El enthroned forever will hear and let be afflicted
those who never allow themselves to change,
who do not fear God,
who send hands against friends,
and violate covenants.

This one's mouth is smooth as butter,
yet war is in the heart,
speaking words more soothing than oil
that are yet drawn swords.

Cast your cares on Adonai, who will sustain you
and to forever let not the righteous fall.

But you, God, will bring the bloody and deceitful
into the pit of corruption, not living half their days.
And I will trust in you.

Glory...

Antiphon Cast your cares on the Lord
who will sustain you,
alleluia.

PSALM 51

Antiphon Dec. 17-23 Our King will come from Zion;
the Lord, God-is-with-us,
is his mighty name.

Have mercy on me, God,
in accord with your unfailing love;
in accord with the greatness of your compassion
blot out my transgressions.

Wash me of my many iniquities
and cleanse me from my sin,
for I know my transgressions
and my sin is before me always.

Against you yourself I sinned;
what I did is evil in your eyes.
You are proven right when you speak
and justified when you judge.
Surely we are sinners from birth,
from conception in a mother's womb.

Surely you desire truth in our inner parts;
in my inmost place you teach me wisdom.
You cleanse me with hyssop and I will be clean;
you wash me and I will be whiter than snow...

You let me hear joy and gladness;
let the bones you let be crushed now rejoice.
Hide your faces from my sins
and blot out all my iniquities.

A pure heart create in me, God!
Renew inside me a spirit to be steadfast.
Do not cast me from your presences,
nor take from me your Holy Spirit.

Restore to me the joy of your salvation
and sustain in me a willing spirit.
I will teach transgressors your ways
and sinners will turn back to you.

Save me from bloodguilt, God,
God of my salvation;
my tongue will sing of your righteousness.
Lord, open my lips
and my mouth will declare your praise.

Sacrifices give you no delight;
I could bring a burnt offering,
but it would give you no pleasure.
The sacrifices, God, you will not despise
are a broken spirit and a contrite heart.

Make Zion prosper in your pleasure,
and build up the walls of Jerusalem.
Then you will delight in the sacrifice of the just,
burnt offerings and whole offerings,
bulls offered on your altar.

Glory... Repeat antiphon.

TOBIT 13:8-11,13-15

Antiphon Dec. 17-23

Wait for the Lord
who will come with saving power.

Acknowledge the Lord in Jerusalem.

You Jerusalem, Holy City,
will be scourged for what your children have done.
The Lord will again have mercy
on the children of the righteous.

Acknowledge the Lord as is deserving
and bless the King of the ages,
that your sanctuary will be built in you again
with joy and cheer by all who were exiles,
and love for all generations
those who were distressed.

A bright light will shine to all the ends of the earth;
many nations will come from far away.
The inhabitants of the most remote parts of earth
will come to your holy Name
bearing in their hands gifts for the King of Heaven.

Generation to generation will give joyful praise
and the name of the Lord will be great forever...

Then, children of the righteous, rejoice and exult;
be gathered together and bless the Lord of the ages.

Happy are those who love you
and happy will be those who rejoice in prosperity.

Happy also are all who grieve over your afflictions
for they will rejoice with you
and give witness to your joy forever.

My soul, praise the Lord, the great King.

Glory...

Antiphon
Dec. 17-23

Wait for the Lord
who will come with saving power.

PSALM 147:12-20

Antiphon
Dec. 17-23

Eagerly I watch for the Lord;
I wait in joyful hope
for the coming of God my Savior.

Extol Adonai, Jerusalem!
Zion, now give praise!

Your God strengthens the bars of your gates,
blesses your peoples within you,
grants peace to your border,
and satisfies you with finest of wheat.

Your God sends a command to the earth,
and in swiftness runs a word,
spreading snow like the wool
and scattering frost like the ash.

Hail is hurled like pebbles;
who can stand before the icy blast?
The word of the Lord is sent, and they melt;
wind stirs up and the waters flow.

The word of the Lord is revealed to Jacob,
decrees and laws of the Lord to Israel.
Not for any nation did the Lord do this;
they do not know these laws.
Hallelujah! Praise Adonai!

Glory…

Antiphon
Dec. 17-23

Eagerly I watch for the Lord;
I wait in joyful hope
for the coming of God my Savior.

WEEK IV
FRIDAY EVENING

PSALM 133

Antiphon The multitude of believers
was heart and soul one. Acts 4:32a

See how good and how pleasant it is
to live as brothers and sisters,
united together.

Like the precious oil running down
on the head and on the beard of Aaron,
running down on his collar and robes,

as if the dew of Hermon
was falling on Mount Zion,
there Adonai bestows
the blessing of life to forever.

Glory…

Antiphon The multitude of believers
was heart and soul one. Acts 4:32a

PSALM 140: 1-9,13-14

Antiphon Rescue me from evil, my God;
you protect me from violence.

Rescue me, Adonai, from humans doing badness;
protect me from humans of violence
who devise bad things in their hearts
and stir up wars every day.
They make their tongues sharp as a serpent;
viper poison is on their lips.

Keep me, Adonai, from the hands of bad doers;
protect me from humans of violence
who plan to trip up my feet.
Proud ones have hidden a snare for me,
spread a net of cords,
and set a trap for me at the side of the path.

I say to Adonai, "You are my God!"
Hear, Adonai, the cry of my cries for mercy!
Lord Adonai, strength of my deliverance,
you shield over my head in the day of battle.
Grant not, Adonai, the desires of bad doers;
let not their plans succeed
or they will become proud...

I know that Adonai secures justice for the poor
and the cause of the needy.
Surely the righteous will praise your Name;
the upright will live before your faces.

Glory... Repeat antiphon.

PSALM 145

Antiphon Dec. 17-23

Our King will come from Zion;
the Lord, God-is-with-us,
is his mighty name.

I will exalt you, my God the King,
and I will praise your Name to forever and ever.

In every day I will praise you
and I will extol your Name to forever and ever.
Great is Adonai, and greatly being praised,
an unfathomable greatness.

Generation to generation commend your works
and tell of your mighty acts
and the glorious splendor of your majesty,
and I will meditate on your wonderful deeds.

They will tell of the power of your awesome works
and I will proclaim your great deed.
They will celebrate and remember
the abundance of your goodness
and they will sing of your righteousness.

Gracious and compassionate is Adonai,
slow of angers and rich in love.
Good to all is Adonai,
whose compassions are on all who are made.

PSALM 145, continued

All whom you have made will praise you, Adonai,
and your saints will extol you.
They will tell of the glory of your kingdom
and speak your might to make known

to sons and daughters of humanity your mighty acts
and the glorious splendor of your kingdom.
Your kingdom is the kingdom of all the everlastings
and your dominion is through all
generation and generation.

Adonai is faithful to all the promises
and loving to all who are made.
Adonai upholds all who are falling
and lifts up all who are being bowed.

The eyes of all look to you
and you give them their food at their time,
opening your hand and satisfying the desire
of every living thing.

Righteous is Adonai in all ways,
and loving to all who are made.
Near is Adonai to all who call,
to all who call in truth.

Fulfilled is the desire
of all who fear and love Adonai,
who hears their cry and saves them
and watches over them.
But wicked ways will be destroyed.

My mouth will speak praise of Adonai.
Let every creature praise the holy Name
to forever and ever.

Glory...

Antiphon Dec. 17-23 — Our King will come from Zion;
the Lord, God-is-with-us,
is his mighty name.

REVELATION 15:3b-4

Antiphon Dec. 17-23 — Eagerly I watch for the Lord;
I wait in joyful hope
for the coming of God my Savior.

Great and wonderful are your works,
Lord God Almighty.
Just and true are your ways,
King of the nations.

Who will not fear, O Lord,
or glorify your name?

Only you are holy.
All the nations will come and worship before you;
your ordinances are shown to all.

Glory...

Antiphon Dec. 17-23 — Eagerly I watch for the Lord;
I wait in joyful hope
for the coming of God my Savior.

WEEK IV
SATURDAY MORNING
and
December 24 Morning

PSALM 50

Antiphon Our God will be made manifest
and will not come in silence,
alleluia.

El Elohim Adonai
speaks and summons earth
from the rising of the sun to its setting.
From Zion, perfect of beauty, God shines forth.

Our God comes and will not be silent,
before whom a fire devours,
around whom a storm is great.
The heavens at above are summoned,
and the earth to judge the people:

"Gather the ones consecrated to me,
 the ones making my covenant by sacrifice."
The heavens proclaim the righteousness of God,
the One who judges.

"Hear, my people, and I will speak, Israel,
and I will testify against you;
God, your God, am I.

Not for your sacrifices do I rebuke you,
or your burnt offerings ever before me.
I do not need a bull from your stall
or goats from your pen,

for every animal of the forest is mine,
cattle on the hills, the thousands.
I know every bird of the mountains,
and every creature of the fields is mine.

Were I hungry, I would not tell it to you,
for the world is mine and all in her.
Do I eat the flesh of bulls?
Do I drink the blood of goats?

Sacrifice to God thank offerings!
And fulfill your vows to the Most High!
Call upon me in the day of trouble;
I will deliver you and you will honor me."

But God says to those who do wicked,
"What to you to recite my laws
or to take my covenant on your lip?
For you hate instruction
and you cast my words behind you.

When you see a thief, you join in,
and cast your lot with doers of adultery.
You use your mouth for evil
and harness your tongue to deceit.

PSALM 50, continued

You sit and speak against your brother and sister
and give slander against your mother's children.
You did these, and I kept silent;
you thought me to be like you?

...Consider now this: ...there is no one to rescue
...those who insist on forgetting God.
One sacrificing a thank offering honors me
and prepares the way,
and I will show that one
to the salvation of God."

Glory...

Antiphon

Our God will be made manifest
and will not come in silence,
alleluia.

PSALM 92:1-9,11,13-16

Antiphon
Dec. 24

Bethlehem in Judah's land,
how glorious your future!
The king who will rule my people
comes from you.

It is good to praise Adonai,
to make music to your name, Most High,
to proclaim in the morning your love
and at night your faithfulness,
on the ten-string and on the lyre,
and the melody of the harp.

For you make me glad by your deeds, Adonai;
at the works of your hands I sing for joy.
How great are your works, Adonai;
very profound are your thoughts.
The senseless human does not know
and the fool does not understand.

Though wickedness springs up like grass
and doers of bad things seem to flourish,
their ways will be destroyed to forever.
But you, Adonai, are exalted to forever...

You gave me strength like a wild ox
and I was anointed with fine oil...
The just will flourish like the palm tree,
and grow like a cedar of Lebanon.

Planted in the house of Adonai,
in the courts of our God they will flourish.
In old age they will still bear fruit,
fresh and green they will stay,
to proclaim, "Adonai is upright,
in my Rock there is no wrong."

Glory...

Antiphon Dec. 24

Bethlehem in Judah's land,
how glorious your future!
The king who will rule my people
comes from you.

EZEKIEL 36:24-28

Antiphon Dec. 24 — Lift up your heads and see;
your redemption is now at hand.

I will take you out of the nations
and I will gather you from all the countries,
and I will bring you back into your land.

I will sprinkle on you clean waters,
and you will be clean from all your impurities,
and from all your idols I will cleanse you.

I will give you a new heart
and I will put inside you a new spirit,
and I will remove the stone-heart from your flesh
and I will give you a flesh-heart,

and I will put inside you my Spirit
and I will move you to follow in my decrees
and my laws you will be careful to keep,

and you will live in the land I gave your ancestors,
and you will be my people
and I will be your God.

Glory…

Antiphon Dec. 24 — Lift up your heads and see;
your redemption is now at hand.

PSALM 8

Antiphon Dec. 24

The day has come at last
when Mary will bring forth
her firstborn Son.

Adonai, our Lord!
How majestic is your name in all the earth!

Your glory is set above the heavens!
From lips of children and infants
you ordained strength to bring to silence
enmity, opposition and vengeance.

When I consider your heavens,
the works of your fingers,
the moon and stars which you set in place,
what is a human that you would be mindful,
a child of Adam and Eve that you would care?

And you made us little lower than a "god"
crowning us with glory and honor,
making us to rule over works of your hands,
putting everything under our feet,

flocks and herds, all of them,
and also beasts of the field,
birds of the air and fishes of the sea,
swimming through the paths of the seas.

Adonai, our Lord!
How majestic is your name in all the earth!

Glory...

Repeat antiphon.

(also indicated with the antiphons for Morning Prayer)

ADVENT

The Sunday nearest to November 30:

Sunday - Week 1

A	Matthew 24:37-44
B	Mark 13:33-37
C	Luke 21:25-28,34-36
Mon	Matthew 8:5-11
Tue	Luke 10:21-24
Wed	Matthew 15:29-37
Thu	Matthew 7:21,24-27
Fri	Matthew 9:27-31
Sat	Matthew 9:35-10:1,5a,6-8

Sunday - Week 2

A	Matthew 3:1-12
B	Mark 1:1-8
C	Luke 3:1-6
Mon	Luke 5:17-26
Tue	Matthew 18:12-14
Wed	Matthew 11:28-30
Thu	Matthew 11:11-15
Fri	Matthew 11:16-19
Sat	Matthew 17:9a,10-13

Sunday - Week 3

A	Matthew 11:2-11
B	John 1:6-8,19-28
C	Luke 3:10-18
Mon	Matthew 21:23-27
Tue	Matthew 21:28-32
Wed	Luke 7:18b-23
Thu	Luke 7:24-30
Fri	John 5:33-36

Sunday - Week 4

A	Matthew 1:18-24
B	Luke 1:26-38
C	Luke 1:39-45
Dec 17	Matthew 1:1-17
Dec 18	Matthew 1:18-25
Dec 19	Luke 1:5-25
Dec 20	Luke 1:26-38
Dec 21	Luke 1:39-45
Dec 22	Luke 1:46-56
Dec 23	Luke 1:57-66
Dec 24	Luke 1:67-79

ACKNOWLEDGEMENTS for HINGE HOURS for ORDINARY TIME

The "hinge hours," also called *Morning Prayer* and *Evening Prayer,* come every day, during the first hour of the day, and in the evening near sundown or at night. For the benefit of those familiar with the *Liturgy of the Hours,* there is a method of sort to this layout. Many psalms from the *Office of Readings* are inserted in front of *Morning Prayer,* and many psalms and canticles from *Daytime Hours* and *Night Prayer* are inserted into *Evening Prayer.* Some of the repetition of psalms and canticles in the *Liturgy of the Hours* is minimized here.

The official translation approved by the Catholic Church for the *Liturgy of the Hours* is a beautiful translation for chanting in monasteries and seminaries.
As a parish priest, almost all of my time with the Psalter is with the church universal but alone with God, whether in my room, in the chapel, or in the woods. Praying in *Lectio Divina,* trying to listen to the Lord, I have found much prayerful fruit in several translations.

This meditation rendering follows consciously these four choices:

1. For the name *Yhvh,* or *Yahweh,* the Hebrew word ***Adonai*** (ah-duh-nigh') meaning *My Lord,* is used. In several places the words *El* or *Elyon* or *Elohim* are retrieved, as is *Sabaoth* instead of *Mighty* or *Hosts.*
2. Following the Christian understanding of one God in the three persons of the Trinity, masculine pronouns for God are avoided, except when God is referred to as Father, or in specific references to Jesus.
3. In an admittedly imperfect effort to pray the gospel as well as the psalms, the word *enemy* is most often rendered as *enmity.*
4. Where people are referred to as *evil,* the emphasis is shifted to those who *do* evil, or *ways* that are evil or bad.

There are problems with all four of these choices, and these would be reasons to not consider this compilation in public liturgy. Still, in my judgment, the benefits overwhelm the problems.

The primary characater of this rendering is from the grace of decades of praying with the Psalter. May the Lord grant more of this grace. Any errors in this rendering are entirely my own. Let us be grateful for all those who do the real work of translating sacred scripture.

Again, the primary source for this work is the grace of two decades of praying the psalms, canticles and readings from several translations, including these:

(*This is my favorite translation of the Psalms.*)

(*This is the newest Catholic translation.*)

I am especially grateful
to all those who worked on the *New American Bible*
and to Mr. Kohlenberger and Mr. Marshall.

These other works were consulted:

The New Jerome Biblical Commentary
edited by Raymond E. Brown, S.S., Joseph A. Fitzmyer, S.J.,
and Roland E. Murphy, O.Carm.
Copyright © 1990, 1968 by Prentice-Hall, Inc.

The following volumes from the Anchor Bible:
Psalms I (1-50); Psalms II (51-100); Psalms III (101-150)
The Anchor Bible, Volumes 16, 17, and 17A
by Mitchell Dahood, S.J.
Copyright © 1965,1966, © 1968, © 1970, Doubleday
The Wisdom of Ben Sira; The Anchor Bible, Vol. 39
by Patrick W. Skehan
Copyright © 1987, Doubleday & Company, Inc.
Tobit; The Anchor Bible, Vol. 40A
by Carey A. Moore
Copyright © 1996, Doubleday
The Wisdom of Solomon; The Anchor Bible, Vol. 43
by David Winston
Copyright © 1979, Doubleday & Company, Inc.
Daniel, Esher and Jeremiah, the Additions;
The Anchor Bible, Vol.44
by Carey A. Moore
Copyright © 1977, Doubleday & Company, Inc.

And a stack of dictionaries.

Stephen Joseph Wolf
Nashville, Tennessee
www.idjc.org

Come, Holy Spirit, take hold of our lives.
Sign us with your holy love.
Give us your gifts. Confirm us in faith.
Spirit come.

Serafina di Giacoma, altered

PSALMS

The cycle of weeks 1, 2, 3, and 4 continues (week "1" for week 5; week "2" for week 6; etc.)

Psalms of Morning and Evening Prayer are consistent with the Liturgy of the Hours.

Italicized Morning Prayer psalms (i.e. *Sun MP*) are from the Office of Readings.

Italicized Evening Prayer psalms (i.e. *Mon EP*) are from either Daytime or Night Offices.

Some of the italicized psalms are moved to different days of the week. "Sunday Vigil" is Saturday Evening.

OLD TESTAMENT CANTICLES

OLD TESTAMENT READINGS

NEW TESTAMENT CANTICLES

NEW TESTAMENT READINGS

Come, Redeemer of our Race: 7 7 7 7 HEINLEIN - Advent Thu MP, 26

Come, Thou Long Expected Jesus: 87 87 D, STUTTGART - Advent Mon MP, 14

Comfort, Comfort, O My People: 87 87 77 88, GENEVA 42 - Advent Wed EP, 24

Creator of the Stars of Night: CONDITOR, LM - Advent Sunday Vigils EP, 6

Draw Near To Your Jerusalem, O Lord: 10 10 10 10 10 10 UNDE ET MEMORES - Adv Mon EP, 16

Faith Of Our Ancestors: ST. CATHERINE, LM with refrain - Advent Thu EP, 28

Immaculate Mary: 11 11 LOURDES HYMN with refrain - Advent Tue EP, 20

O Come Divine Messiah: 78 76 VENEZ DIVIN MESSIE - Advent Fri MP, 30

O Come, O Come Emmanuel: VENI EMMANUEL, LM with ref.-Adv Sun MP, 8

On Jordan's Bank: WINCHESTER NEW, CM - Advent Sun EP, 12

Take, Lord, Receive My Liberty: TALLIS CANON, LM - Advent Fri EP, 32

The Advent Of Our King: 66 86 ST. THOMAS (WILLIAMS) - Advent Tue MP, 18

The Angel Gabriel From Heaven Came: 10 10 10 10 10 10 UNDE ET MEMORES -Advent Sat MP, 34

The King Shall Come When Morning Dawns: MCKEE, CM - Advent Wed MP, 22

Each new liturgical year begins on the First Sunday of Advent with is always the Sunday nearest to November 30.

YEAR & SUNDAY CYCLE	ASH WED.	EASTER	PENTECOST	MONDAY & WEEK ORDINARY TIME RESUMES
2014-A	Mar. 5	April 20	June 8	June 9 Week 10
2015-B	Feb. 18	April 5	May 24	May 25 Week 8
2016-C	Feb. 10	March 27	May 15	May 16 Week 7
2017-A	Mar. 1	April 16	June 4	June 5 Week 9
2018-B	Feb. 14	April 1	May 20	May 21 Week 7
2019-C	Mar. 6	April 21	June 9	June 10 Week 10
2020-A	Feb. 26	April 12	May 31	June 1 Week 9
2021-B	Feb. 17	April 4	May 23	May 24 Week 8
2022-C	Mar. 2	April 17	June 5	June 6 Week 10
2023-A	Feb. 22	April 9	May 28	May 29 Week 8
2024-B	Feb. 14	March 31	May 19	May 20 Week 7
2025-C	Mar. 5	April 20	June 8	June 9 Week 10
2026-A	Feb. 16	April 5	May 24	May 25 Week 8
2027-B	Feb. 10	March 28	May 16	May 17 Week 7
2028-C	Mar. 1	April 16	June 4	June 5 Week 9

Gospel Canticle For Morning

CANTICLE OF ZECHARIAH (The Benedictus)

Luke 1:68-79

+ Blessed be the Lord the God of Israel
who chose a people,
visited them to bring redemption,

and raised salvation in the house of David,
saving strength from God's own servant,

speaking from the age of the prophets
through the mouth of the holy prophet:
Salvation out of enmity,
even out of those who hate us,

to show our ancestors how mercy works,
and to remember the holy promise of the Lord,

the covenant made for our father Abraham,
calming our fear and making us free
to serve God as holy and righteous and just
in the Lord's presence all our days.

And you also child
will be called a prophet of the Most High
for you will go before the Lord to prepare his way

and give to his people a knowledge of salvation
known in accepting forgiveness of their sins.

From the deepness of God's mercy on us,
a sun rising from the height will visit to appear
to those who sit in the dark or shadow of death,
and to guide our feet into the way of peace.

Gospel Canticle For Evening

CANTICLE OF MARY (The Magnificat)

Luke 1:46-55

+ My soul is stretched full with praise of the Lord,
and my spirit, beyond joy in God, my Savior,
who chose to lay eyes on this humble servant.

Behold, now and forward,
each and every age will call me blessed,
for the Mighty One did great things to me.

Holy is the name and the mercy
to generations and generations,
the ones fearing the One,

Who scattered the haughty of mind and heart,
pulled the powerful off their high place,
and lifted with dignity the humble in need.

The hungering are filled with good things,
the rich are sent away empty,
and servant Israel is given relief

with a memory of mercy to remember,
the promise spoken to our ancestors,
to Abraham and his descendants forever.

Traditional Doxology

Glory to the Father and to the Son
and to the Holy Spirit,
As it was in the beginning, is now,
and will be forever. Amen.

MORNING PRAYER PETITIONS FOR THE CONSECRATION TO GOD OF THE DAY AND ITS WORK

For the Church and her ministry and apostolates...
For secular authorities and all serving as stewards...
For people who are poor or sick or in sorrow...
For peace and the basic needs of each human being...
In gratitude for blessings and grace...
For those who have asked for my prayer...
For those for whom I have promised to pray...
For those who weigh on my heart...

EVENING PRAYER INTERCESSIONS

In gratitude for blessings, Abba thank you...
For the sins of this day, Lord Jesus have mercy...
With concerns over tomorrow, Holy Spirit help...
For respect for the dignity of each human person...
For those who have died...

CLOSING PRAYER FOR MORNING AND EVENING

Our Fa-ther, who art in heav-en,
hal-lowed be thy name.
Thy king-dom come, thy will be done
on earth as it is in heav-en.
Give us this day our dai-ly bread
and for-give us our tres-pass-es,
as we for-give those who tres-pass a-gainst\ us,
and lead us not in-to temp-ta/-tion,
but de-liv-er us from e\-vil. A-men.

CPSIA information can be obtained at www.ICGtesting.com
Printed in the USA
LVOW11s0512071214

417597LV00001B/1/P

9 781937 081171